Theology for Better Counseling

Trinitarian Reflections for Healing and Formation

VIRGINIA TODD HOLEMAN

IVP Academic

An imprint of InterVarsity Press
Downers Grove, Illinois

InterVarsity Press
P.O. Box 1400, Downers Grove, IL 60515-1426
World Wide Web: www.ivpress.com
E-mail: email@ivpress.com

InterVarsity Press® is the book-publishing division of InterVarsity Christian Fellowship/USA®, a movement of students and faculty active on campus at hundreds of universities, colleges and schools of nursing in the United States of America, and a member movement of the International Fellowship of Evangelical Students. For information about local and regional activities, write Public Relations Dept., InterVarsity Christian Fellowship/USA, 6400 Schroeder Rd., P.O. Box 7895, Madison, WI 53707-7895, or visit the IVCF website at <www.intervarsity.org>.

Scripture quotations, unless otherwise noted, are from the New Revised Standard Version of the Bible, *copyright 1989 by the Division of Christian Education of the National Council of the Churches of Christ in the USA. Used by permission. All rights reserved.*

While all stories in this book are true, some names and identifying information in this book have been changed to protect the privacy of the individuals involved.

Chapter 4 was previously published as "Wesleyan Holiness and Differentiations of Self" in Wesleyan Theology and Social Science. Published with the permission of Cambridge Scholars Publishing. All rights reserved.

Sections of chapter 6 are taken from Reconcilable Differences: Hope and Healing for Troubled Marriages *by Virginia Todd Holeman. Copyright © 2004 by Virginia Todd Holeman. Used by permission of InterVarsity Press PO Box 1400 Downers Grove, IL 60515. www.ivpress.com.*

Cover design: Cindy Kiple
Images: David Elliott/Getty Images
Interior design: Beth Hagenberg

ISBN 978-0-8308-3972-8

Printed in the United States of America ∞

Library of Congress Cataloging-in-Publication Data has been requested.

| P | 20 | 19 | 18 | 17 | 16 | 15 | 14 | 13 | 12 | 11 | 10 | 9 | 8 | 7 | 6 | 5 | 4 | 3 | 2 | 1 |
| Y | 29 | 28 | 27 | 26 | 25 | 24 | 23 | 22 | 21 | 20 | 19 | 18 | 17 | 16 | 15 | 14 | 13 | 12 |

Contents

Preface   7

1 Is All This Fuss About Theology Really Necessary?   9

2 A Metamodel of Theologically Reflective Counseling 37

3 A Theologically Reflective Counseling Relationship 61
The Triune God and Therapeutic Common Factors

4 Responsible Living 81
Personal Holiness and Theologically Reflective Counseling

5 Out of the Office and into the Streets 101
Social Holiness, Social Justice and Theologically Reflective Counseling

6 Just Forgive? 131
The Atonement and Theologically Reflective Counseling

7 Seeing Now in Light of the Not Yet 157
Eschatology and Theologically Reflective Counseling

Postscript 179

Notes 183

Bibliography 201

Index 206

Preface

I ONCE ASKED AN ARTIST HOW LONG IT TOOK HER to paint a particular picture. Her reply was instructive. She said, "It took me thirty years and three days." My thoughts about this work are something like that. I have been swimming in integration waters since I took my first pastoral counseling course in the mid-1980s, and have been thinking about the integration of theology and counseling ever since. What does it mean to bring theological reflection into one's work as a counseling practitioner? What shapes might theologically reflective counseling take given the broad sweep of theological thinking and counseling theories and techniques that exist today? How does theological reflection in turn shape counselors so that their hearts are even more fully aligned with God's heart? Does one's membership in a particular theological stream (e.g., Baptist, Lutheran, Pentecostal, Reformed, Wesleyan) make a difference in how one integrates theology and counseling? Many excellent books and journal articles have been and are being published about the integration of theology and the practice of counseling. I offer my voice to this growing conversation through this book, and in your reading of it I seek to be in dialogue with you about the ways that counseling practitioners can bring theological reflection to their work with clients.

Throughout this book I use several phrases interchangeably to refer to Christians who are also engaged as counseling practitioners as either licensed mental health professionals or as pastoral counselors. Sometimes I write about "Christians who counsel." Other times I comment on "Christian counselors." Some paragraphs will simply address "counselors" or "mental health professionals." I am not staking a claim on a definition of "Christian counseling." That is a different conversation than the one I wish to have with you, the reader.[1] Instead, I suggest a roadmap for those who live, move and breathe a Christian worldview, and who desire to live and think Christianly in their work as counseling professionals. Sometimes the cases I present are loosely based on particular clients. In those instances where an individual is indeed the basis for the case scenario, I have secured written informed consent to use his or her story, and have changed that person's name and other identifying information to protect his or her confidentiality.

Several people read early drafts of this book and offered helpful feedback. My thanks go to Ken Collins for sharing with me his expertise on John Wesley's theology. Many thanks to Tracey LeGrand, Richard Landon, David Thompson, Chuck Gutenson, Steve Stratton and Jennifer Ripley for your insightful words. I also want to express my gratitude to Gary Deddo, my editor at IVP, and the anonymous reviewers whose feedback improved the manuscript. A research grant from the Wabash Center for Theological Education (Mid-Career Faculty Workshop) launched my focused thinking about teaching and integration, which eventually resulted in this book. A sabbatical from Asbury Theological Seminary provided the time I needed to think and write. Finally, a word of deep appreciation to my counseling faculty colleagues at Asbury—Anne, Russell, Tony, Tapiwa, Javier and Steve—you inspire me, and this book is dedicated to you!

Is All This Fuss About Theology Really Necessary?

Give me the enlarged desire,
And open, Lord, my soul,
Thy own fullness to require,
And comprehend the whole;
Stretch my faith's capacity
Wider, and yet wider still
Then, with all that is in Thee
My soul forever fill!

CHARLES WESLEY (1707–1788),
"Give Me the Enlarged Desire"

I CONFESS. FOR THE YEARS THAT I WORKED as a licensed professional counselor, I gave no thought to *serious* theological reflection. I had been trained in Christian counseling. I was biblically literate. What more did I need? To me serious theology was dry, dull, boring and seemingly irrelevant to my everyday life. The topics that I assumed interested *real* theologians held no interest for me. I found little place for serious theology in the midst of my clinical work. God forgive me for my ignorance and naiveté.

A little background information will help you appreciate the full extent of my confession. Before I became a licensed professional coun-

selor, I had earned a degree in Christian ministries. I had to take a few
courses in theological and biblical studies as part of my curriculum.
The theology courses covered the major doctrinal categories in a systematic way. That is, I learned about the doctrine of God (theology
proper), of Christ (Christology), of the Holy Spirit (pneumatology), of
the church (ecclesiology) and so forth. My biblical studies classes presented overviews of Old and New Testament. Upon graduation I was
hired to work in a local church as their director of Christian education
and youth ministries. I used the biblical knowledge and skills I had
obtained in graduate school, but I rarely thought of myself as engaging
in theological reflection, because in my mind I wasn't a theologian. I
could state what I believed about God the Father, God the Son and
God the Holy Spirit. I could even spell and define the "big" theological
words like *omnipotence, omnipresence* and *omniscience,* and even some of
the "-ologies"—like *soteriology* or *eschatology.* Yet I was far more interested in practical and concrete application than systematic and philosophical theology. If one of my professors *had* told me that there was
nothing more practical than good theology, *which they probably had,* I
had forgotten their exhortation.

Fast forward a few years, and I have now decided to pursue a degree
in pastoral psychology and counseling at a nearby seminary. My goal
was to learn all of the counseling theories and techniques that I could
absorb and to waive as many of the required Bible and theology classes
as I could get away with. I already had earned a degree from a Christian
graduate school in Christian ministry, *and* I was a relatively biblically
literate Christian! What more did I need? In spite of my best efforts, I
did have to take several regular seminary courses as part of my counseling curriculum. I approached them begrudgingly. I did not come to
study doctrine or church history. I could not possibly imagine how
these classes could relate to my career as a licensed professional clinical
counselor. Classes on specific books of the Bible were okay. I could see
how additional biblical knowledge could fit into my counseling tool
bag. But I had no room for more formal theological studies and I was
not challenged to read theological works within my counseling courses.
I thought that it was enough that I had mastered the model my program

taught to me that integrated Christianity and counseling.

Upon graduation, I worked in a Christian counseling practice. As was appropriate and with my clients' permission, I used the Bible, the Christian counseling model I had learned and books written by other Christian mental health professionals to augment my work with clients. If asked, I would affirm that I counseled from a Christian worldview or that I was a Christian counselor. For the most part that was adequate for the day. Yet there were times when my clients pressed me for more—when they asked important questions that arose from their life circumstances. "Where was God while I was being raped when I was a missionary?" "How could God let this tragedy happen to my loved one?" Some of my clients struggled with *wanting* to forgive someone who had hurt them deeply and unjustly, but *could not do so* at that time. They wondered if God would reject them. Other clients no longer wanted to be threatened or beaten in their own home. They knew that God hated divorce, and they felt guilty for contemplating divorce from their abusive and unrepentant spouses. They desperately wanted to obey God but they also wondered if that implied that God had assigned "spouse abuse" as their particular cross to bear.

These clients labored to make Christian sense of their suffering and they were asking for my help. They were not asking for a seminar on theology *but were, in fact, asking hard theological questions*. They agonized over a disconnection between their assumptions of what they believed God *could or should* do for them and their present painful circumstances. Some wrestled with the problem of evil and the justice of God, or the question of theodicy. Others were confounded by a theological dissonance between their understanding of God's sovereignty and their experience of being "trespassed against" severely and unjustly. From one perspective these clients were living with a conflict between their explicit knowledge of God and the Christian life and their implicit knowledge of living as followers of Jesus. What had happened to them or their loved ones just did not fit with their "in the bones" understanding of God. As a result they experienced a kind of *theological disequilibrium* or a *theological cognitive dissonance*, which left them discouraged, disoriented and often distraught.[1] By the grace of God I was able to walk beside my clients as they journeyed through these unexplored and unwelcome theological places. I wish I could say that these experiences drove me to read theology more deeply and more personally. They didn't. I was at a point in my professional development where I had a greater craving for more techniques in my counseling toolkit than I had a desire for more theology for clinical reflection.

A few more years and a doctoral degree later I accepted a faculty position at Asbury Theological Seminary. Here I met my theological Waterloo. I came face to face with the realization that I had skated by with *thin* theological reflection for years. If I was going to teach in a counseling program that took theological integration seriously, then I had some important study and personal growth ahead of me. The language of theology is different than that of therapy, and I applied myself to learn this new lingo and to let this new language seep into the core of my being to help me become more of the person (and clinician) that God was calling me to become. Broadening my explicit study of theology and biblical study went hand in hand with deepening my relationship with God. I experienced a kind of conversion of my imagination, a "transformation of ideals and perceptions, and a resocialization into a new community of reference and faithfulness."[2]

I began to read books written by *real* theologians. I also formed friendships with faculty colleagues whose areas of expertise were theology or biblical studies. Many of these friends also were interested in interdisciplinary dialogue, so while I helped them to understand my world of counseling, they helped me to understand their world of theological and biblical study. Several of them were kind enough to review things that I wrote for publication. I wanted to be sure that I represented their discipline correctly. I was becoming more theologically fluent and was able to translate thick theological concepts into everyday language and life for myself, my clients and my students. Finally I began to think and live theologically at an enriched level.

Lest I misrepresent the scope of my theological forays, I didn't read *everything* in theology (I still find philosophical theology most challenging to understand). Instead I attended to theological topics that resonated with clinical issues and personal interests. The theological and therapeutic turn toward relationality is an example of this kind of convergence.[3] As postmodern therapies and neuroscientific discoveries deepened my understanding of self-identity as "person-in-relationship," theologians expanded my understanding of the Trinity as "divine-person-in-relationship."[4] Theological perspectives on human relationships enriched my study of individual, couples and family counseling.[5] Several theologians explored theologies of Christian forgiveness at the same time that I was involved with empirical studies on psychological forgiveness.[6] Biblical and theological work on God's justice resonated with my interest in counseling as a form of advocacy for social justice.[7] Other theologians wrestled with human suffering in light of the goodness of God, which contributed to my work with crisis and trauma counseling.[8] Today I could no more think of counseling without a solid theological foundation than I could imagine consulting a medical doctor who had only a rudimentary understanding of anatomy!

Perhaps aspects of your story are similar to mine. You might be a counseling student in a Christian counseling program. You love your counseling classes and you may tolerate classes outside of your discipline (especially if they happen to be theology, biblical study or church history). Or you could be a licensed mental health professional or a pastor, and you want to strengthen your ability to weave your Christian faith into your counseling practice. On the other hand you could be a person who is keenly interested in anything related to the integration of counseling and theology. My first goal in this book is to awaken in you a desire to drink deeply from theological wells so that you will be as well-formed theologically as you are clinically. To that end I encourage you to read broadly to become as fluent as possible in your own theological tradition and become as knowledgeable as possible about others. That way you may have a better sense of which theological stream a particular author swims in (e.g., Anabaptist, Baptist, Lutheran, Reformed, Catholic, Wesleyan).[9] If you think through the content of the books on your shelf that speak to the integration of Christian theology and psychology or counseling, authors may or may not make their theological home-base explicitly known. And most readers do not mind this at all.

Yet I think that paying closer attention to the particularity of one's theological roots has benefits. In this way you not only know the degree of commonality that different theologies share, but you also become more alert to their distinctiveness (some subtle and some not so subtle)—which can become a therapeutic hidden bias, especially when clients give consent for the integration of spirituality in their counseling. It is beyond the scope of this work to highlight the uniqueness found in the major or minor streams of Christianity. But I can use information from my own theological home to serve as an example. I hope that you will be inspired to deepen your own spiritual walk as you learn more about mine, and that you will be challenged to turn to some of the primary sources from your theological home base.

So in the interest of informed consent—my theological orientation is found among the family of theologies that arose from the teachings of John Wesley (1703–1791). Wesley was an eighteenth-century Anglican clergyman who called attention to "practical divinity," or practical theology in today's lingo. Some readers may remember that Wesley's Methodist movement brought about a revival of sorts in eighteenth-century England. Where Wesley's own Anglican Church concentrated its ministry on the well-to-do, Wesley risked their ecclesial wrath and took the gospel message *to* the common person, *to* the highways and byways, *to* the poor as well as the rich.[10] He emphasized the importance of interpersonal relationships for spiritual growth. He developed discipleship groups and trained the laity (men and women) to be small group leaders.[11] These commitments resonate with twenty-first-century therapeutic commitments to social justice and community counseling models.[12] Since the 1990s a number of mental health professionals have been writing about the relationships between psychology/counseling and Wesleyan theology.[13]

John Wesley was a man of God with an overarching concern for *lived* Christianity. His dual emphasis on "knowledge and vital piety" combined his unswerving commitment to the significance of scriptural truth in the believer's life (personal holiness) with his unswerving commitment to the centrality of *communal* practices of a lived faith in the church's life and mission (social holiness). Although Wesley read widely and wrote ceaselessly, he never published a theological "magnum opus." Instead Wesley embedded his theology of God in his sermons and tracts, in his notes on Scripture and in his copious correspondence with his colleagues, congregants and critics. Wesley discussed theology in everyday terms, highlighting the concrete difference that being a follower of Jesus *should and could* make in one's life. Wesley considered theology a matter of "practical" or "experimental divinity." Do not confuse Wesley's use of the term *experimental* with our notion of hypothesis testing. Think more of *experiential* than experimental. A notation in the Wesley Study Bible provides this comment on John Wesley's use of experience:

> John Wesley's theology, while grounded in Scripture, grew from experience—his and that of others. In the Church of England during Wesley's time, Christians drew upon three sources to discern questions of faith and life: Scripture, tradition (particularly the early history of the church), and reason. To these three, Wesley added, or at least emphasized, experience as a source, highlighting awareness of God's presence and work in the lives of individuals.[14]

Contemporary Wesleyan scholar Ken Collins clarifies that for Wesley "experimental or practical divinity is participatory and engaging. It entails nothing less than the actualization and verification of the truths of Scripture with respect to inward religion (by grace through faith) within the context of the Christian community."[15] Wesley longed for people to experience the *objective reality* of God's amazing love for humanity as revealed to us through the living Word (Jesus Christ) and the written Word (the Bible), and as made known to us through the Holy Spirit. When people received God's love, transformation happened—God's love spilling over in the lives of ordinary men and women in acts of love for their neighbor as a testimony to and as a result of their love for God.

Wesley's emphasis on *practical* divinity is a good fit for theologically reflective counseling. Counseling is one avenue through which Christian mental health professionals can assist others in the process of opening their lives more fully to God *by helping them remove the barriers*

that get in their way of receiving and sharing God's love. We typically refer
to those barriers as counseling goals. Counselors are *specialists in applied
sanctification* when they help Christian clients to conform their lives
more closely to the image of God. To borrow a Wesleyan term, counseling can function as a *means of grace*, a process through which God
can pour God's love into human lives.[16]

The "early Methodists did not emphasize beliefs that differed from
other Christian traditions."[17] Like John Calvin (1509–1564), Wesley
believed that theology was meant to affect the extent to which Christians were able to love God and others *in this lifetime*. And like Calvin,
Wesley called people to repent of their sins, receive God's forgiveness
through the cross of Jesus Christ and to be filled with the Holy Spirit.
Wesley was keenly interested in people experiencing the assurance of
salvation in their life *and* conforming their life to the heart of God (and
not the world [Rom 12:1-2]).[18] However, unlike Calvin, Wesley never got
around to organizing his theological teaching in a systematic way (e.g.,
Calvin's *Institutes of the Christian Religion*). Instead Wesley liberally
wove theology into his sermons, hymns and many letters. He was so
steeped in theology and biblical study that it oozed out when he responded to everyday questions from parishioners. Thinking theologically was as natural to Wesley as breathing. And while we would expect
this kind of theological fluency of clergy (like Wesley), my hope is that
Christians who counsel would aspire to a greater degree of "theological
fluency" after reading this book.

In each chapter ahead I develop a section on theological concepts
that resonate with clinical concerns. I dip into Wesley's writings at this
point. Christians are theologically situated in the same way that they
are culturally situated. And unless you work in a theological setting
(such as a church or seminary) few of us have had the time or resources
or opportunity or obligation to heighten our awareness of the roots of
our theological beliefs and to see how these roots shape our theology.
So rather than offer you only "generic Christianity" in the theological
sections, I model how a particular theological starting point brings
richness to clinical thinking.

I certainly have not arrived—that is, I am not "bilingual." But I have been working on increasing my theological "vocabulary" and "conversational skills"—personally and clinically. To give you an idea of what this looks like in therapy, I include a section on theological reflection in the chapters that focus on application (chaps. 3-7). In these sections I explore theological foundations in general and highlight some Wesleyan perspectives in particular. This explicit use of theology may be a new experience for some readers, and John Wesley is one theologian who does not usually get much "air time" in Christian counseling texts. Trust me, I am not trying you convert you to Wesleyanism! Instead, I am trying to demonstrate how one's theology does shape counseling. So when you come across a theological concept that is new to you or newly framed, I invite you to name and to consider what your own particular theological understandings are and to reflect on how they may influence your work with clients, especially Christian clients.

My second goal is to present a process model for theologically reflective counseling that will help you to bring theological insights into your work with clients. This model is not based in any specific theological tradition, nor is it attached to any particular theory of counseling. However, one's openness to the work of the Holy Spirit, one's own spiritual formation and one's theological, ethical and therapeutic commitments are essential prerequisites for its implementation. I will discuss each of these components more fully in a later section of this chapter. In many respects the model might be considered a type of *meta*model of integrative counseling. I have based the therapeutic scaffolding for it on a common-factors model for couples and family counseling developed by Sean D. Davis.[19] What is new is the way that this metamodel, which Davis applied to systemic therapy, provides means for the practical integration of theology into counseling. The model does not dictate the specific therapeutic moves one makes. Instead, it highlights general therapeutic processes that become avenues through which you may hear a client's presenting problem, frame that problem in light of salient theological categories or themes, and bring those theological reflections to bear upon in the client's work (with the client's permission). In chapters three through seven I highlight selected therapeutic issues that resonate with theological categories and show you how I would apply the model to these client concerns.

A PEEK INTO THE EDUCATIONAL PROCESS FOR CHRISTIAN PRACTITIONERS

Christians pursue training as professional counselors, social workers, marriage and family therapists, psychologists and so on. The skills for theologically reflective counseling in any of these allied fields often begin in one's master's program. I knew what I had experienced as a master of arts student and I knew what we did at Asbury Theological Seminary to help our counseling students to become theologically reflective practitioners. I was curious to know how other counselor education programs taught their students how to do "on the ground" theological integration. A few years ago I had the privilege of interviewing faculty and students at seven Christian institutions of higher education (universities or seminaries) that offer master of arts degrees in counseling or marriage and family therapy.[20] I asked faculty how they defined *integration* and how they went about teaching students to be integrative practitioners. I asked students where they experienced integration in their counseling program, how they learned how to do integrative counseling, and what additional educational experiences they would like to have before graduation.

Common teaching strategies emerged from my interviews. Counseling faculty offered prayer and devotional readings in the classroom. Instructors used these practices to heighten students' awareness of the presence of God in their midst as a way to model integration.[21] The counseling students I interviewed identified these as important practices in their own spiritual development. Professors assigned textbooks which had been written by other Christian mental health professionals that combined theology and psychology. Faculty engaged students in theological reflection through classroom discussion and written course assignments. This gave students an opportunity to stretch their theological wings prior to working directly with clients. By and large, counselor education faculty affirmed that practicum and internship were critical locations for learning practical integration skills. Discussion

about on-the-ground integration took place in on-campus practicum/
internship group supervision as program faculty reviewed students'
counseling audio or video tapes. Research by Randall Sorensen and
colleagues supports the importance of personal relationship with
mentors who model integration for counselors who are developing integration skills.[22] Faculty also acknowledged that the integrative skill
levels of the onsite practicum or internship supervisors varied greatly,
and that the students who had field placements in secular settings had
little or no opportunity to practice overt integration on site.

Differences in programs surfaced. While all counseling programs
tracked students' clinical development, two of the schools had additional processes in place to mentor students' personal and spiritual formation. Although all programs claimed that they wove integrative perspectives throughout students' counselor education program, some
schools offered a specific course on the integration of theology and
counseling. At seminary-based counselor education programs students
were required to take courses in biblical studies, theology and church
history (the seminary equivalent to general education courses). Seminary-based counseling faculty relied on these courses to introduce students to the content they would need from these disciplines so the students had something more to integrate than what they brought with
them into their program. Nevertheless, seminary-based counselor edu-
cators acknowledged that in spite of these course requirements, students' ability to build bridges between theology and clinical practice
was rudimentary at best.

Differences among students also emerged. Entry-level students had
a dissimilar picture of integration than graduating students. New students longed for less theory and theology, and more specific how-tos.
They wanted to know how to explicitly integrate Christian beliefs and
practices with counseling. Their desire for more distinctly Christian
counseling interventions was most likely a reflection of their level of
professional development.[23] More advanced students voiced an inter-
nalized process of integration and were more likely to report that integration happened "within the person of the counselor." These students
had moved from a focus on explicit "Christian" strategies to a concen-

tration on an implicit embodiment of theological realities in terms of *who they were* as counselors and in *how they related* to clients. This represents a shift in emphasis from an accumulation of *Christian information* to the personal and *spiritual formation of the therapist*. These findings reflect those reported by M. Elizabeth Lewis Hall and colleagues. These researchers conducted a qualitative study to discern student perspectives on integration. They discovered that integration was facilitated through a caring, open-minded faculty, the intentional inclusion of integration within the curriculum, and an institutional climate that modeled the integration of faith and learning. Students embraced integration as a concept through its presentation as propositional content, as an embodied reality and as a practice.[24]

One thing that stood out to me throughout these conversations was that little, if any, theological reading, *written by theologians*, arose as an important ingredient in counseling courses on the master's level. Two explanations for this come to mind. First, I can testify to the difficulty of finding theologically oriented books to use in counseling courses that were (1) written by a theologian, and (2) readily understandable by my nontheologian counseling students.[25] Theology has its own language and style of presentation, and many of my counseling students find theology books difficult to digest (not impossible, just more challenging than their counseling books). Second, sophisticated integration demands that one develop expertise in three disciplines: counseling theories/techniques, theology, and biblical studies. Counseling faculty would love to include additional course work in theology and biblical studies within their degree plans, but they find this just about impossible to do. Within a sixty-semester-hour degree plan, state licensure requirements may account for all sixty hours—and theology and biblical studies courses are not on state licensure boards' radar screens.[26] Students want to become skilled counselors, eligible for licensure. They do not necessarily see themselves as theologians even though they want to become Christian counselors. This places the burden for growing in theological sophistication upon the graduate.

I acknowledge that my institutional sample was small (N = 7) and confined to master's level programs. The schools that I visited were not obscure institutions of Christian higher education but schools that tend to be well-known and well-respected in the Christian counseling and psychology community. Nonetheless, these conclusions must be held lightly until further study supports or challenges them. The bottom line: Academic preparation provides a *baseline* for theological reflection and integration. Implication: To develop greater proficiency, counselors need to read theology *after* graduation, and they need a process for transferring theological insights into clinical practice.

WHAT KIND OF THEOLOGIAN ARE YOU BECOMING?

Perhaps one of the reasons why theology is not more fully embraced (and studied) by counseling professionals is that they may not have developed a large enough picture of theology's sweeping landscape.[27] That certainly would have been my story. My counseling professors during my master's program clearly were theologically proficient (the majority having seminary education), but I did not know *what theological source material* they drew upon to construct the models that were presented in class. I learned the models but not their process for bridging the gap between the disciplines of theology and psychology. The only theology I had been introduced to formally in my counselor training was systematic theology, and in my myopic view that boiled down to the memorization of doctrine. What I had not remembered was the classic definition of theology: *faith seeking understanding.* This is indeed what many clients struggle to do when they are angry at or disappointed in God.[28] So my restricted definition of theology limited my interest in learning more.

Today I have a broader picture of theology, its purpose and its tasks. For example, Stanley Grenz and Roger Olson define theology in this way: "Christian theology is reflecting on and articulating the God-centered life and beliefs that Christians share as followers of Jesus Christ, and it is done in order that God may be glorified in all Christians are and do."[29] Christian theology has a particular content (God and the God-centered life) that is derived from particular source materials (the Bible, church history and Christian traditions) for particular purposes (so that God may be glorified through the way that Christ's followers live). In the broadest sense, *theology shapes who we are and how we live* by helping us to better understand who God is and how we can live together as members of God's family in this world that God created and loves. Missiologist Andrew Walls offers this insightful summation:

> Theology springs out of mission; its true origins lie not in the study or the library, but from the need to make Christian decisions—decisions about what to do, and about what to think. Theology is the attempt to think in a Christian way, to make Christian intellectual choices. Its subject matter, therefore, its agenda, is culturally conditioned, arising out of the actual life situations of active Christians.[30]

Walls's definition highlights the dynamic relationship between theological reflection and Christian living—*real life* is the context out of which a practical theology arises. To help our Christian clients make Christian decisions about "what to do and what to think," counselors need to be able to think theologically.

Grenz and Olson describe theology's two tasks. The first is a *critical* task. Theology analyzes and appraises existing beliefs about God, humanity and the world in light of the biblical message and historic Christian traditions.[31] Some of these beliefs are affirmed by orthodox Christians throughout the ages, while others become salient to one denomination but not another. This is the stuff of systematic theology and doctrine—to which I had been exposed in my master's education. However, theology has a second *constructive* task. This is the "how shall we then live" side of theology. And this is the task that connects so well to theologically reflective counseling. It is theology that speaks to one's present situation, which helps to connect what we believe with how we should live as the people of God during our times of trouble in our various culturally bounded contexts. This makes theological reflection relevant to people in the culture they live in, and it allows Christian truths to challenge and change the very culture it speaks to. Mark D. Baker and Joel B. Green clarify this task as follows: "The theological task is in some ways a balancing act, in which we are asked to go beyond the insights of Scripture in order to address ever-unfolding challenges while at the same time ensuring that our extensions of the biblical witness are consonant with the central insights of Scripture."[32] This is a description of what we do as Christian counselors when we consider how theologically oriented clinical conversations may help *this* client who lives in *this* cultural setting at *this* period of time (historically and developmentally), bringing spiritual and theological resources to bear on their specific presenting problem so that Christian truths have an opportunity to challenge those aspects of clients' lives which need to be addressed.

Grenz and Olson also offer a continuum of theological thinking. Points on the continuum include folk theology, lay theology, ministerial theology, professional theology and academic theology. As you read the description of each following point, consider where you currently place yourself along this continuum, and then ask where you might like to place yourself.

At the most basic level is *folk theology*. The folk theologian is highly experiential, subjective, pragmatic and avoids serious theological reflection in favor of simplistic faith formulas. Think of this as "bumper sticker theology." The hallmark of this type of theology is an unswerving commitment to informal spiritual beliefs that can be boiled down to a slogan or sound bite, and a resistance or reluctance to holding these beliefs up to critical examination. Folk theology is not necessarily bad theology. The pithy sayings that weave their way throughout folk theology can be very helpful in certain situations. The spiritual motto "Let go and let God" can help a client to release their cares into God's keeping (1 Pet 5:7). And during times of trouble or emotional turmoil these elementary concepts may ground us in God. I have used the image of being held in the palm of God's hand as a source of comfort and strength (Is 49:16) when I felt like my life was out of control, and I have often repeated to myself my favorite crisis-management Bible verse "And it came to pass . . ." (Lk 2:1 NKJV) to remind myself of the temporary nature of crises (very sophisticated theology—wouldn't you say?).

All of us start out as folk theologians. Folk theology begins in our childhood.[33] These early experiences become part of our "implicit theological memory" when as children we observe, experience and

wonder about the world. If we were raised in Christian faith communities, then we experienced the stories and practices of our church
family, which embedded Christian theology in one's bones through
family participation in a local church. A growing proportion of the
population lacks this kind of experience in our increasingly post-
Christian world. At some point we embraced the Christian faith as our
own and now seek to live in ways that are characteristic of God's redeemed people. Experiences in adulthood then expand our implicit
memory, and exposure to Christian teaching enlarges our explicit theological memory. This combination of implicit and explicit theology
helps to shape the kind of Christian people we become. In contexts
where we have easy access to Christian literature, we have print and
multimedia resources at our fingertips to help us deepen our understanding of the Christian life as we interact with members of a Christian
community. This is the typical case in most areas of developed cultures
(like the United States), but it is certainly not so in all parts of the
world. In some developing cultures, printed Christian resources are
either not available (not translated into their language) or not readily
accessible (translated but expensive). In other contexts the Christian
message is primarily shared orally. In oral-based cultures folk theology
takes its cues from direct observation of nature and the rhythm of the
seasons. So in addition to a normal reluctance or resistance to critical
examination of their faith is an inability to do so because of a lack of
exposure to the more Western style of analysis and logic.[34]

Thank God that growth in grace is not dependent on one's reading
level! Some of us know saints who never learned how to read or never
mastered reading well but who know God intimately, are full of wisdom
and are open channels for the Holy Spirit's work. They are the pillars
of their local Christian community. Their theological education is
based on lived theology, a hunger to know God more deeply and a
desire to live a life more fully aligned with God's purposes. These saints
take advantage of the Christian resources that are available to them
(e.g., guest preachers, radio programs, etc.). Unfortunately, because the
printed Bible may not be available or accessible, they also do not have
an opportunity to compare what they are hearing with the written

Word for themselves (individually and communally), and thereby they may not identify misdirected or even false teaching about God and the Christian life.

Many of our clients are likely to function as folk theologians. Their theological boat *may* be rocking when they call for an appointment. These clients may be like the disciples in Mark 4 who experienced the storm at sea, woke up a sleeping Jesus and asked him, "Teacher, do you not care that we are perishing?" (Mk 4:38). In such cases, folk theology may turn out to be inadequate. The collision of unexplainable suffering with folk theology drives many Christians to doubt their faith. Is the counselor's theological foundation *thick* enough to provide a holding environment for clients during periods of spiritual disequilibrium? Is the counselor's theology *complex* enough to embrace life's relentless ambiguities? Is the counselor *secure* enough in his or her own faith development to allow that counselor to be with the client as the client wrestles with God—without the counselor feeling compelled to defend God or to fix the client's theological perspective?

The next point on the theological continuum is *lay theology*. Lay theologians study theological resources. They are proficient at asking important questions about what, why and in whom they believe, and they are willing to name and face the theological cognitive dissonance that surfaces between what they believe and how they live. Counselors who aspire to the level of lay theology will read books written by other Christian counselors *and* books written by theologians who are engaged in theology's constructive task. This latter reading will require the Christian counselor to build therapeutic bridges between this theology and the practice of counseling.

Next is *ministerial theology*. The ministerial theologian embodies the same commitment to theological reflection as the lay theologian. The difference is that ministerial theologians have received formal training in theology and biblical studies. Ministerial theology understands how theological thinking has developed over time. Ministerial theologians are familiar with biblical languages and their study tools, and know the categories and vocabulary typically used in theological books.

The final two levels, *professional theology* and *academic theology*, are more indicative of individuals whose life work is theological writing and teaching. Professional and academic theologians serve the church by providing the kind of resources that Christian counselors will use to increase their capacities to think theologically and to live a more Christ-centered life.

As you can see, the depth of explicit theological knowledge increases as one moves along the continuum. Most of us began our counselor education as folk theologians with strong Christian commitments. Course work that included theological resources helped us to attain lay theologian status at the time of our graduation. After graduation a portion of us may have pursued additional theological education through additional study. Yet the mere accumulation of theological facts is not enough for solid theologically reflective counseling. And while I am proposing that knowing and understanding explicit theology is important, I am also affirming that there is *more* to theologically reflective counseling than that. As Coe and Hall suggest in their book *Psychology in the Spirit*, theologically reflective counseling challenges us to become increasingly vivid and vibrant representatives of God's love with our clients, through who we are (implicit theology) and what we know (explicit theology).

Borrowing from the literature on critical thinking, Christian counselors can employ weak-sense or strong-sense theological thinking. Weak-sense theological thinking sees the world in fairly clear shades of black and white. Right action is always easy to identify, and sinful action is always easy to name. Theological ambiguity does not exist. Weak-sense theological thinking culminates in a caricature of biblically based counseling—a "take two verses and call me in the morning" approach to weaving God's truth into troubled human hearts. Integration is as straightforward as lining up specific Scripture verses to match particular life needs, based on an assumption that if a client knows what is right according to the Bible, the client will obey.

Several problems exist with weak-sense theological thinking. First, knowing Scripture doesn't necessarily lead to obedience. Human beings are expert in self-justification, and our ability to rationalize known sin is outstanding.[35] Second, weak-sense theological thinking fails to recognize that people engage Scripture from particular social locations, and that this cultural situatedness influences how we understand God and interpret Scripture. It may assume that the counselor's theology is right and other theological perspectives are wrong. Finally, weak-sense theological thinking may fail to recognize the theological position from which one *is* counseling, so it becomes a hidden theological bias. As you may have surmised, weak-sensed theological thinking can happen at any point along the theological continuum and can result in the indiscriminate dispensing of theological information and advice within a counseling session.

In contrast one can engage in strong-sense theological reflection. Here one is aware of a broad range of theological positions, topics and perspectives. One is relatively articulate about one's theological home base and can state why one affirms these theological truths. At the same time a curiosity exists about different theological positions and how theologians wrestle with the kind of contemporary issues that clients bring to counseling. Strong-sense theological reflection is cognizant of tendencies toward theological egocentrism and ethnocentrism, and seeks to correct these inclinations through open-minded dialogue with others. Strong-sense theological reflection acts as one lens through which a counselor sees a client's story, while concurrently listening for the theological framework in which the client placed his or her narrative. One only needs to swallow whole the position of a perceived authority to maintain weak-sense theological thinking. Developing strong-sense theological thinking requires a willingness to tolerate theological disequilibrium as one moves from theological assimilation (making theological round pegs fit into square holes) to theological accommodation (creating new categories to allow for the newly encountered theological pegs). It unfolds through study *and* formative interactions with others. These reflective experiences (intellectual, interpersonal and experiential) can foster Christian spiritual and moral growth.[36]

So far I have proposed that the clinical formation and competency of many Christian counselors outstrips their theological formation and competency. While the reasons for this are understandable (limited space in master's programs, the press for clinical mastery after graduation, limited opportunity for integrative theological reflection after graduation, etc.), this renders counselors vulnerable to weak-sense theological thinking in their work with clients regardless of their location on Grenz and Olson's theological continuum. Four additional factors compel me to urge Christian counselors to commit to ongoing theological reflection. Let's look at each of these factors.

Evaluating systems of therapy. One uses theology when evaluating the degree to which secular systems of therapy align with a Christian worldview. If you received your counselor education at a Christian institution of higher education, then like me you most likely relied on your course texts or your professors to help you determine the degree to which various counseling approaches were compatible with Christianity.[37] With new systems of therapy emerging since graduation, you have to rely on your own understanding of theology to evaluate the degree to which these new approaches fit with a Christian worldview. For example, what theological conclusions have you drawn about mindfulness interventions? On the other hand, if you received your counselor education at a secular institution, then it is unlikely that any theological appraisal was presented by your professors. If spiritual or religious concerns were addressed in your counselor education program, then Christianity was most likely presented within your course on cultural diversity along with other world religions. In this course it was more likely that Christianity *was evaluated* than it was that Christianity served as a source or standard of evaluation.[38] Theology is also useful when you evaluate approaches to *Christian* counseling. Solid theological reflection will help you to determine if you concur with the theological premises that underlie various approaches to Christian counseling.[39]

Establishing professional competency. Professional competency is the second reason for sustained theological reflection. All professional ethics codes (e.g., AAMFT, ACA, APA and state licensure ethics sections) require that therapists work within the scope of their training. Many states also require that counselors display a professional disclosure statement in their offices that includes a list of the areas they are competent to practice in. *Competency*, however, is a vague term. If you were required to justify to a licensure board that you are competent in a particular area, what would you do? Documentation of academic course work, consultation or supervision with expert colleagues, and continuing education units are some of the ways one might substantiate one's competency.[40] What level of theological competency is necessary for one to offer counseling that is Christian? Clients are assured that licensed mental health professionals have met certain standards about therapeutic proficiency, but no such standard assures clients of the counselor's theological proficiency.[41]

Employing theological empathy. Third, theology is part of our work because we are *Christians* who counsel. According to Grenz and Olson, we step into theological arenas whenever we discuss questions of ultimacy. This includes questions about God, ultimate meaning and life's purpose. While few clients seek out licensed professional counselors, marriage and family therapists, social workers, or psychologists to discuss their questions about God (pastoral counselors may see this more often), many clients' concerns revolve around issues of meaning and purpose. Earlier in this chapter I defined theology's two tasks: critical and constructive. We engage in the *constructive* task of theology as we work with theologically tinted therapeutic problems. When theological themes are on the clinical table, Christian counselors and clients seek to discern what God is saying about this *particular* issue to this *particular* client at this *particular* time. The goal is to bring theological reflection to bear upon the client's clinical concerns *in collaboration* with the client.

Engaging in theological discernment. A counselor is not the only one in a counseling session with theological convictions. Christian clients bring their theological perspectives with them. Sometimes their theology helps them to cope. At other times their theology may be toxic. Ronnie Janoff-Bulman observes that when our fundamental beliefs about life collide with our experiences, we are thrown into an emotional tailspin.[42] We can no longer account for what has happened to us with our present understanding, and the result is shattered theological assumptions. Take the couple struggling with infertility. They may ask, "Why does God let women, who abort their babies, get pregnant and we can't?" Or consider the clients who are suffering with clinical symptoms related to childhood sexual abuse. They might demand to know, "Where was this loving God of yours when I was being molested?" At appropriate moments, counselors can use theological reflection to help clients explore how clients' theology is interacting with their presenting problem. According to Grenz and Olson,

> Whatever it may look like, our interpretive framework comprises our fundamental belief system and constitutes our basic theology. Our belief system—our theology—therefore, stands in a reciprocal relationship to life. Theological convictions lead us to look at life the way we do and to experience the world as we do. Our life experiences, in turn, bring our theological convictions into the picture and cause us to reexamine, reevaluate and even revise our convictions about God, ourselves, and our world. . . . In the theological enterprise we consciously bring to light the interaction between beliefs and experiences. This includes exploring our beliefs in the light of our experiences. More importantly, it entails discovering the implications of that belief system for how we look at, live in, and experience the world.[43]

We bring our theological convictions into the session. What you believe about human nature and God's grace has an impact on the kind of therapist you are, the kind of therapy you offer and the kind of meaning that you make of life's trials and tribulations. Your explicit and implicit theology becomes one lens through which you view the client's world. You draw upon these foundations as you walk beside the client toward mental or relational wholeness. I believe that it is possible for Christians who counsel to be therapeutically and *theologically* competent. It may mean that some will choose to take academic courses in theology, while others will read and study on their own. For all of us it means that we are participating in a Christian community that will challenge us to live more Christianly, where theology becomes embodied in real life when emotions *and* reason are engaged.[44]

PREREQUISITES FOR THEOLOGICALLY
REFLECTIVE COUNSELING

While becoming more theologically literate is an important aspect of integrative counseling, knowledge alone does not an integrative counselor make. *Who the counselor is,* is just as important, and this is reflected in the kind of commitments that the Christian counselor brings into the session. Our spiritual, theological and therapeutic commitments provide the delivery mechanisms for theologically reflective counseling (see fig. 1.1).[45]

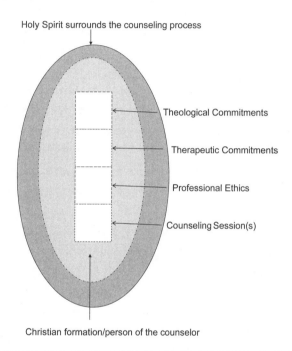

Holy Spirit surrounds the counseling process

Theological Commitments

Therapeutic Commitments

Professional Ethics

Counseling Session(s)

Christian formation/person of the counselor

Figure 1.1. Prerequisites for theologically reflective counseling

Commitment to the ministry of the Holy Spirit. The Holy Spirit surrounds the counseling enterprise. When Christians counsel, the Holy Spirit precedes them into the counseling room. No human counselor can be more interested in a client's well-being than the wonderful Counselor, the Holy Spirit. Christian counselors respond to the presence of the Spirit in their personal lives, rely on the Spirit's support and guidance in their work lives, and remain open vessels through which the Spirit of God can work as they recognize God's fingerprints in their clients' circumstances. Theologically, we would say that it is all God's grace that truly heals. Like the great theologians before him,

Wesley acknowledged and affirmed the priority of God's grace in our lives—captured in Wesley's concept of "prevenient grace." Prevenient grace is the grace from God that prepares the way for God's work in God's world, particularly God's work in human hearts. This grace "comes before any knowledge of God and informs our ability to know right from wrong and recognize sin."[46] Prevenient grace prepares Christian clients for God's intervention in the counseling process.[47] When Christian counselors work with clients who are not followers of Jesus, prevenient grace is still at work, wooing the client to take one step closer to the one true God.

Commitment to Christian formation. In biblical terms, here is where Christian counselors "go on toward perfection [maturity]" by ingesting "solid [spiritual] food," so that their faculties are "trained by practice to distinguish good from evil" (Heb 5:14; 6:1). Notice how this mandate from the book of Hebrews combines explicit and implicit theological formation. It includes a foundation of basic teaching (Heb 6:1-2) or explicit theological knowledge, and the subsequent indwelling of this knowledge (training by practice) in one's being so that a particular kind of fruit (discernment) is exercised at the appropriate time—a manifestation of implicit theology. This Christian formation happens within a communal context ("let *us* go on toward perfection" [Heb 6:1]) in which all are pressing on for a greater capacity to love God and love others ("the love that you showed for his sake in serving the saints" [Heb 6:10]).

Discipleship is one church word for this Christian formation process. If you are in Christ and are part of God's new creation (2 Cor 5:17), then you may also desire to have more of yourself transformed to Christlikeness (Rom 12:2); if you are "putting away" hurtful ways of relating to God and others and are putting on "the new self, created according to the likeness of God in true righteousness and holiness" (Eph 4:24), then you are engaging in processes of Christian formation. This is a lifelong process which brings explicit and implicit theology into alignment so that our lives are increasingly a fuller expression of Christlikeness. Explicit theology helps us to know intellectually the foundations of our faith. When we engage in thoughtful reflection on our experiences we grow attuned to the (in)congruence between biblical and theological precepts and our way of being (implicit theology). Ideally this ongoing cycle of action and reflection happens privately and communally.

Individual theological commitments. Theology provides a basic understanding of God and humanity that is foundational for all counseling work. The Bible and our theology help us to understand God's design for human beings and their relationships. They identify the human problem and how humans can change. Christian mental health professionals will differ on the depth of theological resources on which to draw. This component may be quite thin if the counselor is a folk theologian, has little understanding of the Bible or has done little theological study beyond what is available in the popular Christian press. On the other hand it may be quite rich if the counselor has invested time in theological and biblical study, and can function at the lay or ministerial theology level. I want to emphasize at this point that this model does not specify *which* specific theology one embraces. To that end the model is atheological, offering counselors an opportunity to ponder their own theological leanings (explicit theology) and to consider how these theological commitments may or may not influence their work with clients (implicit theology).

Individual therapeutic commitments. For most licensed professional counselors, clinical and counseling psychologists, marriage and family therapists and clinical social workers, this area is well developed. It may be less developed for those with little formal training in counseling, but who have a heart for helping hurting people in one-to-one settings (like lay counselors). Just as the model is atheological, it is also atheoretical. Plug in your preferred way of case conceptualization. At this point counselors can ask: What degree of congruency exists between my theology and my therapeutic commitments? Is there coherence between what I believe to be true about God and God's purpose for human relationships and how I work with clients? How do I navigate the tensions that inevitably arise between theological and therapeutic perspectives?

Professional ethical commitments. Counselors' skill in ethical decision making will vary depending upon (1) how counselors have matured in their moral formation, (2) how knowledgeable counselors are about specifics in their professional code of ethics, (3) how well-versed counselors are in thinking ethically about complex counseling cases, and (4) how competent counselors are to work with a client's presenting concern. Regarding the ethical use of explicitly Christian counseling theories and techniques, counselors must discern the following: Do clients ask for Christian counseling, giving consent for the use of Christian perspectives and interventions in their therapy? Do clients affirm a kind of global spirituality, desire spiritually informed counseling, but do not want counseling that is expressly Christian? Do clients reject the inclusion of religious or spiritual practices, including Christian practices, in which case counselors are limited to private theological reflection? These are salient questions if Christian counselors are to follow ethical counseling practices.

Practical implementation. All of one's Christian formation, theological reflection, clinical training and ethical decision making become the scaffolding that supports the session-by-session and moment-by-moment work with a client. Christian formation provides a perspective on persons and personhood that supports the Christian counselor's capacity to "be with" the client. The counselor is not intentionally wondering what theological point should be brought to bear on the client's problem. Instead, the counselor can lean into the Holy Spirit, trusting that the Spirit will do that which the Spirit does best—that is, seek for ways to remove whatever separates God from God's beloved child, the client. At this point the counselor's focus is on the client's presenting problem and the goals that are collaboratively developed to help this client meet the *client's* goals. Here is where the rubber meets the road, and the nitty-gritty of integration works itself out, implicitly and explicitly.

You will observe that the boundaries between the segments are permeable (see fig. 1.1). The degree of permeability determines the extent to which data can flow. Boundaries that are too closed prevent counselors from accessing implicit and explicit theological insights. Boundaries that are too porous result in indiscriminate and even inappropriate use of explicit theology in counseling. A counselor can start with theological hunches or insights, and then consider how they align with therapeutic inclinations, ethical commitments and ultimately contribute to shaping one's work with clients. Or a counselor might begin with the counseling session and work through the segments by reflecting on the ethical principles that affect a therapist's decisions and by seeking additional therapeutic and theological information. Table 1.1 presents questions that a therapist might use for theologically sensitive case conceptualization.

If there is coherence and congruity within the theologically reflective counselor, then one can imagine that the column will stand *relatively* straight, as pictured in figure 1.1. However, if a counselor's implicit and explicit theology has less connection with his or her therapy, then the segments may be askew. For counselors who have studied in faith-based counselor education programs, or for those who have sought supervision in integration, it is more likely that the segments of the column are in *relative* alignment. Conversely some counselors may have given little thought to how their theological commitments cohere (or do not cohere) with their approach to therapy.

In the following chapters I invite you to think about how *your* theological and therapeutic loyalties shape your work with clients. As I mentioned earlier, at times I will show you how my Wesleyan theological commitments inform my work from family systems, social justice and crisis counseling perspectives as examples. In chapter two I present a model of theologically reflective practice that takes into account the features that I named previously. In chapter three I explore how the connections between trinitarian theology and therapeutic common factors inform our work as theologically reflective practitioners. Chapters four through seven apply the model of theologically reflective practice to four clinical situations. Chapter four explores how personal holiness strengthens the counselor's ability to challenge clients to assume responsibility for self. Chapter five investigates how social holiness can provide a foundation for counseling as advocacy for social justice. Chapter six discusses how the atonement calls Christian clients to consider repentance, forgiveness and reconciliation in the face of interpersonal offenses. Finally chapter seven connects one's view of the end of all things (eschatology) with meaning-making in trauma counseling.

Table 1.1. Theologically Sensitive Case Conceptualization

Client-Presenting Concerns

1. What does an assessment of the client's spiritual/religious affinities reveal?
2. What has been the client's experience with Christianity in general and the local church or individual Christians in particular?
3. What Christian commitments does this client hold that can support his or her clinical work? How might these same commitments set up obstacles?

Ethical Commitments

1. To what degree does the client desire or expect explicit Christian intervention? Has the client given consent for the inclusion of spiritual/religious interventions or conversations?
2. What ethical concerns are present in this clinical situation? In what ways do my personal Christian commitments and the ethical principles of my professional affiliations coalesce or conflict? How will I model responsible and ethical practice with this client given the particulars of the situation?
3. Where am I called by the contours of this situation to act as an advocate on behalf of issues of social justice?

Therapeutic Commitments

1. What treatment approach will best serve the needs of this client?
2. What clinical practices will help clients meet their goals?
3. What spiritual/religious strategies will help this client meet his or her goals? Are they evidence-based approaches?[a]

Theological Commitments

1. Where might God be already at work in this client's life, especially within the context of the presenting problem?[b]
2. What theological themes relate to the client's counseling concerns?
3. What view of God does the client endorse? What does the client think about God's presence in the midst of his or her life as it relates to the presenting problem?
4. What Christian practices will help this client achieve his or her counseling goals and grow in Christian maturity?[c]
5. What characteristics of the client challenge my perception of this person as a child of God and a person of worth and tempt me to respond in ways that do not reflect the Spirit of God living in me?

---

[a]Joshua N. Hook et al., "Empirically Supported Religious and Spiritual Therapies," *Journal of Clinical Psychology* 66, no. 1 (2010): 46-72, doi:10.1002/jclp.20626.

[b]Howard Stone, "Theodicy in Pastoral Counseling," *Journal of Pastoral Psychotherapy* 1, no. 1 (1987): 47-62.

[c]Sharon E. Cheston, and Joanne L. Miller, "The Use of Prayer in Counseling," in *Integrating Spirituality and Religion into Counseling: A Guide to Competent Practice*, ed. Craig S. Cashwell and J. Scott Young, 2nd ed. (Alexandria, Va.: American Counseling Association, 2011), pp. 243-60; Chet Weld and Karen Eriksen, "Christian Clients' Preferences Regarding Prayer as a Counseling Intervention," *Journal of Psychology and Theology* 35 (Winter 2007): 328-41; Sherry Johnson, "One Step Closer: The Implicit Use of Scripture in Counseling (Clinicians' Columns)," *Journal of Psychology and Christianity* 20 (Spring 2001): 91-94; James B. Hurley and James T. Berry, "The Relation of Scripture and Psychology in Counseling from a Pro-Integration Position," *Journal of Psychology and Christianity* 16 (Winter 1997): 323-45.

A Metamodel of Theologically Reflective Counseling

To serve the present age,
  my calling to fulfill;
O may it all my powers engage
  to do my Master's will!

Arm me with jealous care,
  as in thy sight to live,
and oh, thy servant, Lord,
  prepare a strict account to give!

CHARLES WESLEY,
"A Charge to Keep I Have"

ANNA WAS ALWAYS THE LAST CLIENT OF THE DAY. She was a plain woman in her mid-thirties. She was working in a job for which she was appropriately educated but for which she was not particularly well-suited. She was employed as a high school math teacher—yet dealing with adolescents was definitely not her gift. She often described her daily work life as sheer torture. The students were disrespectful to her and she perceived the administration in her high school to be unsupportive of her. She loved the beauty of math and longed to work in a job where she could commune with her calculator instead of engage in daily combat with the students. She had no energy after school for any kind of a social life, so she was lonely. Even when she attended social functions, she arrived and left alone. She could never be described as the life of the party because she was busy filling her spot as a wall flower. Not surprisingly she was moderately depressed and anxious. She came for personal and career counseling because she wanted to make a change in her life.

Imagine what a typical counseling session with Anna might look like. If I were a fly on the wall, I could probably tell what *theoretical* orientation (e.g., psychodynamic, client-centered, cognitive-behavioral, family systems, narrative) Anna's counselor adopted by listening to how he or she interacted with Anna. However, the *theological* commitments that shape the counselor's work might be more difficult to discern. How can counselors and therapists draw upon theology in their work with clients in an ethically responsible way? I began this exploration in chapter one. Borrowing a definition of theology from Stanley Grenz and Roger Olson, I described Christian theology as that which results from "reflecting on and articulating the God-centered life and beliefs that Christians share as followers of Jesus Christ, and it is done in order that God may be glorified in all Christians are and do."[1] Theological reflection not only addresses the "what" of Christian beliefs (the critical task of theology), it also has power to shape daily living when Christians allow Scripture and theology to illuminate those areas where their life *is* conforming to the heart of God *and* to clarify those places where their life *is in tension* with the heart of God. Grenz and Olson identified this as the constructive task of theology. We join professional and academic theologians in their work on the critical task as we study the Bible with others and participate in a local church or small Christian discipleship group. We join them on the constructive task when we explore how theological truths relate to our clients' struggles. In order to show ourselves approved to do such work with clients (2 Tim 2:15), I suggested that counselors would benefit from lifelong theological formation and study. Later in this chapter I will present a metamodel of theologically reflective counseling. Before that, however, I want to take us on a quick tour through the history of integration. This quick side excursion will help us get the lay of the land as we move into integration in the twenty-first century.

A VERY BRIEF HISTORY OF INTEGRATION

Christian counselors and psychotherapists have been pondering the ins and outs of integration for quite some time. In the late nineteenth century, when modernism became a predominant worldview, psycho-analysis, the first force in psychology, emerged as the treatment of choice for emotional problems. Prior to that time, distressed people sought the counsel of the pastor or priest. Now they went to their analyst instead. "Soul care" became secularized and was no longer under the exclusive jurisdiction of local clergy. In the early twentieth century behaviorism ascended in prominence (especially in the United States) as the second force in psychology. Behaviorists considered non-observable influences (such as thoughts, emotions and spiritual matters) to be inappropriate variables for empirical psychological study. The gap between psychology/counseling and spirituality widened. By the middle of the twentieth century counselors working from secular humanistic perspectives argued for the centrality of clients' inner life (those nonobservables) and cast aside schedules of reinforcement in favor of techniques that promoted self-actualization and self-awareness. Humanism became the third force in psychology. From a philosophical perspective these three approaches—psychoanalysis, behaviorism and humanism—offered worldviews that competed with Christianity.[2] From a practical perspective they contributed to the exclusion of spiritual content from counseling. The gold standard was a counselor whose work was value-free, and since religious content was value-laden it was deemed inappropriate therapeutic material. During the final decades of the twentieth century counselors working from feminist and multicultural perspectives successfully challenged the profession's belief in value-neutral therapy. Multiculturalism arose as counseling's fourth force.[3] Ethical counseling practice now demanded that counselors give due attention to the impact of race, ethnicity, gender, social status, sexual orientation and so forth, on all aspects of human development. With this clinical turn toward diversity, the door was opened to (re)admit religion/spirituality into the counseling room. To aid therapists in this integrative effort, the American Psychological Association (APA) and the American Counseling Association (ACA) have published texts showing *how to* integrate spirituality and religion into counseling. Spirituality has been named the fifth force in counseling within the ranks of the American Counseling Association.[4]

Christianity has its own version of an integration story.[5] As previously noted, congregants have sought the help of pastors to deal with emotional and spiritual problems from the beginning of church history. This practice continued even as professional psychology and counseling arose as distinct disciplines in the helping professions in the nineteenth and twentieth centuries. Nevertheless as professional counseling practices grew in popularity and accessibility during the latter half of the twentieth century, Christian people began to seek help from secular licensed counseling professionals, especially when their emotional and psychological concerns exceeded their pastor's skill. Given the values-free stance of many secular therapists (if not outright antireligious attitudes), many Christians were leery of secular counselors. However God called gifted Christians into professional psychology and counseling. These individuals who had been trained as psychologists, psychiatrists and professional counselors resisted the secular separation of spirituality and counseling. Beginning in the mid-1950s individuals who were committed to Jesus Christ and trained in the helping professions wrestled with questions like: Can theology and psychology be integrated? Should theology and psychology be integrated? And if they can and if they should be integrated then, What does integration look like? Three contrasting perspectives on integration arose.[6] Nonintegrationists rejected secular counseling theories and denounced the integration of psychology and theology. They believed that the Bible was a *necessary and sufficient* resource to meet clients' psychological and emotional needs. Moderate positions combine theological and psychological insights but they differ in terms of which discipline (theology or psychology) defined the territory, and how material from the secondary discipline would be incorporated into the first. A third group of Christian mental health professionals included those who promoted the full integration of psychology/counseling and theology. They believed that these disciplines could be woven together with integrity because all truth is God's truth. I place myself within this third category.

While a nonintegrationist voice continues to exist in the therapeutic community (broadly defined), the Zeitgeist is integration. Mental health professionals who profess Jesus as Lord *and* those who do not are writing about how to include spirituality and religion in counseling in ethically appropriate ways.[7] Of particular interest for my purposes are the resources for Christian counseling professionals. At least two peer-review journals exist to disseminate theoretical discussions and empirical research about the integration of psychology/counseling and theology (*Journal of Psychology and Christianity* and *Journal of Psychology and Theology*). Moreover, Christian scholars have developed texts that review and evaluate secular theories and techniques from Christian perspectives.[8] Furthermore, Christian practitioners have produced books to help Christians counsel from psychodynamic, relational cognitive-behavioral and family systems perspectives, or to consider integration from particular theological viewpoints.[9] This work follows in those footsteps. Rather than presenting a model that frames integration from *specific* theological or therapeutic homes, I offer a metamodel of theologically reflective process that encourages counselors to be more keenly aware of the theological threads that are woven into clients' lives and that *may be* followed in their subsequent work with clients. It also encourages counselors to become more sensitive to the interaction between their own theological-therapeutic commitments and those of their clients.

BECOMING A THEOLOGICALLY REFLECTIVE COUNSELOR

Bringing theological reflection into one's work requires a fourfold focus: (1) the *preparation* of the counselor—the degree to which counselors are theologically and therapeutically formed; (2) the *person* of the counselor—the ways that counselors embody their theological commitments through virtuous Christian character; (3) an awareness of the *presence* of the Holy Spirit; and (4) the *practice* of the counselor—how counselors work with clients in session therapeutically and ethically.

The preparation of the counselor. Preparatory work for theologically reflective counseling happens outside of the counseling session in two ways: (1) through formal or informal study of theology, the Bible and counseling theories and techniques, and (2) through participation in theologically formative communities. When counselors dedicate time to becoming well-enough versed in theology, biblical study and counseling practices, including professional ethics, then they have the raw data of integration. The counselors that I know who represent the best of theologically reflective practice are committed lifelong learners. They are willing to learn the specialized language of theologians and biblical scholars, in effect becoming "bilingual." They want to strengthen their theological muscles as well as their therapeutic ones. These counselors are also embedded in communities that help them live more fully as members in God's family so that they "talk the talk" and "walk the walk" Christianly (participation in local Christian community/church) and therapeutically (participation in supervision and in conversation with other mental health professionals).[10]

The person of the counselor. As I alluded to in the previous paragraphs, theology does not just reside in the heads of theologically reflective practitioners. It gets into their hearts. They become shaped by the Word of God (biblical studies) and words written about God (theological studies). Within the context of a local Christian community the practice of Christian being and living is shaped and affirmed. N. T. Wright puts it like this: "Being trained to think 'Christianly' is the necessary antidote to what will otherwise happen: being, as Paul says, 'squeezed into the shape dictated by the present age'" (referring to Rom 12:2).[11] It does little good to "talk the talk" in therapy when counselors cannot also "walk the walk." Philosopher Michael Polanyi refers to this in-your-bones data as tacit knowledge.[12] Tacit knowledge "indwells" you and is expressed through your beliefs and behaviors. You rely on this in-your-bones theology as you attend to your client. That is, you are not wracking your brain to find some theological sound bite that applies to your client. Instead you are spiritually formed to be fully present with the client. At just the right time, from the depths of your theological tacit knowledge, insights emerge that are just right for this clinical situation. What Polanyi identifies as inspiration grounded in tacit knowledge, Christian counselors know as the ministry of the Holy Spirit.

Presence of the Holy Spirit. While counselors need explicit consent from clients to work with spiritual and/or religious themes, the Holy Spirit needs no permission to work in clients' lives. The Holy Spirit of God superintends the Christian counselor's work. The Spirit goes before the counselor into the counseling office, is present with the counselor during the session, and goes with the client when the session ends. The Holy Spirit can empower counselors to speak hard-to-hear truth in loving and respectful ways, to engender hope and to be channels for God's work in the client's life. Christian counselors can testify to those times when the Spirit of God seemed to impress a thought, image or insight on them that subsequently spoke to a concrete client need. I believe that even when counselors are prohibited either by office policy or a lack of permission from a client from overtly addressing spiritual concerns, they can still lean into the Spirit's presence and find strength and help in time of need.[13]

The practice of the counselor. When clients consent to the inclusion of Christian spirituality, their counselors are prepared to work with client issues in a variety of ways that range from implicit to explicit inclusion of theology. If you have an opportunity to observe master theologically reflective practitioners at work, you will see that theological conversations appear to arise effortlessly. These master counselors follow a model of therapy guided by their therapeutic commitments *and* they are sensitive to times when theological themes emerge as clear figures that arise out of the clinical ground. Then they are able to make their tacit (in the marrow of their bones) theological knowledge overt (shared with the client in terms that are salient to the client's goals).[14] Sometimes they may use historic Christian practices (forgiveness, reading Scripture, prayer, participation in worship, membership in discipleship small groups, serving the poor, etc.) with clients.[15] Other times they will help their clients to ponder theological things as part of their counseling conversations. Learning these theologically oriented clinical skills requires supervision and consultation. Supervision or consultation will also sensitize counselors to those moments when their theological biases are threatening therapeutic processes and robbing clients of opportunities to grow spiritually, personally, relationally or emotionally.[16]

A METAMODEL OF THEOLOGICALLY REFLECTIVE
COUNSELING PROCESS

So far I have been laying the foundation for theologically reflective counseling. I have proposed that theologically reflective counseling includes theological, therapeutic and ethical commitments that are embodied in the personal, spiritual and professional formation of the counselor, and the counselor's awareness of the ever-present ministry of the Holy Spirit. Therapeutic common factors will assist me in becoming more concrete about theologically reflective processes. Common-factors researchers Douglas Sprenkle, Sean Davis and Jay Lebow presented a metamodel that shows how model-dependent and model-independent variables combine to create change in couple and family therapy.[17] *Meta* means to stand *above* or *outside* the interaction so that you can take a comprehensive view of what is going on. The metamodel of change developed by Sean Davis describes therapeutic processes that are present in effective couples and family therapies.[18] In a similar vein, this metamodel of theologically reflective counseling process borrows concepts from Davis's template and applies to them to contexts where theological reflection can support therapeutic change and foster spiritual maturation.

This model is pictured in figure 2.1. The major movements in this model include *attending, addressing, aligning and attaining*. Therapists *attend* to the theological echoes in clients' stories and invite the client to *address* those relevant theological themes in their work. As a result of clinical work toward therapeutic goals, clients may subsequently choose to *align* their lives so that how they live is more congruent with what they profess (e.g., Mt 5–7; Rom 12:1-3). As a result they may *attain* a deeper measure of Christlikeness expressed in faithfulness, hopefulness and lovingkindness. Experienced clinicians will recognize the dynamic pattern of leading and following that arises in counseling sessions. Counselors *lead* a client in an exploration of the client's concerns and then *follow* the client as the client engages these matters. In theologically reflective counseling processes, Christian clients not only strive for clinical goals, they are also likely to experience a deepening of their walk with Jesus and grow in Christlikeness (1 Pet 1:15-16), which then creates opportunities for counselor and client to attend to new areas of the client's life where the Holy Spirit may want to do some work.

The material that immediately follows offers a general overview of each phase in the model. Think of this model as a road map for theologically reflective clinical practice. It lays out options for traveling through clinical material that resonates with theological themes. This is something akin to reading a map and knowing that you are entering a metropolitan area or that you will soon be driving along secondary roads over potentially rough terrain. You make specific, strategic decisions based on your understanding of the kind of driving processes that are associated with the terrain ahead (city driving versus driving on unfinished roads). In a similar way, this model highlights processes that bring theological reflection into a therapeutic arena over the course of treatment. The therapist and the client then bring a specificity of theology (Reformed, Lutheran, Wesleyan, etc.) and therapeutic strategy (cognitive-behavioral, psychodynamic, narrative, etc.) to the model. In subsequent chapters I will refer back to the model and show you how you can address theological themes that are commonly present in clinical situations.

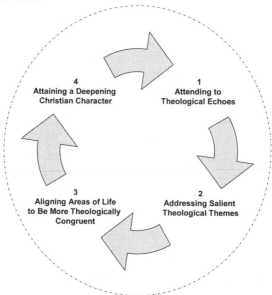

Figure 2.1. A metamodel of theologically reflective counseling process

Attending to theological echoes in client's story. Attending is one of
the basic counseling skills. Attending communicates respect to our
clients and provides the vehicle through which counselors "join" with
clients and build a collaborative therapeutic alliance.[19] We attend to
clients' verbal and nonverbal cues. We listen carefully to clients' narratives to hear not only their story but also to hear the "story behind the
story." Attending includes focused observation to help us see patterns of
behaving and relating that may help or hinder clients' progress. While
attending is the foundation of good listening in general, skilled attending also is guided by the theory counselors work from, which gives
priority to some aspects of the clients' problem over others. For example, cognitive therapists listen keenly for clients' thinking errors.
Behavior therapists closely observe reinforcement patterns. Emotion-
focused therapists highlight the feelings clients express or suppress.
Family systems therapists examine relationship interaction patterns.
Solution-focused therapists listen for the "exceptions" to clients'
problems.[20] So what may seem like a casual conversation to an unini-
tiated observer is in actuality a purposeful use of focused awareness.
The replies that counselors make to their clients are not random statements at all but theory-guided responses that intentionally shape the
therapeutic conversation.

A similar kind of purposeful attending is essential for theologically
reflective counseling. Theologically reflective attending focuses therapists' awareness on theologically related undertones: how clients use
religious/spiritual coping, how clients view God, clients' expectations
of God, clients' experience of their relationship with God (or the lack
thereof).[21] In other words, the counselor is listening for the client's
spiritual and theological frame. This framework may not be well ar-
ticulated and may be peripheral to the client's presenting problem. Because we are "all theologians" clients will have a sense of how such
"ultimate concerns" intersect with their lives.[22] And this intersection
provides a point for theological reflection. Therapists can be on alert
for promptings from the Holy Spirit to attend "here" or "there," and can
use their theologically focused attending to *invite* the client to explore
these matters more fully as part of their work.

While clients may be unaware of how their theological assumptions interact with their interpretation of their presenting problem, this model recommends that counselors remain sensitive to the theological assumptions that may be buried within clients' presenting concerns. Clients enter counseling with a story of what has gone wrong in their lives and have a theory about how their problems came to be. These theories may take a theological shape. For example, do clients believe their presenting problem is the result of personal sin, human biology or spiritual forces (demonic or divine), or is the problem seen as merely a part of the human condition? For instance, certain followers of Jesus attributed the death of a group of Galileans to the Galileans' sinfulness (Lk 13:1-5).

Counselors and therapists may also attend to clients' view of God. Does the client relate to God primarily as a generous Santa Claus, a doting Grandfather, an implacable Judge, a divine Sovereign or a heavenly Father?[23] Clients are likely to have assumptions about the role that God plays in the origin of or the solution to their problems. As counselors listen to clients describe their experience with God, counselors will begin to understand how clients make sense of the relationship between God's goodness, God's power and their situation. The technical theological term for this is *theodicy*. While the philosophical arguments surrounding theodicy may be of acute interest for some theologically reflective clinicians, all counselors will be most interested in clients' conceptualizations.[24]

Counselors initially address questions related to religion and spirituality through the process of securing informed consent. While a counselor can pursue a more formal spiritual or religious assessment, much information can be gleaned at this stage by asking the client two questions: How important is religion/spirituality to your life? Would you like to include religion/spirituality as part of your counseling? This alerts counselors to the degree of explicit integration with which a client is comfortable.[25] If the client is a person of faith and is at ease talking about faith in the first session, a counselor may inquire about the client's theory of God's presence. Clients' approach to Scripture is helpful information to have and counselors will want to know the extent to which clients wish to include the explicit use of the Scripture in their counseling. Do clients and counselors employ compatible enough interpretative stances toward God's Word? This is a question of hermeneutics or one's interpretive strategy. I will say more about this later in this chapter.

Of course therapists bring their own theological framework to therapeutic conversations. Our theological frames become the filters through which we hear the clients' spiritual interpretations. It is important for counselors to include an adequate (although not necessarily extensive) disclosure of their spiritual, religious or theological commitments as a part of securing clients' informed consent and to reaffirm client assent or consent when spiritual or religious resources or interventions are about to be incorporated into the course of treatment. Clients' theological frames may be at odds with those of their counselors. *What is at stake is the extent to which therapists use their own theology as a measure of the degree to which a client's theology is "different than mine," misunderstood, misguided or even toxic* because there is not the theological equivalent of the DSM to which one can refer to make this judgment. This presupposes that counselors are aware enough of their theological commitments.[26]

Addressing salient theological themes. As theological themes emerge, counselors and clients collaborate to name the themes and to agree on the extent to which these themes are central to clinical work. At times theological themes will remain in the wings, waiting for their entrance cue. At other times they will take center stage. And periodically they won't even be on the playbill. I suspect that the scope of themes that could emerge in counseling is rather large! Instead of listing all of the potential themes that one *could* deal with, I will highlight those that seem most readily applicable to a wide range of clients with Christian commitments by raising a series of questions.

First, to what extent does God's loving relationship with us serve as a model for the therapeutic alliance? This question is more focused on the therapist's self, but since no relationship is formed by one person alone, it emphasizes the importance of the therapeutic relationship. Second, to what degree are clients able to take personal responsibility for their contribution to the problem or for their role in resolving the problem? For Christian clients personal holiness is associated with faith in God. This is not about the client's salvation, nor is it necessarily linked to doctrinal affirmations (i.e., cognitive assent or agreement). Instead, it is associated with the degree to which a client relies on and is directed by God's heart and God's agenda for self and the world. Third, to what degree are clients willing to address the ways that they have failed to love others as God would have them love (1 Cor 13; 1 Jn 4)? To what extent are factors related to societal injustice affecting clients' lives (1 Pet)? How can counseling empower clients to confront these issues? Social holiness is associated with the degree to which the love of God is expressed in active love of neighbor—be that neighbor one's spouse, child or community. Fourth, to what degree do issues related to repentance, forgiveness and reconciliation factor into clients' dilemmas? Can clients lean into their experience of being forgiven by God to extend grace-filled forgiveness to those who have wounded them? Do clients need to repent of wrongs committed against others? To what extent can clients achieve reconciliation with children, parents, spouses or neighbors? Fifth, to what extent can clients cling to the hope we have in Jesus, especially in times of distress? Many times clients face situations where preferred options are no longer on the table (e.g., trauma, divorce, automobile accident). Therapists cannot turn back the hands of time for a do-over day. Nevertheless we can help clients appropriate the hope that is embedded in God's promise of a "new heaven and a new earth" (Rev 21).

In each of the following chapters I associate these theological themes with a theological world. W. Paul Jones developed a typology of five theological worlds.[27] David M. Durst observes that "within each person's worldview is a sense of his or her own place in the world and the personal dilemmas that cry out for satisfaction through faith and life. The set of thoughts and emotions that make up a person's sense of self and spiritual need can be described as various theological worlds."[28] Counselors can subsequently ascertain which theological world seems to fit best with this client. Does the client approach his or her spiritual life as a foreigner, one who is faint, a fighter or a fugitive, or have life experiences "flattened" the client? I will provide a fuller description of these worlds later in this chapter.

Aligning areas of life to be more congruent with theological commitments. As counselors and clients collaborate around theological themes, counselors will recommend interventions that can help clients to address the theological issues that are associated with clinical goals.[29] Ethical practice requires counselors to describe adequately the proposed interventions and to secure the clients' consent before implementation. Theologically reflective interventions may be aimed at changing clients' *cognitions* (e.g., Scripture reading), helping clients to *regulate their affect* (e.g., prayer or meditation), or challenging clients to adopt new *patterns of behavior* (e.g., forgiving, repenting, serving the poor). Here counselors may also utilize techniques that are associated with their particular therapeutic commitments that serve these purposes.

The common factors model developed by Sean Davis identified emotional regulation, cognitive reframing and behavioral shifts as three categories of model-specific interventions that helped to change the cycle of couples' interactions.[30] When brought into a process model for theologically reflective counseling, these categories can be either explicitly or implicitly Christian in nature. Examples of explicit interventions can include (1) seeking peacefulness during anxious exchanges through private prayer to strengthen emotional regulation, (2) reading the Bible in service of cognitive reframing, and (3) learning new relationship habits that embody the virtue of love as it is described in 1 Corinthians 13. Interventions may also be implicitly Christian in nature. They may reflect standard emotional, cognitive and behavioral approaches that may also serve ways of living that are consistent with a Christian lifestyle. A counselor with strong-sensed theological reflection will follow the lead of the Holy Spirit into clients' lives, and while the therapeutic work may not be overtly Christian it nevertheless makes space for God to work clients' hearts. For example, a client can become aware of the corroding effect of contemptuous verbal exchanges and the distancing impact of turning away or against another (e.g., spouse, parent, child, friend) when an olive branch of repair had been offered.[31]

The implementation of model-specific interventions altered couples' interaction cycle by helping them to (1) slow down the process, (2) stand outside of self and other, and (3) take personal responsibility.[32] When brought into a process model of theologically reflective counseling, interventions help clients to move toward their goals in three similar ways. First, they will help clients *to slow down* to see the faithfulness of God at work (Ps 46:10). Often the pain of the presenting problem blinds clients so they cannot see God in the midst of their problem (1 Kings 19:11-13). Second, counselors will help clients to *"stand meta"* to their own situations, and place their concerns within a horizon of hope that comes from their faith in the everlasting faithfulness and love of God. Essentially counselors help clients place their problem within the larger framework of God's love and care for them. Third, counselors challenge clients *to assume personal responsibility* to love God and to love others in spite of their current conditions. This does not mean that theologically reflective practitioners ask clients to be doormats for unjust relationships. No. Instead counselors ask clients to do the following: "If it is possible, so far as it depends on you, live peaceably with all" (Rom 12:18).

Attaining a deepening Christian character. If our work with clients achieves any degree of success, our clients will have greater capacities for faith, hope and love.[33] Regarding faith, our clients will be faithful to their promises to others and walk faithfully in their relationships. They will be covenant keepers and trustworthy friends and partners. Regarding hope, our clients will have eyes to see God's footprints walking beside them even in the darkest of times. Their hope is not dependent on transitory circumstances but on the eternal promises of God. Finally, regarding love, our clients will be able to love God with more of their being and will be better able to let the love of God flow over in concrete acts of love for others. The exact shape of this love will depend on clients' cultural, familial, developmental and ecclesial location, although its contours will mirror 1 Corinthians 13.

INTEGRATION ISSUES: THEOLOGICAL WORLDS, HERMENEUTICS AND ETHICS

As you can see, this model of theologically reflective process (attending, addressing, aligning, attaining) provides space for clients and counselors to work within their own theological and therapeutic frameworks. It provides a generic roadmap for developing a theological route through clinical terrain by highlighting how common therapeutic practices can also meet theological goals. An understanding of theological worlds, an awareness of the importance of hermeneutics and adherence to ethical standards affect how counselors implement theologically reflective counseling.

Theological worlds. Worldviews are sweeping stories of how the world works. Steve Wilkens and Mark Sanford point out that worldviews "tell us what we should love or despise, what is valuable or unimportant, and what is good or evil. All worldviews offer definitions of the fundamental human problem and how we might fix it. . . . We don't just think our way into worldviews, we *experience* them."[34] Worldviews hum quietly in the background of our mind, providing the melody line through which we interpret the world. Wilkens and Sanford observe that various worldviews provide an answer to the question "what is the way to the 'good life,'" or put another way, "how then might one be saved?" Of course, each worldview has also to address the question "saved from what?" (what is considered the "good life"?) before that worldview can begin to offer its own path. A client's religious and spiritual commitments become a worldview that is as important to understanding who that client is as is their gender, race, ethnicity and so on.[35]

Clients may profess a Christian worldview. Theologian W. Paul Jones noted that Christian individuals also belong to different "theological worlds." Jones is not referring to one's theological heritage or doctrinal commitments, such as "I am a Baptist" or "I am a Lutheran." Instead, Jones proposes that one's theological world results from interactions between two poles: one's *obsessio* (question, need, ache at a deep level) and one's *epiphania* (those moments, events or relationships that provide an answer to life's questions worth living and dying for). According to Jones, "The dynamic establishing one's World, then is this ongoing interaction of *obsessio* and *epiphania*. One's disposition is determined by whether this dynamic is seen more from the perspective of one's *obsessio*, or if the *epiphania* is the more weighted pole."[36] While Jones acknowledges that a greater number of theological worlds may exist, he concentrates on five particular theological worlds based on the interaction of *obsessio* and *epiphania*. Drawing upon the work of W. Paul Jones, David Durst describes how the five theological worlds shape how Christians may live. As you read Durst's descriptions of the foreigner, the faint, the fighter, the fugitive and the flattened,[37] consider the kind of experiences and memories that might shape this theological world—the *obsessio* and *epiphania*. Imagine how they might present themselves in counseling.[38]

The first worldview is that of the *foreigner*. The foreigner feels like an alien or an orphan in the universe, presently abandoned and isolated, but longing for a true home. Durst describes the theological frame of the foreigner as follows:

> The universe seems arbitrary, huge and small at the same time, and I am lost in it. I want to find solace in meaningful relationships but they are never enough, and I am aware that they are all transitory anyway. I am in this world that is not as it should be, but I find myself unable to either change it or resign and accept its absurdity. Strangely puzzling is that most people seem to accept the order of things and their place in it. Obviously, I'm the odd one. I ask "why?" but find no answers. It almost feels that I used to be at home, almost like I have memories of its tastes and smells, but either home moved or I have wandered too far to find my way back. I'm a bit like Spielberg's E.T., trying to devise a way to "phone home" but not at all sure I'm getting through, or can get through. I wonder if there is really anyone out there to answer.[39]

The foreigner desires fellowship with God and longs to experience God's closeness. Foreigners seek a homecoming, a theological reconciliation with God and others.

The *faint* feels impotent, insignificant and invisible. He or she longs for fulfillment. Durst describes the experience of the faint as follows:

> Really deep down, beneath my public face, I feel empty. I think the people who pass me by with barely a notice probably have the right idea. I don't expect people to honor me or even like me. Let's just get along even if we are pretending. If I were to suddenly vanish, some might notice and a few would care, but their worlds would go on without too much alteration. So, mainly I try to get along, to comply with the expectations of others and thereby make my life worth something.[40]

The faint long to experience God's overflowing love, infusing every pore of their being. They desire wholeness, to become fully themselves, and the capacity to express the fullness of their humanity.

The *fighter* angrily shakes his or her fist at the chaos, oppression, and evil in the world. Durst sums up the fighter's theological world as follows:

> History demonstrates a constant flow of oppression and injustice. I am convinced we must move beyond this. Suffering and death are intruders that must ultimately be defeated. I give no ground to resignation, nor support the hope of fleeing this world for heaven, but work to make this sacred earth a place of peace and justice. Sometimes I have been atheistic, believing that a God could not exist who tolerates such vast amounts of suffering. In my best moments I have believed that God exists and will yet put suffering to an end. In both states of mind, I am compelled to fight for right. I don't expect to cure this world, but I do want to make a positive difference, a lasting contribution that makes things better.[41]

The fighter longs for God's justice to be present in the world today, for God to "set the world right."

Fugitives are wracked with guilt. They feel powerless, condemned, knowing that they have fallen short. Durst paints the heart of the fugitive as follows:

> There is a huge gap between what I aspire to be and what I am. My flaws are displayed in my thoughts and actions, and in my very humanness. I want to be and do good, but I so often do the opposite. Some call it "selfishness," some "sin," but I could just as easily call it "me." And, no, I'm not bragging. I can justify my actions, but I know when other people do similar things to me, I'm angry. I am guilty of violating my own principles, so if there is a God I have surely broken God's commands and expectations. Honestly, I think I do things to try to pay back the world for the wrong things I have done. To a significant degree, I act out of guilt.[42]

Fugitives need forgiveness, a way to take away their guilt so that they are able to please God.

The *flattened* are or have been overwhelmed by life circumstances.

Longsuffering in the face of adversity, the flattened long for fortitude to face the next challenge. Here is how Durst pictures them:

> As often as not, I feel overwhelmed. I have that feeling of being pressed on by threatening situations and conditions. And I am not alone. Some are hit with poverty and some with illness and grief, but an honest look at this world reveals it to be a predatory place. You just get through it. There is some truth to the expression, "Blessed are those who expect nothing, for they will not be disappointed." I look for perseverance more than power, and I admire those who endure suffering more than those who ignore the world's troubles.[43]

Clients occupy more than one theological world at a time. However, Jones notes that one world will tend to take precedence. How might insight into a client's theological world contribute to theologically reflective counseling practice? It is possible that such an understanding gives counselors insight into clients' spiritual longings. Jones proposes that "an *obsessio* is whatever functions deeply and pervasively in life as a defining quandary, a conundrum. . . . Whatever its content or intensity, we are dealing with that primal level of functioning in each of us with which one must make peace, for it will not go away."[44] If the client is living out of his or her *obsessio*, then theologically reflective counseling may help the client to live more fully into *epiphania*. Or it may take the shape of encouraging the clients to increase their awareness of alternative theological worlds, which are at their fingertips but are presently underdeveloped. In subsequent chapters I have linked the five worlds with a clinical concern. These are not the only relevant categories clinical problems may fall into, but I find this conceptualization helpful in framing the kind of spiritual longings that may underlie some client's spiritual concerns.

A client is not the only person in the room who approaches life through theological world lenses. Counselors do too. Do you recognize your own story in one or more of the theological world descriptions? Can you give voice to the *obsessio* and *epiphania* that serve as your meaning world? Just as feminist and multicultural movements insist on counselor awareness of their biases related to gender, ethnicity, race, class and so forth, our explicit theological beliefs and our implicit theological world predispose us to theological biases. Ethical work with clients requires that we become cognizant of these theological predispositions—formal and informal, explicit or implicit—and to see how these tendencies may influence our clinical work.

Hermeneutics. Central to the practice of theological reflection is the recognition that we are engaged in an interpretive or *hermeneutical* enterprise. If you are familiar with this term, you most likely associate it with the disciplines of biblical studies and theology. In these arenas, hermeneutics refers to the system used to ascribe meaning to biblical texts (biblical studies) and then to extend these insights into discussions of how this applies to our lives as the people of God (theological studies).

Professional and academic theologians and biblical scholars can identify the specific school(s) of interpretation to which they adhere, whereas you and I may not be able to do that. This does not mean that we read Scripture without a method of interpretation. *Everyone* who reads the Bible has a method of interpreting Scripture—a hermeneutic. It more likely implies that most of us haven't given any conscious thought to *how* we reach the conclusions that we do reach. LeRon Shults and Steve Sandage link awareness of one's hermeneutic with spiritual maturity. They write,

> Spiritual maturity should include self-awareness about one's spiritual identity, *interpretive tradition*, and social location. This is different from a more immature spiritual grandiosity that fails to recognize that one has a perspective or interpretive vantage point. This requires spiritual humility. . . . Humility is a virtue that promotes a willingness to be self-critical, consider the perspectives of others, and remain open to new discoveries.[45]

Perhaps you are old enough to remember the old computer days of DOS (disk operating system). If so, you will also remember the transition to Windows. Within a Windows platform, "what you see is what you get" (WYSIWYG). Many people adopt WYSIWYG hermeneutics. A major assumption behind WYSIWYG hermeneutics is that any reasonable person would arrive at the same conclusions that I arrive at, because the meaning of the biblical text is right in front of your nose—in plain black and white! While this hermeneutical strategy can work in many circumstances, it raises any number of important questions. How does culture influence your interpretation? How about your gender? What about your status within your culture? Developmental stage in life also influences one's range of interpretative options. And I haven't even begun to list the questions about the accuracy of one's translation of the Bible, or the extent to which social-cultural knowledge about the Ancient Near East shades the meaning of texts. These questions scratch the surface of the kind of issues that arise when counselors or clients adopt a WYSIWYG hermeneutic.

Other systems of interpretation exist beyond WYSIWYG. For example, your interpretation of the Bible may rest on knowing an author's intent (e.g., What did the apostle Paul mean in a specific passage of Scripture?). Or perhaps you are more interested in the reader's response (e.g., What does this Pauline passage mean to me?). Maybe neither of those questions interest to you, and you are most concerned with the social and cultural context within which the biblical authors wrote (What were the different views on divorce that were well-known to Jews when Jesus made his statements about divorce in the Gospel of Matthew?). One common interpretative strategy that we use when reading the Bible is to "let Scripture interpret Scripture." Have you stopped to consider how you decide which Scriptures take priority as the ones through which you view other verses? This is a matter of hermeneutics. Many Christian clients expect counselors to use the Bible. Counselors need to aware of how their hermeneutics compares with that of their clients.

The importance of theological and psychological hermeneutics came home to me during my work with one particular family. Forgiveness was a salient clinical issue in this case. I had just completed a research study on psychological forgiveness so I felt that I was equipped theologically and clinically to help this family. Understanding forgiveness as a process fit with my interpretation of Scripture, my theology and my psychology. The parents in this family saw forgiveness quite differently—biblically, theologically and therefore psychologically. The parents believed that when Jesus commanded us to forgive, that is what you did, here and now. No questions asked. No discussion required. No "process" about it. Based on their hermeneutic, the parents expected their estranged adult child to forgive an offending family member and to reconcile—immediately. The parents' loyalties lay with the family member who was the alleged wrongdoer, who had spoken the right words of repentance but evidenced no changed behavior in the opinion of the primary injured party. These parents had little empathy for the aggrieved family member. At one point I found myself caught in an intense discussion with these parents about the appropriate view of forgiveness. Try as I might, I could not convince them of the error of their thinking. They were not buying the premise that psychological research might shed light on an important biblical practice (forgiveness). Because the Bible did not unfold any kind of forgiveness process, these parents were not buying what I wanted to offer. I was therapeutically and theologically stuck—until I stopped trying to change their minds about their view on forgiveness. This was not one of my finest clinical hours. Nevertheless, I learned a great deal about navigating the in-between space when the hermeneutics of counselor and client differ.

Ethical issues. Ethical practice associated with this model *minimally* includes adhering to the legal and ethical guidelines for counseling and psychotherapy in general. These include (but are not limited to) the following: practicing in a manner that is respectful of diversity, avoiding bias, doing good, doing no harm, remaining mindful of role-related obligations that arise from one's professional identity (e.g., maintaining confidentiality, minimizing dual relationships, avoiding sexual relationships with clients), seeking supervision as required by law and consultation as needed.

It is tempting to assume that because one *is* a Christian that one is *automatically* competent to incorporate religiously based or spiritually based interventions in Christian counseling. This is a false assumption. Two research findings make a compelling case for paying close attention to ethical practice in theologically reflective counseling. One study found that licensed mental health professionals approached clients' religious and spiritual issues based on the *counselor's* experiences. Other researchers observed that *clients tended to drift toward their coun-*

selor's values, including their spiritual values, over the course of therapy.[46] These research findings underscore the care that counselors must take not to impose their theology on clients. What precautions can Christians who counsel take to avoid such unintended imposition? Christians who desire to practice theologically reflective counseling should first evaluate their competency to do so. The following questions will aid in this personal assessment:

1. Do I have the ability to create a spiritually safe and affirming therapeutic environment for my clients?

2. Do I have the ability to conduct an effective religious and spiritual assessment of my clients?

3. Do I have the ability to use or encourage religious and spiritual interventions, if indicated, in order to help clients access the resources of their faith and spirituality during treatment and recovery?

4. Do I have the ability to effectively consult and collaborate with, and when needed, refer to clergy and other pastoral professionals?[47]

Second, Christian counselors can employ written informed consent to make counselors' theological commitments explicit. If a counselor's setting allows for work from Christian perspectives, disclosure and discussion of this option *before* beginning formal treatment is appropriate. Areas that may be covered in an expanded informed consent may include disclosure of counselor's religious views and other information related to cultural and spiritual diversity, assessment of client's openness to the use of religiously based interventions or other theologically congruent interventions, acknowledgement of possible change in locations when implementing religiously based interventions if applicable (e.g., going to a prayer chapel), acknowledgement of newness of many religiously based treatment options, the possibility of other similar services at reduced rates (e.g., seeking help from their clergy) and reimbursement fee options.[48]

Counselors may also secure clients' informed consent for the use of theologically reflective interventions during the course of treatment. For example, a Christian counselor has gained a client's consent to work from an explicitly Christian perspective. During one session the counselor discusses therapeutic benefits of prayer or Scripture reading with the client, and then assigns daily prayer or recommends reading specific Bible passages as homework. This discussion may be accompanied by the client's signature acknowledging his or her willingness to use these interventions and the counselor makes a note of this discussion in the case file. It goes without saying that counselors employ only those spiritual interventions that they are competent to use, and which are directly in service of helping the client reach his or her goals.

Fuller Seminary psychology professor Siang-Yang Tan highlights further hazards that Christian counselors face when working with spiritual issues in counseling. He cautions against arguing over doctrinal issues rather than clarifying them. He notes that counselors must avoid abusing or misusing Christian practices during counseling. Because it is likely that Christian counselors and their clients may attend similar religious functions, it is possible that counselors may fail to maintain boundaries that are necessary to sustain a professional therapeutic relationship. In our zeal to help hurting Christians, we must guard against usurping ecclesial authority instead of making a referral to an appropriate church leader. Finally he warns us of using only religious interventions for problems that require medication or other medical treatments.[49]

SOME CLOSING THOUGHTS

I hope that this model of theologically reflective process can help Christian counselors bring theology into their work with Christian clients. It requires counselors to commit to developing theological competence as well as clinical excellence. With ethical guidelines in hand, counselors can confidently meet with clients, hear their story and look for the ways God is working in the client's life.

A Theologically Reflective Counseling Relationship

The Triune God and Therapeutic Common Factors

⅏

Come, Father, Son, and Holy Ghost,
Whom one all-perfect God we own,
Restorer of Thine image lost,
Thy various offices make known;
Display, our fallen souls to raise,
Thy whole economy of grace.

Soon as our pardoned hearts believe
That Thou art pure, essential love,
The proof we in ourselves receive
Of the three witnesses above;
Sure, as the saints around Thy throne,
That Father, Word, and Spirit, are One.

CHARLES WESLEY,
"Come, Father, Son, and Holy Ghost"

I GREW UP IN AN ERA WHEN HYMNS were the music of the church. In the 1970s the "worship wars" had not yet commenced and contemporary Christian music was nonexistent in the local church I attended. As a teenager I grumbled about that. Then a funny thing happened on the way to adulthood. I fell in love with hymns! One of my favorite hymns was and still is "Holy, Holy, Holy," with lyrics by Reginald Heber (1783-1826). I'll say more about holiness and counseling in chapters four and five. Right now I want to highlight the final line from verses 1 and 4: *God in three persons, blessed Trinity!*

I never gave much thought to an association between the Trinity and Christian counseling until a few years ago. It was not a topic that was covered in my Master's of Pastoral Psychology and Counseling program. It has never come up in any of my counseling sessions. So why do I bring it up now? Because I think that the relationship between the members of the Godhead exemplifies the kind of relationship that theologically reflective practitioners can offer to their clients. When we focus on the quality of the counseling relationship, we are asking about the extent to which Christian counselors can reflect the love of the triune God to clients, particularly those clients who are more challenging to love. The issue is not about liking or not liking one's clients, but about the capacity to fulfill Jesus' command to "love one another" under the best of circumstances (1 Jn 4:11), or the challenge to "love your enemies" under more trying clinical conditions (Lk 6:27-36). Christian counselors represent the triune God's love for the world when the counseling relationship mirrors God's love for clients.[1] Some clients put our capacity to do that to the test.

THEOLOGY UNDER FIRE

Cynthia was a single woman on the verge of a promising career in finance. She had recently accepted a position with a prominent firm. While her professional life was blossoming, her private life was spinning out of control. Cynthia struggled with bulimia. This problem had plagued Cynthia since her early adolescence. During her junior year in high school she had completed an inpatient treatment program for eating disorders. While she remembered many of the coping strategies she had learned in her teen years, she had never fully given up the thought and behaviors patterns that characterize bulimia. She had completed her undergraduate degree without a repeat hospitalization. The pressure of her recently completed MBA and the demands of her new job had triggered a resurgence of this disorder to such a degree that Cynthia worried it would ruin her chances for professional success.

On one hand Cynthia brought notable strengths into her therapeutic work. She already understood the dynamics of bulimia. She was smart and focused. Nevertheless, Cynthia was not the easiest client for me to connect with. Her self-presentation had a subtle whining quality to it and she replied with "yes, but" more often than not. I knew that if I didn't improve my therapeutic alliance with her then it was probable that she would drop out of therapy. Throughout the opening stage of counseling, I prayed for God to help me see her as God saw her—*as a child of God and a person of worth*. I recognized that Cynthia was caught between her desire for freedom from bulimia and her reliance on it as a way to maintain an illusion of control. As I began to empathize with her terror about giving up her bulimic thoughts and behaviors, God helped me to see her through a new set of lenses, and with this new vision I was able to be a more open channel through which the holy love of the triune God might flow.

If I want to be salt and light in the midst of my counseling, if I want to be a theologically reflective practitioner in action, not just in knowledge, then I need to find a way to connect with all the "Cynthias" on my case load. At this juncture therapeutic common factors provide the how-tos for these particular theological commitments. Common factors are variables that cross all schools of counseling that are related to clinical outcomes. In 1992 Michael Lambert identified four factors that account for therapeutic change, and he estimated the proportion each factor contributed to positive clinical outcomes.[2] These four factors are (1) factors that are unique to the client over which the therapist has no control (40%), (2) factors related to the therapeutic alliance (30%), (3) client expectance or hopefulness (15%), and (4) the specific school of counseling employed by the clinician (15%). As you can see the relationship between the counselor and client is a major asset! A common-factors approach provides a roadmap to ways that theologically reflective counselors might reflect the holy love of the Trinity. In this chapter I explore how a theological commitment to trinitarian theology and a therapeutic commitment to common factors support theologically reflective counseling.

THEOLOGICAL COMMITMENTS: TRINITY

According to Stanley Grenz and Roger Olson, an integrative motif is the central or orienting idea through which a theologian views all other aspects of his or her theology.[3] For John Wesley that orienting idea was God's holy love. Wesley's eighteenth-century focus on the priority of God's love mirrors a twentieth- and twenty-first-century interest in the Trinity. This focus, old and new, forms a strong theological foundation on which we can stand for a theologically reflective counseling relationship. As a theological thinker, Wesley is not alone in his belief in a triune God of holy love. An understanding of God's love for humanity is an essential feature of all streams of Christian theology.

The holy love of the Trinity. Twentieth-century theologian Mildred Bangs Wynkoop claimed that "love is the dynamic of Wesleyanism."[4] No matter what theological category John Wesley began with, eventually his thinking returned to his central theme of divine holy love. The systemic principle of equifinality (many ways exist to reach a clinical goal) applies to Wesley's theology: any entry point eventually led Wesley back to God's holy love. Whenever Wesley preached or wrote about the triune God, the theme of holy love reverberated through every page. The adjective *holy* described the quality of relationships in terms of purity, integrity and "rightness"; the noun *love* expressed the nature of the relationship itself. Given Wesley's concern with practical divinity, one could parse the phrase as *holy loving*, emphasizing love's vibrant (as opposed to static) character. The phrase is paradoxical. *Holy* is linked with being set apart, separated from, for the sake of purity, whereas love moves toward the beloved seeking intimacy and communion. Without love, holiness degenerates into rigid, uncompromising, judgmental and harsh rule-keeping. Without holiness, love defaults into self-indulgent, self-focused and self-serving sentimentality. The holy love of God calls us to become a people that follow after the heart of God and to become imitators of Jesus in all that we say and do. Only through the grace of God and the power of the Holy Spirit are we empowered so to do!

Like theologians before him John Wesley's view of God was thoroughly trinitarian. In his sermon *On the Trinity* (sermon 55), Wesley wrote:

> But surely there are some [fundamental truths] which it nearly concerns us to know, as having a close connextion with vital religion [alive and active faith]. And doubtless we may rank among these that contained in the words above cited: "There are three that bear record in heaven, the Father, the Word, and the Holy Ghost: And these three are one."[5]

Wesley preferred descriptive language to refer to the triune God, specifically, the "Three-One God."[6] He held to the classic understanding of this "Three-One God" as Father, Son and Holy Spirit. For Wesley the truth of the Three-One God is seen through the changed lives of believers.

Contemporary insights about the Trinity. Wesley was more concerned with how the Trinity was revealed to humanity through salvation than he was with thoughts about the nature of the relationships *within* the Godhead. This task has been taken up by contemporary theologians such as Jürgen Moltmann, Wolfhart Pannenberg, Miroslav Volf and Stanley J. Grenz, and they have deepened our understanding of intratrinitarian life in meaningful ways. A *social* view of the Trinity emphasizes the lively relationships of love shared among members of the Godhead.

The Godhead exits in a social matrix of Father, Son and Holy Spirit. The Trinity is a perfect model of unselfish, other-centered, loving relationships. In the Middle Ages trinitarian theologian Richard of St. Victor observed that the extreme goodness of the Godhead must involve love. Divine love needed an "other," one who is equal to the lover and who is the object of the lover's love. This kind of love is dynamic in that it is given and received. If this supreme love were not to collapse into itself, it is shared with yet a third—hence, the loving relationships shared among Father, Son and Holy Spirit. The members of the Godhead are in relationship with one another, and they comprise these relationships. Instead of thinking of a person as an autonomous, independent self (the modernist idea of "self"), the Trinity more closely models the postmodern concept of self as constituted through relationship with others. That is to say, "*person* should be defined as that which enters into relationships and does not exist apart from them. The key to its meaning is intersubjectivity along with mutuality and reciprocity."[7]

This perspective on the Trinity focuses our attention on God as divine "persons-in-relation" and on the interpersonal community of counselor-client as a basis for theologically reflective counseling. When the Christian counselor steps into his or her office, God is already there. Even though informed consent may limit the counselor to implicit integration, God remains present. When Christian therapists engage Christian clients, the dialogue between counselor and counselee becomes a trialogue, with God as the third member of the conversation. This expanded "therapeutic community" (counselor, counselee, God) serves as a way station where clients may experience God's love through their interactions with their counselors. For example, Cynthia gave consent for explicit integration of Christianity and counseling. We discussed the extent to which she would be comfortable using Scripture and prayer in therapy sessions. She appreciated being consulted about this because she was able to define her preferences, which I subsequently honored. She struggled with shame about her bulimic relapses, wondering how God could love a person such as her. Through our therapeutic work she realized a relationship in which she was accepted "just as she was" and she began to voice an awareness of being accepted and loved by God. I encouraged her to remain active in her local church and to seek the support of others in her congregation so that she would have less of a sense of being alone and have additional opportunities to belong.

Love is the sine qua non of divine relationality (Jn 3:16; 1 Jn 4:8, 16). The Father, the Son and the Holy Spirit give love to one another and receive love from one another. Dennis F. Kinlaw observes that self-giving love is key to understanding the Trinity. This kind of love is less concerned with what the beloved can do for the lover, but what the lover can offer to the beloved. It is "other centered" or "other oriented" love, that is sustained by the being of the lover, not by the beloved one's reciprocity.[8]

Dance is one image that captures the essence of the loving triune relationship. Early theologians referred to this as "perichoresis." This divine dance of love features Father, Son and Spirit circling one another and moving in perfect harmony. No prima donna exists here! There is no upstaging. Instead, there is gracious giving and receiving, a coming and going, a stepping forward and yielding space to the other, maintenance of personal identity while sharing intimate connection with the others, an ideal of "attached separation" and "separated attachment," an ecstatic dance of love.

We might restate Kinlaw's quote as *self-giving love is key to understanding the therapeutic alliance.* Theologically reflective counseling is less concerned about what the client can do for the counselor than it is with what the counselor can offer to the client, which the client can receive, reject or modify. The therapeutic relationship is other centered or client centered. It is not there to meet the needs of the counselor. Under the best of circumstances counselors adopt a collaborative stance in relationship to their clients so that a sense of equality (not hierarchy) permeates the counseling relationship. The counselor does not hog the therapeutic space. In the clinical perichoresis therapists move between leading their clients and following their clients. *Together* client and therapist choreograph the "dance" of therapy. For example, my work with Cynthia moved between support and challenge. We celebrated her moments of success over bulimic behavior. Yet this was also followed by tempered confrontation when her bulimic thinking patterns interfered with her forward movement. We collaborated around strategies that would help her to challenge her disordered thinking during her hectic work day. At times I led in this therapeutic dance and at other times I followed Cynthia's lead.

You will recall that in chapter one I stressed that therapists are theologically situated, and in chapter two I emphasized that counselors will be assisted in theologically reflective counseling practices as they come to understand the influences that shaped clients' spiritual worlds. While nurturing a collaborative and supportive therapeutic relationship applies to all five categories of theological worlds (i.e., foreigner, faint, fighter, fugitive, flattened), I believe that the counselor's capacity to develop a strong therapeutic alliance is especially salient to those who experience themselves to be theological *foreigners*.[9] W. Paul Jones describes the felt theological world of the foreigner as follows: "Somehow separation should not be, for one cannot be content in lonely unconnectedness. . . . One's state is that of an alien—a streetwalker of the Spirit. One simply does not belong—that's it. And yet, deeply within, one senses beyond sensing that one was 'made' to belong, somewhere, to 'something.'"[10] The world of the foreigner is one that longs for belonging, for acceptance, for connection. The therapeutic relationship can be one place where foreigners find belonging, acceptance and connection.

Cynthia belonged to the theological world of the foreigner. In spite of her academic and professional achievements she felt like an outsider who longed to become an insider. She had few friends growing up. She felt uneasy in her family of origin. She never had a steady boyfriend throughout high school or college. She knew how to look like she fit in. But inside herself, she knew she was faking it. Knowing this about Cynthia, and recognizing my own experience of not easily connecting with her, heightened my intent to nurture as solid a therapeutic alliance as possible.

Jones notes that foreigners move to a rhythm of separation and reunion. Consider the parable of the prodigal son (Lk 15:11-32). This sense of not belonging (separation) but longing to belong (reunion) may be one way to describe the relationship of the loving father and his wayward son. The father "belonged" to his younger son, was separated when this son moved to a far-off country, and finally experienced reunion in the son's homecoming. Note that the process was reversed with the elder brother—a movement from union to separation—and the hearer of the parable is left wondering about the prospect of reunion between these two brothers. Clients who also live in the world of the foreigner perceive themselves to be spiritual orphans. These clients carry within themselves a sense of abandonment. Perhaps this is the client who was the neglected child in his or her family. Maybe this is the client with poor social skills who never fit in, who always was the "last kid standing" when teams were chosen by classmates. They long for a place to belong or a people to belong to.

Through work with a caring therapist the theological foreigner can experience the love of God and may come to know that he or she belongs to God and therefore may be more open to fellowship with God and God's people. The theologically reflective counselor will want to attend carefully to the client's experiences that have contributed to shaping the client's theological world as a foreigner. Recalling that theological worlds emerge out of a dynamic of *obsessio* and *epiphania*, counselors may get clinical mileage by watching for patterns of separation and reunion, in general, and within the therapeutic relationship in particular. This involves attending to the tear and repair cycle that regularly happens in clinical work.[11] It is likely that ruptures in the therapeutic relationship will trigger feelings of not belonging (*obsessio*) within the theological foreigner. Therapists' efforts to repair these clinical tears will help the client reduce his or her sense of isolation and restore a sense of belonging (*epiphania*).

One's theology of the Trinity provides an orienting perspective for work with clients. Christian counselors can embrace the model of other-centered love when they encounter clients like Cynthia. Counselors can rely on the Holy Spirit when they meet clients that are particularly hard to love. But loving clients is not enough. Counselors also must attend to the reasons why clients come to therapy. A common-factors perspective will help us to act in ways that will promote a trinitarian approach to counseling.

THERAPEUTIC COMMITMENTS: COMMON FACTORS

For the past several decades researchers have explored the factors that influence therapeutic outcomes. As a result of these efforts we know that a number of factors exist that are common to successful (or unsuccessful) counseling. A common-factors position on change highlights mechanisms of change that are present in successful therapy. While some common-factors proponents would argue that the common factors alone contribute to positive therapeutic outcomes, making allegiance to any school of therapy irrelevant, others contend that the different counseling theories are the delivery systems through which common factors work. This moderate position is the one advocated in a model of theologically reflective counseling. Earlier I highlighted the four common factors that Michael Lambert identified (client factors, therapeutic alliance, client expectancy, therapeutic model). Building on Lambert's work and empirical research, marriage and family therapists Douglas Sprenkle, Sean Davis and Jay Lebow identified five major categories of common factors.[12] They are client characteristics, therapist characteristics (which includes the therapeutic relationship), dimensions of expectancy and hope, non-specific mechanisms of change, and the role that models play. Let's look at each of these components more closely.

Client characteristics. In the 1990s Michael Lambert highlighted the important role of the client in the outcome of counseling. Lambert's best guess was that 40 percent of the outcome variance in counseling had to do with such things as clients' motivation, commitment, inner strength and religious faith/spiritual commitments. These are things that the client brought to counseling. Lambert also included aspects of the client's life that happened outside of the counseling room—things such as social support, community involvement and fortuitous events. Notice how the items in the list of client characteristics have *nothing to do with what the counselor does in session!* Counseling may thus be viewed as a process that (1) enhances clients' capacities to tap into their own resources and strengths, and that (2) increases their ability to capitalize on everyday serendipities as an opportunity for change (those fortuitous events). Karen Tallman and Arthur Bohart speculate that the reason that many models of therapy seem to work is not because of the model but because *clients take what models offer and find ways to use them for their own purposes.*[13] A study by Karen Helmeke and Douglas Sprenkle supports this. These researchers asked clients and counselors to identify the "pivotal" moments in counseling sessions. They discovered that clients typically named different important moments than did their counselors.

During the final session of counseling I typically ask clients for feedback on their overall experience. I am especially curious to know of ways that we worked together that made an important difference to them. One client shocked me when she reported that my walking into the door frame was a turning point in her therapy. I remembered the event. I had offered to get her a drink of water as we began our work together (I offered this to all clients as an act of hospitality). I misjudged my step as I opened the office door, and indeed I walked right into the door frame as I left the office. What made a difference for her was not my bruised ego or my bumped forehead, but the fact that I laughed at myself for my lack of "grace," returned with her glass of water and then promptly launched into our session. She said that in contrast she would have died a thousand deaths of humiliation and shame. I have not had another occasion to practice "door frame therapy" and I have never forgotten her testimony either! Just as the common-factors research suggests, my brilliant interpretations were less important to her than this fortuitous event. If God can use a talking donkey as a method of divine intervention (Num 22:1-35), there is nothing to stop him from using a door frame!

Counselors of faith do not need to be surprised by such reports, nor should they feel that their labors are in vain. Instead we can rejoice that God is doing what God does best—working in the hearts and minds of his beloved children. In these moments I see the hand of the triune God at work. Theologians affirm that we respond to God only because God has empowered us to do so. From the first, it starts with God. Without God initiating a relationship with us, we could not or would not be able to respond to God's loving invitation "to come unto him." Wesleyans call this *prevenient grace*—the ever-present grace of God that prepares the way for life change. This is the grace of God at work before we even know that we are in need of it. Prevenient grace goes before client and counselor into the counseling room. And this same grace accompanies the client home. Prevenient grace was at work when the Father sent the Son into the world to make a way for humanity to be reconciled to God. God's grace draws us to him. Those who put their faith in the resurrected Christ then receive the Holy Spirit. God's grace lives in them. The Holy Spirit works in mysterious ways in the lives of God's children so that we may go on to maturity (Heb 6:1). These ways can include counseling—and all of the other serendipities (a.k.a. moments of prevenient grace) that help clients reach their counseling goals.[14]

I was working with William and Marge in couple's counseling. They were struggling to alter the dynamics of their underfunctioning (William) and overfunctioning (Marge) relationship. One time William came into the session with great excitement. The men's group at church announced that they were planning a trip to a Promise Keeper's conference and were going to offer scholarships to husbands in need. An elder at the church had submitted William's name, and William received a scholarship. He looked forward to learning about "keeping promises" as a man of God and to participating in a men's accountability group after the conference. Marge had been trying to get William to look at Promise Keeper's literature for months. When it came from Marge, William reacted by distancing from her suggestion. When it came from other men in the church, he took them up on their offer!

Therapist characteristics. The therapeutic relationship is subsumed under the common factor of "therapist characteristics." Counseling "models work through therapists."[15] *Who* the counselor is and *how* the counselor interacts with clients is of utmost importance when it comes to creating a strong therapeutic alliance. Research has found specific aspects of the counseling relationship that contribute to better clinical outcomes. The therapeutic alliance is collaborative. A strong alliance is constructed by the counselor *and* the client. The participation of both parties is required. Alliances are affected by a therapist's skill in connecting with clients. This includes such factors as warmth, congruence, genuineness and respectfulness. An emotionally and socially intelligent counselor will build stronger connections with clients than those unfortunate counselors who fall short in these areas. Skillful counselors will match their method of engagement to the client instead of expecting the client to change to fit the counselor. For example, does this client expect a therapist who will give direction or one who will be more indirect? While counselors must be genuine, their genuineness can be channeled in ways that meet clients where they are.

Building a strong therapeutic alliance begins the moment that counselor and client meet. It is essential that theologically reflective counseling includes providing a Christlike welcome to clients. This not only includes welcoming clients into the therapist's space, it also includes the therapeutic processes of securing informed consent and information gathering. Securing informed consent demonstrates counselors' respect for clients' autonomy as therapists discover the extent to which clients desire explicit integration of Christian spirituality. Your printed informed consent form can notify clients about your spiritual and religious commitments, and it invites them to stipulate the degree to which religious and spiritual conversations or interventions may be introduced in their work.[16] Clients may experience the information-gathering phase of counseling as an intrusion into their private lives—even if that is why they sought counseling! If you use a standardized form to gather background information about clients, you can smoothly include a section that gently asks about their religious and spiritual preferences, experiences and expectation. Recall how Jesus' interaction with people was tailored to the individual. Jesus engaged Nicodemus (Jn 3) in a level of theological discussion that was commensurate with Nicodemus's education. Contrast this conversation with the one that Jesus had with the Samaritan woman (Jn 4) or with the man who had been born blind (Jn 9). Jesus shaped the theological aspect of each discussion to meet the spiritual needs and religious sophistication of each one he spoke with. With the crowds, Jesus used stories (parables). With the Pharisees, Jesus used Scripture and explicit theological propositions. As counselors and clients *collaboratively* specify the goals for counseling, counselors begin to imagine what spiritual and clinical practices could help this couple achieve their goals. Counselors may privately reflect on theological themes that are implied by the client's presenting problem.

Counselors also remain cognizant of the client's culture. We live in a multicultural society, and it is essential that counselors know about and respect the client's culture. This includes spiritual and religious cultural backgrounds in addition to racial and ethnic backgrounds. Often counselors must become students of the client if the counselor is unfamiliar with the client's background and a referral is not possible or practical. For example, members of a conservative Mennonite church came to the counseling center I worked in. Men and women dressed "plainly." They had the chrome removed from their black cars. When I worked with members of this church, I was a learner. I could not assume that my understanding of the Christian life was identical to theirs, and so I frequently adopted a one-down position when we talked about matters that were at the intersection of faith, life and their counseling goals.

The person of the counselor is a fundamental part of the alliance. Counselors must be authentic, avoiding phoniness. They are curious about clients and how clients make sense of the problems that bring them to counseling. Clients react to us as people of a certain age, gender, ethnicity and spiritual heritage.[17] These factors, while not necessarily determinative, can impact the therapeutic alliance—for better or worse. For instance when clients learn that you counsel from a Christian worldview as you discuss informed consent, they may be reassured that your counseling will be biblically consistent, or they may become more guarded, wondering if you will be judgmental and rejecting once you get to know them.

Three interrelated factors are woven into the alliance: goals, tasks and bonds. The alliance is affected by the degree to which counselors collaborate with clients on these three important factors. Do counselors follow clients' goals or impose their own goals on the client? Do counselors help clients understand the tasks of counseling that contribute to goal attainment? To what degree do clients and counselors feel connected and engaged with one another? The creation of a solid therapeutic relationship at the beginning of therapy is predictive of positive outcomes.[18] Counselors can repair a poor early connection with work, but this assumes that the counselor is aware that the connection is weak and that the client returns for additional sessions. So counselors must remain sensitive to the ebb and flow of the counseling relationship over the course of time. Many sessions will inevitably involve confrontation and challenge that can threaten the therapeutic relationship. When these moments of "tear" occur, counselors must follow-up with actions of "repair."

Without belaboring the point, I hope that you can see how these aspects of the therapeutic alliance echo properties of the Trinity in terms of the relationships between members of the Godhead and God's relationship with us. The match is not perfect—no human prototype accurately describes the life of God, but it is close enough to provide a solid foothold for the theologically reflective practitioner. Being a theologically reflective practitioner includes the capacity of *living theologically* throughout your clinical work. When theological reflection gets in your bones, it shapes who you are with others, including your clients. Theological integration at this level happens in the person of the counselor and is made manifest in the counseling relationship. Just as the triune God invites us to trust him, counselors invite clients to trust them by relating to clients respectfully and graciously. Just as God welcomes us into relationship with him, counselors provide welcome to their clients. Just as self-giving love and mutuality characterize the inner life of the Three-One God and the life God extends to God's children, so too counselors relate to clients in self-giving and mutually respectful ways. The quality of the counseling relationship is a theological *and* a therapeutic matter.

Dimensions of expectancy and hope. So far we have reviewed how client characteristics and counselor characteristics contribute to theologically reflective counseling. The third major area of contribution is the extent to which counselors can ignite *hope* within the hearts of their clients. From a common-factors perspective, client hopefulness (the expectancy that counseling will work) is a consistent theme in successful therapy. Clients often enter therapy when their previous efforts have failed to bring sufficient change in their presenting problem. When they come into our offices they are like people without hope. Most systems of therapy spend their opening movements fanning into flame the client's hopefulness. Counselors augment this through their own attitude toward clients' situations and as they share information with clients that shows how counseling interventions will be helpful. Counselors remind clients of God's continued care for them when clients are emotionally, relationally and spiritually demoralized. At times counselors hang onto this hope for their clients.[19]

Cynthia had not begun counseling with a great deal of hope. She had been through a previous treatment program and had "failed" because she had relapsed. I wondered aloud why she had returned to therapy. She said that she remembered feeling totally hopeless and helpless before she entered the treatment program and that with her work in that program she was able to regain control over her life. She felt that God was telling her to trust him in this therapeutic process and she would once again experience true freedom. When she compared her current level of hopelessness with that former experience, she observed that she was more hopeful now about the potential for therapeutic change than then. So she had two voices trying to prime her for counseling. One was her hopeless voice and the other was her hopeful voice. Cynthia soon began to associate the hopeful voice with the prompting of the Holy Spirit. She decided that whenever her hopeless voice became too demanding she would tune down the volume on this hopeless channel by reading Scripture passages that spoke of God's faithfulness and hope.

Nonspecific mechanisms of change. Common-factors scholarship has highlighted the fact that all schools of therapy include mechanisms of change that address (1) emotional regulation, (2) cognitive reframing, and (3) behavioral shifts.[20] Different schools of systemic therapy call them by different names and prioritize them in different ways. Nevertheless, these nonspecific therapeutic change mechanisms end up achieving similar clinical results, even when therapy models propose contrasting assumptions about what causes dysfunction and about what will bring effective therapeutic change.

These change mechanisms find a home in theologically reflective counseling when they become avenues through which counselors help clients to address applicable theological themes and subsequently help clients to align areas of their life to reflect clients' theological commitments. On one hand they can refer to interventions that are explicitly

Christian, which target change in actions, thoughts or feelings. For example, counselors may ask clients to engage in specific Christian practices (forgiving or repenting) to affect their behavior, to use Scripture as a way to evaluate their thought life (cognitive reframing), or to practice prayerful contemplation during times of anxiety (emotional regulation). On the other hand they can refer to a more global transformation that can occur as Christian clients remove the obstacles from their lives that prevent them from more fully aligning their hearts with God's heart. Ephesians 4:17–5:4 or Colossians 3:1-17 describe behavioral, cognitive and affective changes that can be characteristic of those who follow Jesus, as empowered by the Holy Spirit, and for the glory of God.

Models of therapy. If you were wondering when I will address the advantage of one model of therapy over another, then here it is—sort of. One perspective on common factors would argue that common factors render counseling models irrelevant. Lambert estimated that a mere 15 percent of change could be attributed to the school of therapy employed by the counselor. Following Sprenkle, David and Lebow, my position is that we don't need to throw the theoretical baby out with the clinical bath water. Sprenkle, Davis and Lebow explain it like this:

> Effective models are *mostly* effective because they do a credible job of activating or potentiating the common factors that are primarily responsible for therapeutic change. . . . Common factors work through models. . . . Models are needed for the therapist to filter the information most relevant for successful treatment of the client.[21]

Theologically reflective practice is not a treatment-model-specific approach to integration because, I believe, God is not limited to one model of counseling. Nevertheless, the moderate common-factors position acknowledges the value of models as the mechanism through which the common factors are delivered. Provided that theologically reflective practitioners remain grounded in God, seek to be open to the inspiration of the Holy Spirit, and conduct their work in a manner that is God-honoring, client-respecting and ethically appropriate, then the Holy Spirit can do what the Holy Spirit does best—help people more fully embody the image of God in their daily lives.

SUMMARY

In this chapter I have discussed the Trinity as the ideal for understanding the counseling relationship. Then I expanded this perspective by placing the therapeutic relationship within the context of common factors: client characteristics; therapist characteristics, including dimensions of the therapeutic relationship; dimensions of expectancy and hope; nonspecific mechanisms of change and the role that models play. To complete the model of theologically reflective counseling, one more item needs to be added which reflects this chapter's emphasis on common factors. If you look at figure 3.1 you will see that these common factors are represented in the box that covers the entire model. To borrow a computer analogy, this is the operating system that runs in the background, and which powers all that counselors do.

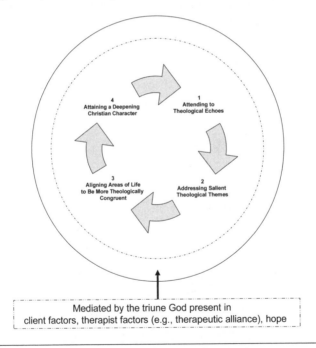

Figure 3.1. Metamodel of theologically reflective counseling

Few of us will instinctively become theologically reflective practitioners. You will need time and energy to develop eyes to see the theological threads woven into your clients' stories and to sharpen your ears to hear the whisperings of the Holy Spirit that nudge you to work in this or that way. A commitment to lifelong theological and biblical formation will deepen and enrich the theological resources that you bring to your work.

4

Responsible Living

Personal Holiness and Theologically Reflective Counseling

From thee that I no more may stray,
No more thy goodness grieve,
Grant me the filial awe, I pray,
The tender conscience give;
Quick as the apple of an eye,
O God, my conscience make!
Awake my soul when sin is nigh,
And keep it still awake.

Charles Wesley,
"I Want a Principle Within"

Holiness may be what God wants from me, and it may indeed be something that I need, but is it *really* something that I long for?[1] Unattractive stereotypes of holiness abound. For example, you may picture someone with a gaunt face who engages in extended periods of fasting. Maybe you equate holiness with an ever-expanding and legalistic list of dos and don'ts. Or perhaps you may think of someone for whom the unpleasant label "holier than thou" might apply. I certainly do not long for those forms of holiness. Yet as people of God we *do* want to be like Jesus; that is, we want to be holy like Jesus is holy. But getting there is another story. We are not the first generation with that desire and dilemma. The Holiness Movement began in the 1840s and 1850s by those who embraced John Wesley's teaching on sanctification.[2]

Unfortunately, stereotypes of holiness contain a kernel of truth. As one branch in the Holiness Movement sought to follow God with their mind, heart, soul and strength, *outward* manifestations of holiness became the yardstick for *inward* spiritual maturity. Today we would call that legalism. Following the rules became the measure of whether one's heart was following Christ. Rather than breathing life into one's soul, these behavioral stipulations often choked the life out of it. Fear of condemnation replaced holy love as a motivation for spiritual growth, and to paraphrase 1 John 4:18, "Perfect fear casts out love." Even today counselors may work with individuals who have been abused by oppressive, legalistic behavioral regulations imposed on them by a church.[3] I want to be clear that such legalistic approaches to holiness are *not* what I am talking about in this chapter, *nor* am I alluding to Christian counselors acting as the holiness police for Christian clients.

Nonetheless holiness remains a central motif in Scripture. As early as the book of Leviticus the people of God were commanded to "be holy" because God is holy (Lev 11:45; 19:2; 20:7, 26). The phrase "be holy, for I [God] am holy" is repeated in 1 Peter 1:16. Holiness is what differentiates believers from the surrounding nonbelieving world in Leviticus and 1 Peter. By associating holiness with the *everyday* act of setting the dinner menu in Leviticus to setting one's mindset for meeting the challenges of a hostile and pagan environment in 1 Peter, holiness penetrates sacred and secular space. Other theological streams capture the essence of holiness with an emphasis on Christ's *lordship* in one's life. Christ's lordship and personal holiness challenge us to commit all areas of our life to Jesus and to live in ways that are faithful to this commitment in ever-increasing measures. It is a call to love God with all of our heart, soul, mind and strength, and to love our neighbor as ourselves. When individuals seek spiritual guidance from pastoral counselors or spiritual directors, they often target areas of their lives where Christ's lordship or their own holiness (or the lack of it) may be presenting concerns.[4] It is *highly* unlikely that any client comes to *professional* counseling with holiness issues as a clearly stated clinical goal. In my twenty-five years in counseling, I have had only two clients who even came close. One was delusional and the other struggled with obsessive-compulsive disorder—both presenting symptoms with religious overtones. It is far more likely that Christian clients present with normal problems in living and relating that impede their development of a lifestyle consistent with Christ's lordship. Holiness, therefore, will most likely be a *byproduct* of your work with clients rather than a direct clinical goal. So if holiness is central to our identity as children of God, and if holiness *should* affect how we live, then I suggest that holiness can be a metagoal in theologically reflective counseling. In this chapter I explore the contours of personal holiness. Then I will examine differentiation of self as one therapeutic channel for nurturing holiness. Finally, I present a case study as an example of integrating holiness with the model of theologically reflective counseling process developed in chapter two.

THEOLOGICAL COMMITMENTS: PERSONAL HOLINESS

If holiness is not the negative stereotypes that I have already listed, then what is it? According to the *Interpreter's Dictionary*, "wherever God's presence is felt, there men [and women] encounter the wonder and mystery of holiness. . . . While it often denotes a state or condition, it is for ancient Israel primarily an *activity and a speaking which eventuate in relationship*."[5] The *Dictionary of Pastoral Care and Counseling* defines holiness as "fundamentally a *relational* term and refers not only to *right relations* to God *but to fellow human beings.* . . . It is closely associated, therefore, with justice."[6]

Holiness—a term that describes relationships and not just a state of being? This expands our view of holiness. Holiness is no longer limited to one's individual relationship to Jesus Christ. It *also includes* one's ability to relate rightly with others. So if holiness denotes "relating rightly," and if many presenting problems in counseling center on relationship problems, then expanding one's capacity for holiness can go hand-in-hand with therapeutic outcomes.[7] When counselors help clients to live truthfully, faithfully and justly in their relationships with others, then counselors are helping clients to live more holy lives—lives that honor Jesus Christ as Lord. This does not take the form of a list of dos and don'ts. For some people it may start out as such, but ultimately it is about developing a desire to relate responsibly toward others. Therapeutic work in holiness may take the form of better parenting strategies, improved marital dynamics, increased self-control over addictive behaviors or improved self-regulation over relationship-threatening emotions such as rage.

My friend Steve Martyn and I pick up on this when we encourage Christians to develop *relational holiness*.[8] We believe that relational holiness is revealed in how one relates to God, in how one manages one's emotional reactions, and in how one relates to others, especially during difficult interpersonal exchanges. The hallmarks of relational holiness include a vibrant and deepening relationship with God, a greater ability to identify and manage intense negative emotions, and an expanded capacity to respond thoughtfully, rather than react automatically, to others in the midst of intense emotional exchanges. Steve and I suggest that work in these three areas deepens one's capacity for relational holiness and that interpersonal problems may arise when one of these components is out of whack. Pastoral counselors and spiritual directors are more likely to work with individuals on improving their relationship with God than are licensed mental health professionals. Nevertheless, all manner of counselors may help individuals learn how to manage their negative emotions more effectively and how to respond to interpersonal challenges more thoughtfully. When we do this kind of work we are also helping clients to increase their capacity for holiness—even if we haven't mentioned the word!

John Wesley described holiness as the here-and-now embodiment and enactment of God's love *within* the church and *to* the world.[9] Holiness not only made us fit for heaven, *it made us fit to live with each other on earth*. Wesley often used the terms *holiness* and *love* interchangeably, so strongly did he see the link between holy living and loving others.[10] For Wesley and his theological successors, holiness was ultimately about relationships. It started with the triune God who created and loved humanity. It continued with God's relentless pursuit of intimacy with humanity, a relationship made possible only through Jesus Christ. Through grace God invites us into a loving relationship with him. Colloquially we say that we invite Jesus into our hearts. Yet Jesus issued that invitation long before we were aware that we needed him. When we respond to God's love—which was made known through the life, death and resurrection of Jesus Christ, and was imparted to believers through the Holy Spirit—then the holy love of God indwells and fills us to such an extent that it spills over into everyday life and transformed relationships. Wesley labeled the inward transformation *personal* holiness. When it overflowed into benevolent actions on behalf of others, he called it *social* holiness. Wesley pictured holiness as a mutually reinforcing dynamic between the two great commandments: Love the Lord your God with all your heart, soul, mind and strength, and love your neighbor as yourself. Wesley declared that when we realized the extent of God's love for us, we could do nothing more *and* nothing less than to respond to God's offer of love by giving our entire self to God and by dedicating our entire self to being shaped by God's love for the world.

Mid-twentieth-century Wesleyan theologian Mildred Bangs Wynkoop vividly describes the dynamic, relational qualities of holiness.[11] Wynkoop invites us to see holiness as a *godly capacity* in which a Christian can grow and develop though the power of the Holy Spirit over a lifetime. Wynkoop argues that we are created in the image of the triune God, whose very essence is love, and when we respond to God's love then the Holy Spirit empowers followers of Jesus to make God their life's orientating point. Evidence of this new orientation is seen in the degree to which the people of God love one another as God has loved them. Wynkoop's picture of holiness is a far cry from the stereotypes this chapter started with. It is less about outward behavior and more about the heart's desire.

Twenty-first-century Wesleyan theologian Mark H. Mann helps us to see more clearly how this interpretation of holiness as a *capacity* can bring holiness into the counseling room.[12] Like Wynkoop, Mann asserts that God created humanity with the capacity to center human life on God and to orient one's life around God's heart for the world—just like a compass orients to the North Star. However, sin, viewed as a disordering and decentering of our life *away* from God, destroys our relationship with God *and one another*. Sinful behaviors are the upshot of this decentering. As a result humanity's "capacity to reflect God's love for Creation in our acts of responsiveness to God's call to holiness" was undone.[13] Yet through God's grace comes the invitation to participate in God's plan for our world. If we accept this invitation to participate in the life of God, we find that *by grace* we are now free to choose, and empowered by God to choose, ways of relating to God, others and the world that reflect the love of God, which has been demonstrated for us in all of its fullness by Jesus Christ. Yet we know all too well that we fall short of this goal. This results in disruptions in our relationship with God and with others. And the effects of these disruptions can eventually end up in a counselor's office.

An emphasis on holiness as a Spirit-supported capacity to orient one's life around God provides a way for counselors to see the role that holiness can play in theologically reflective counseling. For example, counselors can wonder to what degree clients' presenting problems are a form of decentering from God's purposes. If the client is a Christian and open to exploring this, fruitful clinical discussion may follow. Clinical acumen is needed to discern when a client's concern relates to such decentering and when it does not, when this kind of conversation would be helpful, and when it would be off-putting and tear the therapeutic relationship. Such clinical discussions require the judicious use of our skills. We are *not* called to judge our clients, so direct confrontation skills may not be the best way to go. But we can become curious about how a client justifies to himself or herself some troublesome behavior (like having an affair) and the desire to follow Jesus as Lord, or how he or she reconciles harmful interactions with others and his or her understanding of Scripture. The key, I believe, is to be *truly curious* and not to use curiosity as a ploy to judge. We can empathize with their struggles (haven't we all justified poor behavior at one time or another?) and collaboratively develop plans to help them reach their goals.

To what extent can counseling help Christian clients increase their capacity to love God and love others?[14] Christian counselors can develop sensitivities to the factors that limit clients' capacity for holiness. Mann explains, "Different persons will be capable of expressing such transcendence in varying capacities: a child differently from an adult, . . . one who is healthy differently from one who is a victim of an addiction or malady like schizophrenia or Down syndrome."[15] Theologically reflective processes help clients to nurture their capacity for holiness by helping them to remove the obstacles that stand in their way of relating rightly to others.

THERAPEUTIC COMMITMENTS:
DIFFERENTIATION OF SELF

Having discussed a relational understanding of holiness, the stage is set to explore the ways in which this metagoal plays out in a therapeutic context. Consider how your preferred way of case conceptualization and intervention may assist clients to relate rightly to God and to others. While your clinical work may not encompass helping a client to love God more, it more likely will include helping clients to have better relationships with others. Limits may exist on clients' capacity for holiness. Case conceptualization can reflect avenues for understanding how these limits came about and the degree to which clients may be open to remediation and change. Counseling interventions represent ways to help clients increase their capacity for relational holiness.

Let's look briefly at a few examples. From a psychodynamic perspective, you may view the client's situation as one of disordered attachment, which originated in a dysfunctional family environment.[16] You may wonder about the extent to which this client can develop a secure attachment to others, and subsequently you implement strategies to help this client experience others differently, including God. From a cognitive perspective you may identify cognitive distortions that keep unhelpful schemas in place. If the client can challenge unhelpful schemas, then the client may be freer to relate to others because the client is no longer interpreting their behaviors through that lens. From a narrative perspective, you may wonder how you can help the client live more fully into God's story of redemption rather than a story of sinfulness (their own sin or the consequences of being sinned against) that presently shapes the client's life. Who can be a witness to the reality of God's work in the life of this client so that the client can more completely embrace God's call upon his or her life? I work from a family-systems orientation. Following a brief introduction to Murray Bowen's differentiation of self, I will show you how I use differentiation of self as a way to help clients increase their capacity for relational holiness.

Differentiation of self is a central component in Bowen Family Systems Therapy.[17] At its core differentiation of self is about taking responsibility for the self when one is closely relating to others. Bowen identified two components of differentiation: (1) the degree to which a person can balance feeling and thinking, and (2) the capacity for intimacy and autonomy in interpersonal relationships. Intrapersonally, Bowen proposed that people had two primary operating systems: the thinking system and the feeling system. Differentiation of self refers to one's ability to distinguish between thinking and feeling, and the ability to choose which system directs one's behavior. People with lower levels of differentiation are driven by their feeling system. Internal alarms go off when they sense anxiety rising. These alarms are usually out of their awareness. Instead of thoughtfully chosen responses to difficult interpersonal interactions, persons with lower differentiation react automatically. These habituated reactions *temporarily* lower their anxiety. Interpersonally, differentiation of self refers to the capacity to express intimacy and independence in important relationships. Bowen contrasted two competing forces in this regard: a force for togetherness and a force for differentiation. Please do not confuse Bowen's term *togetherness* with healthy human connection or interdependence. The togetherness force compels one to give up personal goals, dreams, desires, hopes and the like—in Bowen's words a person gives up being a "distinct self"—to keep a connection with a significant other intact. In contrast to this, the force for differentiation supports being a "distinct self." But this does not mean that no regard for connection with others exists. Differentiated selves can maintain their own position *and* remain appropriately connected to important others (even when those others are pressing for change).

Anxiety and emotional reactivity play important roles in Bowen Family Systems Theory. When relationship tension exceeds one's set point of tolerance (wherever that point was in terms of closeness and distance, power distribution or intimacy), individuals react to this triggered anxiety. Typical response patterns include *fusion* (giving up self to the other), *cutoff* (giving up the other as a way to maintain a self) or *differentiation* (the capacity to maintain an "I" position when others are exerting pressure to change). Bowen identifies several mutually reinforcing relationship patterns that emerge as partners experience emotional reactivity, fusion and cutoff. Those patterns include an overresponsible and underresponsible pairing, pursuit-distance dance and so forth. The goal in Bowen Family Systems Therapy is to increase one's functional level of differentiation.

Differentiation of self is a way of taking responsibility *for* the self while acting responsibly *toward* others. In therapy this means looking for the extent to which clients can differentiate thinking from feeling, manage and modulate their emotional reactivity, calm themselves down, and claim their own voice without reverting to fusion or cutoff. Differentiation is not about overpowering one's partner or cutting off one's parents. It is about holding onto oneself in the midst of relationship tensions, and showing up and being counted when important relationship events occur.

A DIFFERENTIATING HOLINESS

In a model of theologically reflective counseling Bowen's terminology of *differentiation of self* can be adjusted in such a manner as to serve the goal of increasing clients' capacities for holiness. When the intrapersonal and interpersonal components of the differentiating self are brought to bear upon holiness, the result is a *differentiating holiness*.[18] What then does this look like? I will highlight three coordinates that follow from the preceding theological and therapeutic discussions: (1) a Christ-centered self supplies a firm foundation for taking "I" positions based on the telos set by holiness (1 Pet 1:3-5, 13-16); (2) the peace of God, which transcends all understanding (Phil 4:7), enables, one to soothe anxiety, thereby reducing tendencies for emotional reactivity in the forms of fusion or cutoff (1 Pet 4:8, 12-19); and (3) the grace of God supplies the courage to accept responsibility for the impact of one's actions and words instead of defaulting to self-justification (1 Pet 3:8-9; 4:8-11).

First, one is empowered to take clear "I" positions when the self is centered on Christ. As a result, who I am, what I believe, what I want and what I value are no longer shaped by the demands of the world or the sinful desires of the self (1 Pet 1:14-15), but instead I am transformed so that through the grace of God I can be formed in the image of Christ and participate in expressing God's love for the world. Holiness centers one's life on the triune God—God the Father, God the Son and God the Holy Spirit. The differentiating self reflects the image of God to the world. Because the self has a firm center in Christ, clarity about who I am exists, and now love can characterize my responses to others (1 Pet 4:8). As Christ-centered selves we can rest secure in our value as children of God and persons of worth, and we can extend this same assurance to others. As we grow in Christ, differentiating holiness supports our capacity to love others, especially when they are acting in annoying ways. We can take a stand for how we prefer to be treated (i.e., Christian relationships are no place for abuse). We can accept others for where they are and who they are instead of trying to make them over into our own image. We no longer need to demand conformity from others as a way to reduce our anxiety.

Differentiating holiness also challenges us to increase our capacity to distinguish our thinking from our feelings, rather than to be driven by knee-jerk reactions (1 Pet 1:13; 2:1-2; 3:9; 5:8-9). This capacity is critically important for self-control. We do not need to become emotionally reactive when others fail to meet our expectations, pull away from us or demand their own way. Differentiating holiness requires that we are willing to tolerate the pain of taking an "I" position for the sake of growth (1 Pet 4:12-19). It challenges us to speak the truth in love and to express ourselves to others in ways that respect them and honor God. Times exist when this is not easy.

Please do not confuse differentiated holiness with rugged individualism. Differentiating holiness is developed, nurtured and shaped by and within a Christian community. The therapeutic relationship and the Christian community serve as contexts within which the Holy Spirit brings salvation to its fullest expression. Differentiating holiness enhances our ability to live well with our community, be it family, neighborhood or church. As we grow in differentiating holiness we are able to be more emotionally available to others without feeling like we are going to be consumed by them (and resort to cutoff to manage the fear of being swallowed whole) or feeling like we will cease to exist if we are rejected (and resort to fusion to keep this from happening).

Second, the peace of God, which transcends all understanding (Phil 4:7), enables one to soothe anxiety and limit emotional reactivity, fusion or cutoff (1 Pet 4:8, 12-17). Therapeutic interventions are *not* sources of deep peace. Only God provides this kind of safety and security. Differentiating holiness increases one's capacity to live *with an awareness of God's peace* through the grace of God. A variety of practices can augment one's sensitivity to God's peace. This includes meditating on Scripture, prayer, Christian conferencing, worship, journaling, challenging automatic negative thoughts and so on. Wesley referred to such practices as "means of grace" and encouraged his followers to partake of them frequently and regularly.[19]

Differentiating holiness includes the skill of *self-soothing*. Self-soothing is the ability to calm oneself down and to reduce anxiety. This ability is particularly critical when people find themselves in the midst of strong interpersonal disagreements. Self-soothing supports peaceful relationships within the body of Christ. Edwin Friedman referred to this as the capacity to be a "nonanxious presence" in the midst of anxious relationship systems.[20] When people become nonanxious through differentiating holiness they are able to regulate their own intense feelings instead of waiting for someone else to do that for them. This is a behavior (reducing one's own anxiety) and an attitude (self as responsible for reducing anxiety). Self-soothing contributes to the flow of holy thoughts, words and actions because our affections and emotions are grounded in God's peace.

Third, differentiating holiness relies on the grace of God to supply the courage to accept responsibility for the impact of one's actions and words on others instead of defaulting to self-justification (1 Pet 3:8-9; 4:8-11). Wesleyan theologian Randy Maddox discusses this in terms of "responsible grace."[21] Maddox observes that John Wesley's "distinctive concern was that God's power not be defined or defended in any way that undercuts human responsibility."[22] This is one place where Wesley differentiated from the Calvinism of his day.[23] Wesley affirmed that we are created with the ability to respond to God's grace (*response-able*), and so empowered by the Holy Spirit, we bear the responsibility to orient our lives around God as we love God and our neighbors (*responsible* grace). Differentiating holiness challenges us to embrace responsibility, that is, to see how we are *contributing* to the pain within our relationships. Jesus referred to this as taking the log out of your own eye before you remove the speck of dust from another's eye (Mt 7:3-5). Through differentiating holiness our anxiety-driven reactions will have increasingly less power within our relationships. Individuals will be freer to love others as Christ loves them.

Which theological world may have particular salience as clients increase their capacity for personal holiness? I believe it would be those who see themselves as the theologically *faint*. You will remember from the discussion in chapter two that the theological world of the faint is one of self-estrangement. They believe themselves to be insignificant and impotent. They fear rejection, and this fear has the power to paralyze them. They believe there is nothing to themselves. In Bowen language, they lack a distinct self. This sense of self-estrangement may drive fusion in one's relationships as a way to "get a self" by borrowing from the self of the other. The rhythm of the faint moves between an empty self (*obsessio*) and fulfillment (*epiphania*). What the faint desire is to experience love as filling to overflowing. Unfortunately, given enough time, human love is bound to be disappointing. Jones suggests that resolution happens as the faint experience acceptance by God and others, which leads to the ability to take relationship risks and engage in a process of self-discovery.[24] Theologically reflective counseling can track the extent to which clients operate out of a full or a borrowed sense of self, the degree to which clients are able and willing to take appropriate risks in their relationships (e.g., self-disclosure of vulnerable emotions), and can help them to increase their level self-awareness. In these ways clients will move from *obsessio* to *epiphania* as their clinical work will help them also to grow in differentiating holiness.

THEOLOGICALLY REFLECTIVE COUNSELING IN ACTION

As I looked over my case load for the day, I saw the name of a couple that I had seen several years ago. At that time Don and Bernadette had begun their ministry at Faith Central Church. This Euro-American couple had been in their late twenties, had been married for six years and had just left the seminary, where Don had earned his master of divinity degree. The congregation at Faith Central had called Don to be their youth pastor. But church conflict and disappointment quickly replaced the hope and enthusiasm with which they had accepted the call. Bernadette and Don had come for counseling to ensure that their marriage survived even if Don's appointment to Faith Central did not. That period of counseling had ended well. As I recalled our work together, I was curious to know what had brought them back.

Don spoke first. "Bernadette says she is going to divorce me if I don't change." Over the course of the next hour, the couple's story unfolded. For the majority of their married life, Don had felt free to express his anger at full volume. He never became physically violent. He never threatened Bernadette, denied her financial autonomy or isolated her from family and friends. But the intensity of his anger and the power of his voice frightened her. Twelve years and two children later, Bernadette had an epiphany—she deserved better treatment. This was one step in her living into her awareness of herself as a "distinct self in Christ." She believed that Don had a right to express his anger, and she also proclaimed that she had a right to feel safe when he did. Bernadette demanded that he find a new way to express his anger or else she was leaving him. Don voiced his total commitment to their marriage and to making whatever changes he needed to make, even if he wasn't quite sure what it was that he needed to adjust.

Bernadette picked up their story. "I have been telling him for years that his anger frightens me. When we came to see you the last time, I just assumed that his anger was normal and that I was being unreasonable. I have changed my mind about that. I don't like him to scream at me. I have had enough of it. I am not going to go through another twelve years of living in fear." She affirmed that his anger was not a daily occurrence, nor did she ever feel physically threatened by Don. Yet she was intimidated by his intensity. She didn't want their marriage to end. She also didn't want to live in fear the rest of her married life. Either he changed or she walked.

Attending to theological echoes. Bernadette and Don are in marital crisis. Specifically, Bernadette has issued a challenge to Don: shape up or ship out. This couple is committed to saving their marriage, however what remains to be seen is the degree to which each partner will dedicate himself or herself to the hard work of change that will result in a transformation of their relationship. Bernadette and Don are seasoned Christians. They expect their counselor to be fluent with a Christian perspective on marriage (theology) and knowledgeable about biblical passages that can relate to their situation (biblical studies). What a counselor will need to discover is what *model* of Christian marriage does this couple embrace?[25] What biblical and theological support do they bring with them for their current marital structure and to what degree do their patterns need to change to move the client couple to wholeness and holiness? Counselors can frame Bernadette's challenge to Don as a challenge for Don to grow in personal holiness. She will need to increase her capacity for holiness too. For Don this may take the form of repentance; for Bernadette, forgiveness.[26] Also they will need to restore justice and safety in their marriage.[27]

Don and Bernadette have consented to using Christian practices as part of counseling. They explain that they want counseling that is consistent with the Bible. Counselors will need to be sensitive to the hermeneutic this couple employs when discussions of the roles of husbands and wives surface. Counselors must assess for risk of domestic violence and comply with state laws if mandated reporting laws include abuse of adults. It is likely that gender issues will surface. What expectations do Don and Bernadette hold for men's and women's roles in marriage? How does this couple share power? Will the counselor need to advocate on behalf of Bernadette and empower her to make choices for safety? Is the counselor able to work with the client's theology of marriage and its subsequent application in their marriage? How will the counselor confront unfair patterns of marital interaction that clients believe are supported by Scripture? What if Bernadette decides to divorce Don? What kind of theological or therapeutic challenge does this raise for Christian counselors, and how will counselors resolve any subsequent ethical dilemmas?

Addressing salient theological themes. Several themes immediately present themselves. In addition to personal holiness, one can see how themes of forgiveness, justice and grace may be present. Counselors consider how they understand these concepts theologically and how their theological position compares to that of their clients. Regarding personal holiness specifically, Don and Bernadette's marital concerns offer avenues to help them orient themselves more fully around God's agenda for marriage. Sinful marital habits (overpowering anger from Don and persistent cutoff from Bernadette) have weakened their marriage. Each one needs to rely on God to challenge these habits. They will need to extend grace to one another when they make mistakes as they work toward reconciliation. Seeing their partner as a beloved child of God may help to soften their heart toward one another and toward the hard work of reclaiming their marriage. During seasons of struggle during counseling, each one will need to lean into God for strength and endurance. Both Don and Bernadette believe that God desires wholeness for each of them in their marriage because they do see God as a loving Father. They believe that God will equip them to save their marriage.

Aligning areas of life to be more theologically congruent. Behaviorally, the couple will learn different conflict management strategies and improve their communication skills. Interpersonally, Don will need to regulate his anger, not deny it but manage it, while Bernadette will need to increase her tolerance for an appropriate level of Don's intensity. Intrapersonally, each one will need to learn how to calm the self down so that each one can think more clearly during challenging exchanges.

Forgiveness and repentance practices are indicated. The couple will also need to rebuild their friendship. Don and Bernadette can practice forgiveness and repentance as they take Communion. Praying together and for one another can support them during difficult seasons of counseling. The counselor can use Scripture throughout the course of counseling. Research supports the in-session use of religious-oriented interventions for highly religious clients like Don and Bernadette.[28]

It may be instructive to walk through each aspect of holiness for Don and Bernadette, as expressed in its therapeutic version of differentiating holiness. You may recall that differentiating holiness is denoted by three threads: (1) a Christ-centered self, which supplies a firm foundation for taking "I" positions; (2) relying on the "peace of God" to enable one to soothe anxiety, thereby reducing tendencies for emotional reactivity, fusion or cutoff; and (3) leaning into the grace of God for the courage to accept responsibility for the impact of one's actions and words on others. First, through differentiating holiness Christ becomes more fully the "I's" orientation point for the self, and by extension for one's relationship. This requires a reorienting of one's deepest desires around God's kingdom agenda. Through the Holy Spirit, Don and Bernadette can realign their relationship to become one that more clearly reflects the mutual, other-centered love shared among the Trinity, embodied by Christ in his relationship with us and modeled within the therapeutic relationship. How might this unfold in counseling?

Don became verbally intimidating when he became anxious about not getting his own way. At home he failed to self-soothe and keep himself calm enough to control what he said and how he said it. He (and Bernadette) affirmed that he never displayed this kind of behavior at church—even during the most combative administrative board meetings. That self-control evaporated when he came home. Don needed to develop a deeper understanding of the relational nature of holiness. He wanted to love his wife as Christ loved the church "laying down his life for her." Don may be willing to lay down his physical life for Bernadette but would he be willing to lay down his sense of entitlement to unrestrained venting? The counselor will need to be gentle yet firm in helping Don to align this aspect of his life with God's orientation.

Bernadette was cowered by Don's anger. Theirs was a complementary partnership—the more he shouted, the more she withdrew into herself and shut Don out. She had given up her voice in the marriage and now she had to reclaim it. Bernadette will need to manage her anxious fearfulness and challenge herself to stay present and stay involved in heated (but not intimidating) conversations with Don. She also needs to implement a plan to keep herself emotionally safe during the times that Don messes up, as he is bound to do. With the counselor's help she can learn how to take "I" positions when demanding marital safety *and* stay appropriately connected to Don as she does so.

Second, differentiated holiness includes the capacity to be *emotionally-grounded in the peace of the triune God.* Peace is definitely missing in their relationship, especially when they argue. Don permits himself to shout and stomp around the house when he is angry without any thought to how his behavior affects his wife and children. Bernadette needs to know that God wants her to feel safe in her own home and with her husband. Don grew up in a verbally violent home and ironically pledged that he would not have this kind of home for his own wife and children. He also vowed never to be "walked on" by his wife, as he saw his mother verbally berate his passive father. Sadly, Don and Bernadette re-created his family of origin environment. Don needs to forgive his parents for the model that they set for him, and repent for the many times that he has intimidated and verbally overpowered Bernadette. In contrast, Bernadette needs to feel safe in her marriage and her home. She affirms that Don's feelings of anger deserve validation and consideration, but she insists that the validation and consideration *not* come at the expense of her safety. Bernadette's challenge is to learn how to remain present during an argument and not emotionally disappear. She needs to learn how to calm herself down when she is becoming anxious so she can implement her safety plan even as she challenges Don to exert greater levels of self-control.

A final aspect of differentiated holiness is a *Spirit-enhanced capacity for responsibility for self.* I have already touched on some aspects of this in the preceding paragraphs. Perhaps here is the most tangible aspect of theologically reflective counseling during a session. Secular and Christian interventions can be used to help Bernadette and Don. For Don this means regulating the intensity of his anger, creating space within himself for Bernadette's voice and listening respectfully and as nondefensively as possible when Bernadette offers a complaint, and above all, repenting, which *must* include his dedication to demonstrating consistent changed behavior over time. For Bernadette this means regulating the intensity of her urge to withdraw, creating a space within herself for Don's voice and listening respectfully and as nondefensively as possible when Don shifts to criticism.

Attaining a deepening Christian character. Because Don and Bernadette had assented to using interventions consistent with their Christian faith, we began to explore the theological and biblical contours of their marital makeover. Clinical work with Don included (1) helping Don to become aware of his tendency to demand his way in a childish and hostile manner, (2) teaching Don to self-soothe, (3) practicing nondefensive listening, and (4) maintaining consistent changed behavior over time (i.e., changing his way of expressing anger). Holding himself responsible for the impact of his words and actions, calming himself down when he became anxious, and learning how to speak for what he thought, wanted and desired in his marriage in a respectful manner, as well as listening to Bernadette's thoughts, wants and desires helped Don to increase his functional differentiation. Clinical work with Bernadette included (1) holding on to her perspective during intense conversations with Don, (2) learning how to take "I" positions in her marriage, (3) calming herself down when she sensed that Don was getting angry and remaining in the conversation rather than withdrawing, and (4) forgiveness. Taking "I" positions when her opinion differed from Don's and when she had a marital complaint, managing her anxiety so that she responded to Don rather than reacted to him, not withdrawing in their discussions and forgiving Don helped Bernadette to increase her functional differentiation.

Theological themes wove in and out of more clinically oriented conversations. Theological themes of love and justice, forgiveness and repentance, grace and mercy were continually present. Each partner reflected on how his or her actions and words did or did not reflect an orientation toward God's kingdom. In session I was able to challenge Don and Bernadette to bring their best responsible self to their marriage as a way that they could reflect the power of God in their life. Regularly they reaffirmed their commitment to making their marriage last a lifetime as a way to align themselves with God's kingdom agenda and to make their marriage one that reflected a love that mirrored God's love for them.

CLOSING THOUGHTS

In this chapter I have leaned upon John Wesley's understanding of personal holiness. Perhaps your theological home identifies this spiritual reality in other terms. "Sanctification" and living fully under the "lordship" of Christ are other ways of talking about holiness that may be more familiar to many readers. In this chapter I applied the model of theologically reflective practice to a marital case in which increasing each mate's capacity for personal holiness was facilitated through the therapeutic avenue of differentiation of self. I hope that you considered how your therapeutic home base could be employed in the service of helping clients to align their hearts more completely with God's heart as you thought about Don and Bernadette. In chapter five we will investigate how social holiness and counseling as advocacy for social justice go hand in hand in theologically reflective counseling.

Out of the Office and into the Streets

Social Holiness, Social Justice and Theologically Reflective Counseling

The scepter well becomes His hands;
All Heav'n submits to His commands;
His justice shall avenge the poor,
And pride and rage prevail no more.

With power He vindicates the just,
And treads th' oppressor in the dust:
His worship and His fear shall last
Till hours, and years, and time be past.

Isaac Watts,
"Jesus Shall Reign Wherever the Sun"

CHAPTER FOUR AND THIS PRESENT CHAPTER are set against the theological horizon of *holiness*. Chapter four revealed how an emphasis on personal holiness maps onto calling clients to assume personal responsibility. You will recall that submitting to Christ's lordship is the process of orienting all of one's being around God and God's agenda for our world through the power of the Holy Spirit, who first calls to us to respond to God's loving invitation and then empowers us to do so. It is all grace—"response-able" grace and "responsible" grace. When counselors who are followers of Christ help Christian clients to reach their counseling goals, they are also helping clients to remove impediments to holy living. As "specialists in applied sanctification," counselors committed to theological reflection help clients to increase their capacity for holiness. This is in fulfillment of the first part of the Great Commandment (Mt 22:37): Love the Lord your God with every fiber of your being . . . so that clients can live like resurrection people. Chapter five addresses more fully the second part of the Great Commandment (Mt 22:39): "Love your neighbor as yourself." John Wesley refers to this neighbor love as *social holiness*. Social holiness takes personal holiness out of one's prayer closet into the community of believers *and* into the world. To put it in John Wesley's words: "Solitary religion is not to be found there [in the gospel of Christ]. 'Holy solitaries' is a phrase no more consistent with the gospel than holy adulterers. The gospel of Christ knows no religion, but social; no holiness but social holiness."[1]

Wesley was arguing against individualized, disconnected-from-the-body-of-Christ spirituality. He was arguing primarily for Christians in loving (agape) relationship with one another, and by logical extension Christians in service to the world.[2] Wesley could not imagine full-throttle love of God that didn't also morph into full-throttle love for others. Wesley's concern for the well-being of those within the body of Christ and those beyond it resonates with a current theological emphasis on orthopraxis—working for social justice in the midst of complex world situations. N. T. Wright observes that

> The church has been divided between those who cultivate their own personal holiness but do nothing about working for justice in the world and those who are passionate for justice but regard personal holiness as an unnecessary distraction from that task. . . . What we need is integration.[3]

This theological emphasis on mercy and justice ministry is echoed by the mental health field's stress on social justice counseling and advocacy. According to Courtland C. Lee, "social justice relates to counselors' sense of social responsibility. It involves counselors taking stands on social issues and working to eradicate systems and ideologies that perpetuate discrimination and disregard human rights."[4]

Some counselors are born with a heart for *social* holiness and a passion for social justice. They love Jesus and have joined Christ in his mission of proclaiming freedom for the prisoners (of injustice, domestic violence or child abuse) and release for the oppressed (by poverty and abuse) (Lk 4:18-19) through the practice of social-justice counseling and social action. Some therapists, like Bonnie, can do this openly as Christians. They work in settings where explicit integration of theology and counseling is supported. In contrast Taunya and Elizabeth work in secular settings and must respect the regulations that limit the extent to which Christianity is introduced in their work. While they cannot practice explicit integration, they can lean on the theological foundations for what many in the past may have called the Social Gospel as a source of spiritual support.

Bonnie is a Christian who is a licensed professional counselor in private practice. Her clients laugh their way into mental wholeness. But issues of injustice are no laughing matter to Bonnie. Her justice radar is set on high alert. Whether it is in the counseling office or on the street, Bonnie will step up and step in on behalf of the person who drew the short end of the justice straw. Through her work as a Christian mental health professional, she is a voice for social action and social justice.

Taunya is the victim's advocate in a nearby county. Her job is to support women, men and children who have been affected by domestic violence. She is the only victim's advocate in her county of forty-eight thousand souls. Her job is demanding and emotionally exhausting. Yet her sense of being a voice for those whose voice has been silenced by violence compels her to continue in this job with energy and dedication. She is infused with the love of God for her clients. Through her work at this secular position, she is a voice for social action and social justice.

I first met Elizabeth as a student in my counseling classes. She was working full time in the banking industry to pay her tuition. Elizabeth was not set on fire by balancing credits and debits, but by balancing the scales of justice. During her master's program she became a volunteer victim's advocate through the local rape crisis center. Then she completed her counseling field placement at an urban counseling center whose primary mission is to provide support to women, children and families in crisis through the prevention of family violence and abuse. She is now a staff counselor there. Through her work at this secular agency she is a voice for social action and social justice.

Justice is a challenging construct to define because definitional nuances are culturally conditioned. One can identify at least three categories of justice. Retributive justice is where wrongdoers get what they deserve. Distributive justice is where all get what they are rightly entitled to in order to survive, if not thrive. Restorative justice hopes to bring peace and perhaps reconciliation between offender and offended parties.[5] But who determines what the standard for justice is? *Whose* justice are we talking about? For Christians the "whose" in question is the God who created the cosmos with all creation in right relationships, who heard the cries of his oppressed people and delivered them from Egyptian slavery (the exodus). This is the God who held these same ransomed-from-Egypt people accountable for their failure to worship the one true God wholeheartedly and exclusively, *and* for the injustices that they inflicted on others, which resulted in their exile from their homeland. God in his mercy restored a remnant of his exiled people to Jerusalem, with a promise of a coming Messiah who *would set all things to rights*. This one true God then came to live among us, died on a cross and rose from the dead, destroying death itself. He now empowers his people through the Holy Spirit to be restorers of right relationships with God and one another (2 Cor 5:11–7:13). God's people continue to look forward to the Messiah's return when God will *ultimately* and *finally* set all things to rights when he comes again (Rev 21).

This chapter takes personal holiness out of the sanctuary and into the streets as it explores social holiness and its relationship to social justice counseling and advocacy. First, I will explore a biblical and theological perspective on the God of justice. Next, I will link Wesley's understanding of holiness with this biblical and theological portrait of justice. Then, I will review counseling's historic and contemporary emphasis on social justice. Finally, I will show how these factors map onto our model of theologically reflective counseling.

THEOLOGICAL COMMITMENTS:
THE GOD OF JUSTICE AND THE JUSTICE OF GOD

In the Old Testament *justice* is a complex term that is associated with making right legal decisions and the laws that guide those decisions.[6] It emphasizes one's conformity to God's revealed will in its personal and *social implications*. It is correlated with *shalom*—everything in the created order as God intended—with *righteousness*—everything related rightly according to God's design—and with *faithful love, truth* and *fairness*. Justice is not denoted by oppression, violence, bribery, extortion or actions that take advantage of the powerless and poor, especially those represented by the categories of widows, orphans and sojourners. In the Old Testament, God's character is the basis of Israel's way of understanding justice. Justice is grounded in creation as the newly created humans are charged to rule (to bring justice and God's shalom to creation). Justice is based on God's revelation of himself as a God who attends to the needs of the widow, orphan and sojourner (Deut 10:18), and who expects his people to mirror this characteristic in their interactions with one another. But the nation of Israel had a justice problem! They regularly failed to enact God's justice on behalf of the marginalized, and so God judged them for their injustice. Eventually this resulted in Israel's exile. Israel's Messiah, the long-expected one, is to bring God's justice upon the earth.

Justice is a central biblical theme. It is associated with the very being of God and by extension it should be associated with God's people. Theologian Theodore Jennings Jr. observes that "the being of God is constituted as a relationship to the violated and humiliated."[7] We see this in Genesis 4 as God challenges Cain about his brother's whereabouts. We see this in Exodus 3:7-10 when God reveals himself to Moses as the God who sees the misery of God's enslaved people and who hears them crying out because of their suffering. Subsequently, throughout the Old Testament God is identified as the God who rescued the children of Israel from Egyptian slavery. In sum, God is a

God of justice who loathes mistreatment of people because all people are created in God's image and are of inestimable value to God. God does take sides! He sides with the poor, the oppressed, the weak and the marginalized. When we battle injustice, there is hope because God promises that he will ultimately set things to rights. Steven Roy, professor of pastoral theology, helps us understand God's justice as it is woven throughout four major movements of the biblical narrative: Creation, Fall, Redemption, Consummation.[8]

Creation. Threads of justice initially appear when God creates humanity in God's image. Creation established that all people are worthy of dignity and respect because they are beings who bear the image of God. We therefore carry the responsibility of treating others rightly in accordance with their status as "bearers of the image of God" and of promoting contexts such that these same individuals can fully live into their calling as God's image bearers. The image of God also sets a standard for human behavior. Humanity is to rule the created world in ways that reflect God's values and purpose. God intends the human community to bear the image of the divine community, the loving, self-giving relationships shared within the Trinity (Gen 1:26-31).

When Christian mental health practitioners treat clients with dignity and respect, we do so in part because we can see all human beings as bearers of the image of God. You may not have associated this professional-ethics-code-supported standard with theology—but there it is! All clients have been created in God's image, even if that is sometimes hard to envision for certain clients who are particularly unlovely in their thoughts, words and behaviors. When Christian practitioners work with clients to bring more justice to their relationships or situations (e.g., fairer distribution of power in families, challenging contexts that disadvantage clients from vulnerable populations, etc.), they help clients to move one step closer to living with one another in ways that are more likely to reflect God's purposes and values.

Janice is a Christian counselor who works in a faith-based residential home for single mothers. Janice often goes with her clients when they visit their case worker at the local office of the Department of Human Services. Before Janice identified herself as Cindy's counselor, the case worker approached Cindy as just one more client to see and process. After Janice allied herself with Cindy, the case worker's demeanor was more welcoming. Janice knows that this worker carries a heavy case load and may likely be close to burnout.[9] Janice's mild intervention may not topple the systemic injustice that disadvantages Cindy, but it did create a more welcoming greeting.

Fall. The first humans failed at establishing God's good and just reign on earth. Their sin ruptured the relationship between God and humanity (vertical dimension) and among human beings (horizontal dimension). Intimacy was replaced with estrangement and alienation. The effects of sin were subsequently seen individually, corporately and structurally. Yet from the moment that Adam and Eve were expelled from the Garden, God sustained his commitment to justice in restorative ways (Gen 3). Roy observes, "It is God's commitment to reestablish 'right order' in the fallen world that he has made. In God's justice, he confronts injustice in all its forms and seeks to restore human communities that are characterized by full inclusion and genuine participation."[10] Christian counselors who work with clients who live on the margins of society will come face to face with systemic injustice. Many clients' environments disadvantage them as individuals or as members of an at-risk group. At times this disadvantage is built into the very social structures that provide the framework for their daily living. When counselors help clients to identify and confront these structural injustices, counselors are joining God's commitment to reestablish right order in the fallen world.

The Violence Intervention Program (VIP) is housed at the University of Kentucky. This program is also known as the "Green Dot" strategy. The Green Dot strategy seeks to reduce the bystander effect.[11] According to their website,

> The Green Dot strategy is a comprehensive approach to violence prevention that capitalizes on the power of peer and cultural influence across all levels of the socio-ecological model. . . . The program proposes to target socially influential individuals from across community subgroups. The goal is for these groups to engage in a basic education program that will equip them to integrate moments of prevention

within existing relationships and daily activities. By doing so, new norms will be introduced and those within their sphere of influence will be significantly influenced to move from passive agreement that violence is wrong, to active intervention.[12]

Individuals who have received VIP training are awarded a green dot pin. Yes, the pin is a green dot. This dot represents one individual who will take a stand against violence in any relationship. Green Dot training happens in high schools, on college campuses and in local churches. The Green Dot is not a faith-based program, but its goals are consistent with the heart of God.

Redemption. God's restorative justice involves delivering the widow, orphan, sojourner and poor from exploitation, liberating the dominated and oppressed from the power of their tormenters, eliminating violence and establishing peace, and "restoring the outcasts, the excluded, the Gentiles, the exiles, and refugees to community."[13] Christian mental health practitioners can view their daily work as a way to participate in God's redemptive plan for individuals and families. Counselors can use their skills to advocate on behalf of their clients by attending to social policies that negatively affect clients' welfare.

Ked Frank, an ordained minister, is pursuing his license as a clinical mental health counselor. Ked is the founder and executive director of Refuge for Women. This multifaceted residential ministry seeks to help women escape from the adult entertainment industry. The home offers a safe place for women to recover and redirect their lives within an explicitly Christian environment. According to their website,

> The Refuge for Women offers a new beginning to women who wish to leave the adult entertainment industry. There is no charge to guests as they live and work together as a family towards healing. We are a faith-based non-profit. Although not licensed as a treatment facility by the state of Kentucky, our dedicated staff and volunteers utilize a highly successful curriculum and mentoring approach to help each guest progress through their unique challenges. We ask each woman for a minimum three-month stay, with many women choosing to stay longer.[14]

Consummation. In the end, God will reestablish his just kingdom when the new heaven and the new earth are a reality (Rev 21). Then all things will be set to rights—right with God, right with one another in community, and even right with the created world. Roy concludes, "Social justice in Scripture is creational, restorative, and eschatological. Such is its nature and importance."[15]

The children of Israel anticipated God's justice with earnest expectations—especially when they were on the receiving end of injustice. Sadly, their memory was short-lived and God's people acted unjustly toward one another by neglecting the plight of the widow, the orphan and the sojourner (see Amos 5:10-15). The prophets regularly warned Israel of the judgment they would face if they continued to act unjustly. The Bible is clear that humans bear responsibility for their acts of injustice. The people of God cannot rest on their laurels of offering worship when they are participating in acts of injustice at the same time (see Malachi). Roy notes that God calls us to a holistic ministry, one that pursues justice on behalf of the widow, the orphan, the sojourner and the poor, and that worships the Lord in spirit and in truth.

Justice can be viewed as each one having those resources that are necessary to sustain life physically, emotionally, relationally and spiritually. This is highlighted in the work of Old Testament scholars M. Douglas Meeks and Donald E. Gowan. Meeks notes that the Torah, the Scriptures for the Israelites, established five justice-oriented rules for Hebrew households. First, don't charge interest to the poor (Ex 22:25-27; Lev 25:35-38). This can lead to debt. Debt results in slavery. God has delivered his people from the slavery of Egypt, and they are not to relate to each other in ways that return them to slavery. Even when interest was allowed, creditors were prohibited from taking anything that the poor depended on for life. Second, farmers were instructed to leave the gleanings in the field as they harvested their crops (Lev 19:9-10). The poor would go to the fields and gather whatever the harvesters left behind. In this way the poor's right to a livelihood is asserted in the Torah. Meeks observes that the commandment prohibiting stealing means "do not take what belongs to the poor because the poor belong to God."[16] Third, Israelites were to practice tithing. While modern people think about tithing in terms of supporting religious institutions, the tithe was also meant as a means of livelihood for the poor (Deut 14:22-29; Mal 3:7-12). It represents a redistribution of God's power for life to the poor. Fourth, the Torah household was to practice hospitality. Hospitality was an essential facet of life as it offered safe shelter to those who had no place to live, especially the widow, the orphan, the stranger and the alien. Meeks explains, "True worship is living the economy in which God invites into the household all those who are excluded by the denial of God's righteousness. Almost all of the prophets are concerned with the replacement of hospitality in God's household by empty worship and malicious feasts."[17] Finally, Torah households were to practice the sabbath. Meeks frames sabbath keeping not in terms of rest from work but in terms of God's justice, as sabbath interrupts means of exploiting the powerless through ceaseless work expectations, loss of property and excessive consumption.

Gowan highlights how the Old Testament narratives link the health of a community with its care for those who are powerless, specifically widows, orphans, sojourners and the poor (Zech 7:9-10), who lacked social status, social respect and therefore were easy targets for the unscrupulous in their community (Ps 82:3; Is 1:17). They did not have enough power to insist on being treated rightly. Gowan comments, "For the Old Testament writers the cause of poverty which produced the most concern and true indignation was not what the poor do or do not do but what others have done to them. . . . Those people who do not have the power to insist on justice for themselves are thus held up as a special concern for the whole community."[18] The Israelite community's motivation for caring for the powerless arose from the degree of their awareness that the widow, orphan, sojourner and poor have dignity and value in God's eyes (Deut 10:18-19), and from identifying with them "for [the Israelites] were strangers in the land of Egypt" (Deut 10:19).

God's justice project continues in the New Testament through the life, death and resurrection of Jesus Christ, and through the body of Christ, the church. Israel failed as the representative of God who would bring God's justice to the world in spite of repeated warnings by the prophets. The Gospels tell the story of how God's redemptive plan now rested squarely on the shoulders of God's Son, Jesus Christ. God himself was now taking responsibility for what humanity could not accomplish. Jesus announced his ministry as that of bringing God's justice to earth (Lk 4:18-19). Jesus taught and modeled God's special interest in the poor. To be poor in Jesus' day made one vulnerable to oppression and helplessness. Jesus proclaimed that the poor would inherit the kingdom of God (Lk 6:20). While this beatitude is regularly interpreted as referring to the spiritually poor, Jesus' relationship with the poor, the beggars, the widows and the lepers indicates that it may have also carried a literal meaning. It is the poor, maimed, blind and lame who attend the messianic banquet (Lk 14:21). Jesus challenged those with resources to spend their wealth ameliorating the suffering of the poor (Lk 18:18-25). Through his life, death and resurrection, Jesus took on the forces of evil, absorbing them into himself and draining them of all power. He proclaims that God's justice can be restored to the earth through the body of Christ, the church.[19] Therefore true holiness is not just about relating rightly to God; it is also about relating rightly to others. Holiness is wedded to justice. Biblical justice is concerned with the organization of a just society, not just the saving of individual souls. Throughout the biblical narrative the God of justice intervenes in individual lives and social situations *and* challenges unjust political structures.

JOHN WESLEY, SOCIAL HOLINESS AND SOCIAL ACTION

Consistent with the biblical message outlined previously, John Wesley proclaimed that true holiness is expressed in how we relate to others. Wesley wrote: "Do all the good you can. By all the means you can. In all the ways you can. In all the places you can. At all the times you can. To all the people you can. As long as ever you can."[20] According to Wesleyan scholar Randy Maddox, Wesley advocated for two ways to increase one's capacity for holiness. The first is through *works of piety*. Works of piety are associated with the individual Christian's relationship with God and worship of God. Works of piety include things such as prayer and Bible study. The North American evangelical Christian community is quite familiar with practices that help believers build personal intimacy with God. The other avenue is *works of mercy*, where one expresses love for God through concrete actions that contribute to the welfare of others. In his book *Responsible Grace,* Maddox observes that a dynamic relationship exists between love of God and love of others—to increase in one is to increase in the other.

John Wesley identified profoundly with the poor. He lived during the early stages of the Industrial Revolution. During that time many families moved from rural to urban centers. The social class boundaries in England were firmly entrenched. The gap between the haves and the have nots was great. Poor families lacked access to education and work opportunities. They experienced higher death rates than the rich. Wesley refused to remain mute in the face of these social injustices. Wesley scholar Meeks notes that "Wesley made clear again and again that the poor belong to the one who has died for them; they may not be treated as if they belonged to another master."[21] In his sermons and publications Wesley called attention to the social dimension of sin. He also called attention to the social dimension of holiness. He argued that holiness was not fostered in isolation. It was practiced and developed through Christian community and in service to the community at large.

Wesley would have nothing to do with "solitary religion," secret Christians or faith which did not show itself in actions on behalf of others (Jas 1–5). Christian holiness was an inward *and* an outward reality. Wesley did not preach works righteousness. But neither could he imagine a deep faith in Christ that did not result in good works as evidence of a transformed heart and as an expression of holy love. For Wesley service to the poor was an integral part of *salvation* and *holiness.* It was a reflection of Christlikeness and of God's heart for the widows, orphans and aliens. Wesley challenged his followers to have face-to-face interaction with the poor to prevent deep isolation from, and apathy for, the poor. This kind of interaction raised firsthand awareness of their destitute condition and created a bridge of sympathy. It broke down the dividing walls of social boundaries. At a time when rich families "bought pews" (and only those family members could sit in their pew), Wesley installed benches in his chapels, taking down one barrier between rich and poor. Wesley wrote,

One reason why the rich, in general, have so little sympathy for the poor is because they seldom visit them. Hence it is that according to the common observation, one part of the world does not know what the other suffers. Many of them do not know, because they do not care to know: they keep out of the way of knowing it; and then plead their voluntary ignorances an excuse for their hardness of heart.[22]

Wesley worked tirelessly for the spiritual and material welfare of the poor and powerless. He opened a free school for children, a shelter for widows and a free dispensary so the poor could get medical aid. He established a kind of credit union for the poor. He identified and developed leaders among the marginalized. Wesley worked to reform the conditions under which the poor lived and labored. He pressed for major social reforms in his publications. In Wesley's words, "making an open stand against all the ungodliness and unrighteousness which overspread our land as a flood is one of the noblest ways of confessing Christ in the face of His enemies."[23] Wesley called his followers to social action on behalf of the poor. For example, he encouraged them to boycott buying, selling or consuming alcohol. Why? In his sermon *The Present Scarcity of Goods* Wesley observed that the poor went hungry because valuable resources were going to support the lifestyle of the elite that could otherwise have been used to ameliorate the suffering of the poor (corn was used for alcohol instead of food; land was used for horses instead of edible animals like cattle and sheep). Wesley clearly charged his followers to give not only alms, thus treating the poor as mere objects of charitable care, but to go a step further and to become responsible for contributing to their well-being. Wesley had no split between personal salvation and social engagement. He tied "warmhearted evangelism" with active social reform.[24]

THERAPEUTIC PERSPECTIVE:
SOCIAL JUSTICE COUNSELING AND ADVOCACY

A biblical view of justice and Wesley's appropriation of the biblical mandate to pursue justice can compel Christians who counsel to consider the place of social justice counseling and advocacy in their repertoire. Theological and therapeutic perspectives on social justice require that counselors deal with systemic issues on family, neighborhood, city, state, national and even international levels. Theological and therapeutic social justice perspectives call for counselors to see how injustice is embedded into the structures that maintain oppressive status quos, be they in the family, school, work place, church, community or world. Clinical application is found in the current emphasis on social justice counseling and advocacy.

I have been involved in professional counseling since the mid-1980s. While the counseling literature attests to the fact that social action has been a part of professional counseling from its inception, it has only been since the turn of the twenty-first century that I have noticed a notable increase in an emphasis on social action, social justice counseling and advocacy as an integral aspect of professional counseling. A little history is in order. During the 1990s professional counselors and psychologists who embraced feminist and multicultural sensitivities opened the field's eyes to the gender, cultural and racial biases that were embedded in society in general and in traditional theories of counseling in particular. With these social sensitivities heightened, it was only a small step for counselors to become aware of the negative impact that societal and structural inequality, prejudice and oppression had on clients' physical and emotional well-being. In 1998 counselors with strong interests in social justice organized Counselors for Social Justice, a division within the American Counseling Association (ACA), and they subsequently developed competencies for social justice counseling that have been adopted by ACA.[25] Members of Counselors for Social Justice actively promote the importance of social justice counseling and advocacy. A measure of their success may be indicated by one author's suggestion that social justice counseling is an emerging force in professional counseling.[26]

According to the home page for Counselors for Social Justice,

> Social justice counseling represents a multifaceted approach to counseling in which practitioners strive to simultaneously promote human development and the common good through addressing challenges related to both individual and distributive justice.
>
> Social justice counseling includes empowerment of the individual as

well as active confrontation of injustice and inequality in society as they impact clientele as well as those in their systemic contexts. In doing so, social justice counselors direct attention to the promotion of four critical principles that guide their work: equity, access, participation, and harmony. This work is done with a focus on the cultural, contextual, and individual needs of those served.[27]

Social justice counseling is many-sided. It includes direct and indirect services to clients and their communities. *Direct services* to *clients* can encompass traditional approaches to counseling (e.g., one-on-one, group, family counseling sessions). *Direct services* to *clients' communities* can take the form of workshops in service of preventive education (e.g., stress management, parenting skills). In contrast *indirect services* to *clients* include speaking on behalf of a client to an employer or school official (with the client's informed consent). *Indirect services* to *clients' communities* look the least like counseling because they involve counselors taking social action that will influence public policies that affect their clients. Counselors may e-mail or phone their elected officials to encourage them to vote for or against specific legislation, or they may use their skills to lobby directly for the same.[28] Social justice counseling promotes *environments* (familial, communal, societal) that support human flourishing for all people by standing with and by empowering vulnerable populations to fight injustice. Professional counselors use their skills to battle societal inequities on behalf of at-risk clients and the neighborhoods they live in or in support of the "community" that they represent (e.g., single teenage parents).

While professional counseling is moving full steam ahead with a social justice agenda, it appears as if the field of Christian counseling has been slower to embrace this call as a core aspect of its professional identity. Christian counseling certainly isn't opposed to justice, but Christian counseling publications on social justice and advocacy have yet to achieve critical mass. For example, using "social justice" as a search term in PsychINFO database resulted in four articles published in the *Journal of Psychology and Theology* and eight articles published the *Journal of Psychology and Christianity*, two of the leading journals that focus on integrating Christianity/theology and counseling/psychology.

The number of identified articles expanded to ten and twenty, respectively, when "justice" was designated as the search term. An even fewer number of books written to Christian mental health practitioners have addressed matters related to social justice counseling and advocacy.[29]

Perhaps this reluctance is a carryover from earlier theological controversies. In the late nineteenth and early twentieth centuries, Protestants argued vigorously about the correct relationship of the church to society. More conservative or fundamentalist groups argued for the priority of right belief, or orthodoxy, with a special focus on the inerrancy or authority of Scripture. In contrast, more liberal groups argued for the centrality of right action, or orthopraxy, more commonly known as the Social Gospel, with its special focus on concrete practices of mercy and justice at home and abroad. The historic displacement of soul care from the counseling session in the mid- to late twentieth century probably widened the gap in some church circles even more (see the brief review of the history of integration in chap. 2). Given that mental health professionals who championed the Christian integration movement came largely from more conservative and evangelical theological streams, it is not surprising that the inclusion of social justice counseling and advocacy is a Johnny-come-lately within the Christian counseling integration movement.

The history of *world* Christianity compels Christian mental health professionals to take social justice counseling and advocacy seriously. Missiologist Mark A. Noll cites historian Dana Roberts's observation that today's prototypical Christian is no longer a European man but a *Latin American* or *African woman*.[30] Asia, Africa, Latin America and the islands of the South Pacific boast an unprecedented increase in the number of Christians living within their boundaries compared to the declining Christian population in Western Europe and the United States. Many centers of explosive Christian growth have been affected by "colonization, decolonization, and now economic globalization,"[31] and these brothers and sisters in Christ have been subject to their own culturally situated experiences of inequality, prejudice and oppression. Missiologists Andrew Walls and Cathy Ross note that the call "to seek to transform unjust structures of society" is among the five marks of

Christian mission.[32] Valdir Steuernagel, World Vision International Vice President for Christian Commitments adds, "The Gospel always arrives discerning reality, denouncing an enslaving idolatry and oppressive injustice, identifying with the poor and the suffering, and intervening for liberation, wholeness, and peace, even at the cost of a thousand pigs [cf. Mark 5:1-20]."[33] As a result of these factors, it is hard to imagine everyday Christian counseling that does *not* stand in the gap in the name of Jesus Christ on behalf of those who experience oppression, prejudice and injustice within the family, the neighborhood, the community and the world.

What skills do counselors need for social justice counseling and advocacy? Counselors can use their skills of traditional therapy, but they also must develop three new skill sets. First, counselors must be able to assess the degrees to which *environmental* conditionals promote or inhibit clients' well-being. Counselors working for social justice no longer limit case conceptualization to dynamics that are internal to clients. Social justice counseling requires counselors to assess the extent to which gender, ethnicity, race, class, ability and *environmental factors* (e.g., poverty, power, privilege and oppression) impinge on mental health. Urie Bronfenbrenner's ecological model provides a heuristic that mental health professionals can use to explore such environmental factors.[34] The microsystem level represents "the innermost level of the environment, which consists of the individual and any two-person relationship."[35] At this level counselors remain alert to injustice that may be present in the client's family (e.g., intimate partner violence, child abuse) or at the school a child attends (e.g., conflict between child and teacher), or that happens on the playground with peers (e.g., bullying). With a client's informed consent, a counselor may intervene directly with a person in power on the client's behalf, or a therapist may coach a client during the client's regular counseling session on how to advocate for self. The mesosystem "encompasses interactions and settings that exist in a person's immediate surroundings," such as the neighborhood, social services or the justice system.[36] Intervention at this level may take the form of a counselor helping to organize a neighborhood tutoring club or presenting workshops at a local church or community center. The exosystem refers "to structures of the larger community" and includes formal and informal social structures that impact the microsystems.[37] Examples of the exosystem include the educational system, the work world, the mental health system, the mass media and so forth. Accessing the exosystem, counselors can review how social structures such as the world of work and the media influence clients' situations. The macrosystem level "includes a core of cultural, political, legal, and economic influences that shape an individual's development" (e.g., economic, social, educational, legal and political institutions).[38] At the exosystem level and the macrosystem level Christian counselors may engage in political action to influence legislation that would benefit their at-risk clients. Notice how these levels map onto direct and indirect services to clients and their communities. Using Bronfenbrenner's model, counselors can assess the extent to which variables at each ecosystemic level work for or against clients' well-being and represent opportunities or barriers that are related to clients' presenting problems.

Second, counselors must be able to *empower* clients to reduce or avoid stressful environmental factors and assist clients in mastering the skills necessary to confront and challenge stressful aspects of their environment. This may include helping clients to develop skills in confrontation through role playing conversations with persons in positions of power and by providing emotional support when clients risk using these new skills. In addition counselors can develop prevention-focused workshops, such as a suicide prevention program or educational workshops on parenting skills to reach a larger portion of a vulnerable client population. Moreover, counselors can promote and support client self-help groups. These groups can attend to mental wellness concerns as they also engage in social action and community-based planning.

Third, counselors adopt the role of *social change agents* when they use their training to impact clients' social environments. Counselors can intervene in the home, neighborhood, school or community. They may help families to realign the distribution of power in order to create more equitable sharing of burdens and benefits among family members. Counselors pay close attention to situations of domestic violence, abuse of children and the plight of vulnerable adults (e.g., adults with disabilities, elders, etc.). At times state laws of mandated reporting coincide with a social justice counseling agenda, and counselors then follow these ethical and legal stipulations. Counselors can speak to persons in power on behalf of clients or clients' families. School counselors may work with the family and school personnel to bring about just learning environments for at-risk children. Therapists may help groups of disadvantaged neighbors plan, organize and implement programs that will benefit their local community.[39] Furthermore, counselors can use their skills to bring about structural change at the macrolevel in an effort to change social policies and legislation by writing letters to elected officials or by attending political rallies, or contributing funds to political action committees.

Social justice counseling and advocacy takes the view of *person-in-relationship* and extends it to *person-in-environment*. The dynamics between these two views of personhood are mutually reinforcing, and counselors must think systemically and systematically to see how the environment shapes the person and how the person's response shapes the environment. Social justice counseling and advocacy does not dismiss personal responsibility. It promotes it. Harry Aponte's ecosystemic model of family therapy serves as an example.[40] Aponte recognizes that poverty and oppression limit clients' options. The ecosystemic model requires therapists to recognize the ways that the environment affects clients. Concurrently, therapists also challenge clients to accept responsibility for those areas of their lives over which they *do have control*. As counselors and clients evaluate environmental limitations, counselors can help clients to assess the extent to which they possess the resources (intrapersonal and interpersonal) for solving their problems. This approach to counseling does not foster a victim mentality of helplessness. Instead it nurtures an empowered mentality of hopefulness and personal efficacy. When clients are able to name the range of choices that are rightfully set before them, then they can be held accountable for acting on choices that will foster bio-psychosocial-spiritual health.

An example will help to put feet to the preceding discussion. Susan is the cofounder and current executive director for Step By Step, a Christian ministry to single moms ages fourteen to twenty-four.[41] Step By Step was founded to address the spiritual, emotional, physical and developmental needs of young single moms. This is the vulnerable population to which Step By Step attends. These moms are often without the support of their babies' fathers, and regularly they represent a second or third generation of women who are raising children without the benefit of a lifelong marital bond. Typically a mom is living at the poverty level. Step By Step mirrors the multifaceted social justice counseling model just presented. While Step By Step has not been able to offer traditional counseling services to their moms because their budget currently cannot support that position, they work closely with the community mental health agencies in town. In addition they offer mentoring, love and support (in addition to the gospel message) through bimonthly gatherings. These gatherings provide a meal, a time for socialization and fun, important life information (e.g., parenting tips), and small discussion groups (e.g., healthy boundaries) to the mothers while their children are cared for in a concurrent children's program. Step By Step also teaches these moms how to set life goals (e.g., getting a G.E.D.) and how to plan to achieve these goals. On an individual level Susan has accompanied a young mother to a meeting with the mother's case worker at the Department of Children and Families. The mother may be complying with a treatment plan in order to maintain custody of her children. Susan serves as an advocate for this young mom in two ways. She can affirm the steps that the young mother is making toward fulfilling the treatment plan established by the state case worker, and Susan can confront and challenge the young mom to a greater level of responsibility if the young woman is neglecting aspects of the treatment plan (e.g., getting a manicure and pedicure instead of paying the electric bill).

I began this chapter with a review of biblical justice. The biblical narrative describes God as a just God, one who designed creation in such a way that humanity could rightly and justly relate to one another and to their Creator. Sadly, God's people became perpetrators of the injustice that they were intended to overcome, which resulted in their eventual exile. Jesus Christ, God incarnate, destroyed the principalities and powers of injustice through his life, death and resurrection. Christ-followers are filled with the Holy Spirit and are subsequently empowered to establish outposts of God's just society on earth. Then I explored John Wesley's emphasis on social holiness and its logical extension to social justice. Wesley held together wholehearted love of God and others. Social holiness sought to promote right relationships within the church as an overflow of God's love, and by extension the people of God loved the world that God loved (Jn 3:16) by working to confront systems of injustice wherever they existed. Today Wesley's emphasis on social reform converges with social justice counseling and advocacy. In the final section of this chapter I will explore how these streams join together in the work of the theologically reflective practitioner.

THE THEOLOGICALLY REFLECTIVE PRACTITIONER
AND SOCIAL JUSTICE COUNSELING

Theologically reflective counseling with a social justice focus looks quite different from the typical picture of a client-counselor relationship. As I emphasized earlier, social justice counseling and advocacy can and does include individual office sessions. *But* it proposes that these traditional services are ultimately inadequate to address the mental health needs of an increasingly culturally diverse world. Judith Lewis, Michael Lewis, Judy Daniels and Michael D'Andrea argue that "the greatest challenge facing counseling practitioners in the 21st century involves finding new and more effective ways to help people from diverse populations realize a greater sense of individual health and collective well-being."[42] Counselors' efforts will reach beyond office walls and into the street in ways that would not be considered legitimate until the late twentieth century. For example home-based family therapy takes therapy *to* the family. This allows the counselor to work on the family's turf, to see how the family operates *in situ* and eliminates the family's challenge to find transportation to a counseling center.[43] Theologically reflective counselors with a social justice focus pay attention to the different levels of Bronfenbrenner's ecosystem that can to help clients flourish or cause clients to flounder. C.R.O.S.S. Ministry is a Christian support group for persons with chronic mental illness and will serve as an example of theologically reflective social justice counseling and advocacy.

C.R.O.S.S. The ministry began in 1995 as the brainchild of a friend who had a family member that suffered from chronic mental illness. This friend felt called by God to organize a *Christian* support group for family members of persons with chronic mental illness. My friend, a family life practitioner, recruited a Christian psychiatric nurse and myself, a licensed professional counselor, to join her leadership team. The family members who attended the first few meetings created the name for the support group—"Christians Reaching Out in Sharing and Support" (C.R.O.S.S.). C.R.O.S.S. met every first, third and fifth Monday of the month in the hospitality room of a local church (an inviting living room-like space). We followed a simple structure for our ninety-minute gatherings:

- *Opening and welcome.* One of the leadership team opened the meeting, welcomed new attendees and read the purpose statement for C.R.O.S.S. We wanted to be sure to distinguish it from a therapy group. Everyone was invited to wear a name tag (first-name only).

- *Devotional and opening prayer.* One member of the leadership team prepared a brief devotional and offered an opening prayer. If a group member volunteered to do this, leadership was happily ceded to the person.

- *Sharing and support.* Going in a circular manner, participants were invited to update the group on how they had been doing since the last meeting they had attended. This was a time to share joys and sorrows, to ask for support, to seek group problem-solving and so forth. Group leaders alerted attendees to the time limits of the meeting so that all would have an opportunity to share. Participants were invited to pass if they did not want to share.

- *Closing prayer.* A group leader solicited prayer requests. If time permitted, participants were invited to pray for one another. Otherwise one of the group leaders closed the meeting in prayer.

The leadership team viewed C.R.O.S.S. as a compliment to the family and consumer support groups that were offered by the Bluegrass Chapter of the National Alliance on Mental Illness (N.A.M.I.). Over the course of its ten-year existence, C.R.O.S.S. morphed from a Christian support group for family members to a Christian support group for persons with mental illness.

How do C.R.O.S.S. participants represent a vulnerable population in need of social justice counseling or advocacy? When mental illness strikes, those who suffer from its effects feel isolated, powerless and misunderstood by family members, friends and employers. Persons with severe and persistent mental illness grapple with issues of injustice and discrimination in their family, neighborhood, workplace, church and community. Mental illness carries a stigma. Friends and neighbors may fear the person with mental illness. Mental illness is a noncasserole disease. Few friends or neighbors show up at one's front door bearing a warm tuna-noodle casserole when an acute episode happens. Families struggle to regain equilibrium as they cope with the stress and strain of caring for a loved one with mental illness. They are likely to pull in and subsequently all parties become isolated from needed social support. Concurrently, those who *could* provide social support may gradually withdraw from the family with mental illness as fear, stigma and un-flattering stereotypes cloud their perceptions.[44]

C.R.O.S.S. offered acceptance, socialization and support in a non-threatening group atmosphere. Participants could talk about their struggle with mental illness without excessive explanations. They were with others who understood their experience. In addition they could share with one another the regular joys and sorrows of life. Persons who were just beginning their journey of recovery from mental illness gained hope through the testimonies of those who were further along the path. The group became an important part of many participants' month, sometimes representing the only source of acceptance that they had.

The C.R.O.S.S. group empowered its members to confront igno-rance with educational information provided by N.A.M.I. They prayed for extended family members who refused to accept their loved one's diagnosis. The C.R.O.S.S. group helped one another to see the fingerprints of God in the bleakest of circumstances, and members offered forgiveness to friends and family who did not or would not understand the reality of chronic and persistent mental illness. C.R.O.S.S. participants were also encouraged to be active in their own recovery and not to adopt a victim mentality. Many C.R.O.S.S. meetings included members sharing survival strategies, solutions to common problems and daily living tips. They updated one another on which psychiatrists really listened to their patients and which counselors understood psychotropic medications and so on.

C.R.O.S.S. represents a form of direct service to a particular vulnerable population. The majority of C.R.O.S.S. participants had a therapeutic relationship with a mental health provider (direct service to clients). Many were also active in the Bluegrass Chapter of the National Alliance on Mental Illness, which addressed political advocacy on behalf of all persons with chronic mental illness and their families (indirect service to community). This example is a departure from the one-on-one counseling application of theologically reflective practice that you find in other chapters to show you how a social justice focus moves counseling beyond the counseling office.

Attending to theological echoes. While not a focus of every meeting, group members regularly shared their frustration with the injustices they experienced because of their mental illness. They reported that they were ostracized, misunderstood and judged as lazy or crazy by family or friends who lacked an accurate understanding of the complexities of mental illness. Issues of ready access to counseling services and the most effective medications were also typical discussion topics. For example, it was typical for insurance company reimbursement procedures to authorize prescriptions for older psychotropic medications before they permitted prescriptions for newer medications. Older medications were less expensive but also had many side effects. Newer medications were more expensive but had fewer side effects, so clients were more likely to comply with doctor's orders and thereby experience greater benefits from the medications. These do not seem like spiritual topics—but that is only so if you separate life into secular and sacred components. Theologically, we can reflect on what are the needs for well-being and community membership that are represented by the vulnerable population of those with severe and persistent mental illness. Addressing these concrete concerns will take a form different from leaving the gleanings in the harvest field for the poor to collect. Theologically reflective counselors can seek the guidance of the Holy Spirit to give them eyes to see and ears to hear the cry of this vulnerable group, and then the Spirit will also provide the wisdom for appropriate action.

Addressing salient theological themes. At C.R.O.S.S. gatherings awareness of God's justice was more caught than taught. Some participants eventually voiced outrage at the unfairness of losing their hopes and dreams to severe and persistent mental illness. Some were brave enough to direct their lament toward God. They had no idea how God could set things to rights. The outcry of several attendees was not directed at anyone in particular, but was more generally focused on the general injustice of life. Others who had walked with God and lived with their mental illness for a longer time offered testimony of God's goodness that came in the form of other support group members, understanding friends and family, and an open reception in their local church. Notice that justice was nuanced in terms of right relationship to others, acceptance and belonging more than it was about "getting what is rightfully due to me." Certainly conversations about unjust treatment took place—where guilt and innocence were ascribed, and satisfaction was sought or longed for—but for the most part the presence or absence of just and right relationships was foremost in their hearts.

While individual participants could inhabit any of the theological worlds (i.e., foreigner, faint, fugitive, flattened), the theological world of a fighter ascended for the group as a whole. The rhythm of the spiritual world of the fighter is one of conflict and vindication. The *obsessio* of the fighter is a concern for this world. The *epiphania* comes in the form of concrete change. Life can be divided between winners and losers, with death as the final enemy. Because life is a battle, people may grasp for power. The theological world of the fighter includes experiences of being oppressed and opposed. Fighters respond to injustice with anger because they are acutely aware of societal evil. This awareness

and anger can trigger reform or rebellion. Jesus the Messiah is also
Christ the Liberator. Jesus Christ is the one who has come to set the
world to rights. As followers of Christ, fighters show their love of
neighbor by taking the side of the widow, the orphan and the powerless—even if they are also among those ranks. This liberation is not
limited to God's perfected future. The effort to bring God's will to
earth as it is in heaven is a present-tense struggle against structural
evil.[45] Moving between conflict and vindication was a daily reality for
many C.R.O.S.S. participants. They knew that most of society viewed
them as losers, but in this group they were winners. They were some of
the bravest people I have met. They faced a day-by-day struggle with
mental illness and stigma. In C.R.O.S.S. meetings their courage was
recognized, affirmed and applauded. Here they experienced a kind of
vital Christian community that John Wesley desired for his congregations. C.R.O.S.S. did not function as a church. But the communal dimension of sharing life together in love was present.

I suspect that counselors who are drawn to social justice counseling
and advocacy also inhabit the theological world of the fighter. Fighters
see the injustice that is present and feel compelled to do something
about it. One challenge that persons with mental illness face is that of
finding safe housing. Because they are often underemployed or unem-
ployed, they may not be able to afford a nice apartment in a safe neighborhood. Aware of this situation, two members of the C.R.O.S.S. leadership team were instrumental in securing a large grant that helped
them to establish a program which supports safe and affordable housing
for persons with severe and persistent mental illness.[46]

Space was made in C.R.O.S.S. meetings for even the most challenging participant to find a place to belong. One C.R.O.S.S. member
was notorious for a spirit of grumbling and complaint. At each meeting
this participant presented a prepared and detailed list of the affronts
that she experienced since the previous meeting. Early on in her involvement with C.R.O.S.S., no amount of gentle problem-solving
seemed to help. "Yes but" were the two most frequently spoken words
in response to any encouragement from other group members. As
trying as the sharing of this participant could be, the group nonetheless

embraced her for who she was. She had a keen sense of humor, a dry, quiet wit that often emerged amid the laundry list of complaints. The group "loved on her" through their acceptance. Her obsessive rumination of the ills that she experienced was a manifestation of her mental illness. I am happy to report that the group also celebrated with her when a new medication enabled her to manage her ruminations, secure a part-time job and begin to live with less oppressive fear and anger.

Aligning life to be more theologically congruent. With the theological emphasis on justice, alignment takes the form of empowerment of self and confrontation of unjust structures, where possible. Three processes—taking "I" positions, self-soothing and taking responsibility for self—emerged as avenues of empowerment that C.R.O.S.S. participants drew upon to address a variety of issues. Regarding taking "I" positions, participants were regularly encouraged to phone their psychiatrists when problematic changes in their symptoms emerged. Many did not want to bother their doctor or thought it would be fine to wait another two months for their scheduled appointment. Because of the presence of a psychiatric nurse in the leadership team, we were able to offer accurate information about the typical side effects of medications and support participants in taking active steps when amelioration of emerging symptoms was possible through a medication adjustment. Regarding self-soothing, participants talked about how they took care of themselves during anxiety attacks or what they did when family members disappointed them. Several members testified to the benefits of prayer as a way to stay centered during stormy times of life. Regarding taking responsibility, C.R.O.S.S. attendees were encouraged to do what was within their capacity to manage their own life and schedule. When a problem in living was on the table, the group recognized the challenge that faced the participant and also identified avenues of action that that person might consider. Conversations were directed away from a helpless victim theme toward the person-as-overcomer, with a clear recognition of what participants could or could not change.

The C.R.O.S.S. group operated out of the levels of Bronfenbrenner's ecosystemic model. The leadership team worked directly with persons with mental illness and their families, and the group members developed friendships that extended beyond the scheduled meeting time (microsystem level). Group members were active participants in local churches and in N.A.M.I. One local church offered meeting space to us free of charge for the ten years of C.R.O.S.S.'s history (mesolevel). The group supported one another in dealing with the ins and outs of the relating to unsympathetic or ignorant family members (i.e., those who refused to recognize the reality and pain of mental illness), managing the mental health system, applying for Social Security Disability Income, contacting pharmaceutical companies for access to free medication or for medication at reduced cost, navigating interaction with the court system when one member was over-medicated and pulled over for a DUI (driving under the influence) (mesolevel). Many group members joined others who wrote letters to state legislators or rallied at the state capital to influence legislation related to mental health care (macrolevel).

Attaining a deepening Christian character. Each C.R.O.S.S. meeting was an opportunity for participants to step out of the pressure of their daily existence and to refocus on the help that comes to them from God. They experienced God's faithfulness in ways that were often surprising. Yes, many struggled to maintain an experienced awareness of God's love for them, often voicing a fear that God had abandoned them to their mental illness. Yet others were able to counter that those thoughts were their depression talking, and so they helped one another to create a new way of relating to the God whose love is everlasting and faithful. The group provided the "meta" perspective. They could identify God's hand in others' lives more easily than for themselves. They pointed out how God was at work in the circumstances of their lives. They became true agents of change for one another as they respected one another's boundaries, learned to bear one another's burdens without being burdened by them, and offered unconditional love and support to each other. The result was an awareness of God's faithfulness through thick and thin times of mental wellness, a hope that God would set things to rights either through new advances in medication or when Christ returned as we experienced a new body, and a sense of compassion and forgiveness for those in society who had yet to understand the reality of mental illness.

In the C.R.O.S.S. group the mediating factors of *relationship* and *hope*, which energize this metamodel of theologically reflective counseling, deserve special attention. I believe that one key element in this group was the leadership team, all of whom had professional training in a field related to mental health, and who modeled Christian spirituality. Group members reported that the leadership team's presence provided a sense of safety and security for them. Participants knew that help was at hand if their story triggered an emotional crisis for another member. Team leaders did not flaunt their expertise. Instead they encouraged participants to share from their own wealth of experience as a way to empower participants. In addition C.R.O.S.S. became a place for team leaders to share their own personal struggles. Leaders may not suffer from severe and persistent mental illness, but each leader experienced painful life events and sought the support of their brothers and sisters in Christ who participated in C.R.O.S.S. A second key element was that of hopefulness. There was a sense of expectancy and celebration that attended each meeting. Participants were recognized for their courage in living. They were celebrated for their steps toward well-being. They were supported during their dark days. The group held onto hope for those whose only option was to "hope against hope."

CONCLUSION

C.R.O.S.S. did indeed "cross" the bridge between personal and social holiness by helping participants to deepen their relationship with God in nonthreatening ways (devotion, prayer support, encouraging church attendance) and by providing a place of belonging and community (social holiness) as the group sought to deal with social problems they experienced as a result of their mental illness (social justice and advocacy). Within the group there existed a clear call to personal responsibility and an awareness of the environmental factors that made living with mental illness particularly challenging. No member was allowed to wallow in self-pity, but instead they were nurtured in their capacity to experience God's grace in the face of bouts of clinical depression, anxiety disorders or schizophrenia. They became change agents within their family, their church and even in our community. For example several C.R.O.S.S. participants have held leadership positions in the Bluegrass Chapter of N.A.M.I.

I am grateful for my experience in C.R.O.S.S. Today I invite representatives from the Bluegrass Chapter of N.A.M.I to speak in my counseling classes. Many counseling students begin their master's program with little exposure to persons with severe and persistent mental illness, and what exposure they do have through the media is not very flattering of persons with mental illness. When N.A.M.I. representatives come to my classes, my students have an opportunity to see people who look just like them speaking about surviving extraordinary psychological pain and suffering. I am pleased to say that each year a team of students from Asbury Seminary participates in the annual N.A.M.I. Walk to raise awareness about mental illness.[47] Several students have subsequently decided to work with persons with chronic mental illness as their professional calling.

First Peter 1:16 exhorts us to be holy because God is holy. John Wesley proclaimed "The gospel of Christ knows no religion, but social; no holiness but social holiness." Martin Smith and Matt Redman sang about dancers who dance upon injustice.[48] Personal holiness and social holiness mean we are loving God with all of our being and loving our neighbor as we are infused with God's love. Social justice counseling and advocacy fits into the matrix of theologically reflective counseling as Christians who counsel take their love of God and their concern for their clients out of the office and into the streets.

6

Just Forgive?

✺

Five bleeding wounds he bears,
Received on Calvary;
They pour effectual prayers;
They strongly plead for me:
"Forgive him, O forgive," they cry,
"Forgive him, O forgive," they cry,
"Nor let that ransomed sinner die!"

My God is reconciled;
His pardoning voice I hear;
He owns me for his child;
I can no longer fear:
With confidence I now draw nigh,
with confidence I now draw nigh,
And, "Father, Abba, Father," cry.

CHARLES WESLEY,
"Arise, My Soul, Arise"

In all ongoing relationships someone is bound to behave badly. When things get bad enough, people seek counselors to help them deal with issues of forgiving, repenting and reconciling. The Smiths had been married for twenty years when Joe Smith began to wrestle with his latent homosexuality. He began a secret life on the edges of the gay community. Mary Smith accidentally discovered her husband's hidden life one day when she was working on their home computer and found the websites that Joe had been exploring. This finding sent their relationship into a tailspin. Mary felt deeply betrayed by Joe. Joe felt misunderstood and judged by Mary. They decided to go to counseling. At their intake session they affirmed that they wanted to save their marriage. They declared their love for one another. Neither could quite imagine life without the other. Although Joe reaffirmed his original marital vow to "forsake all others," he couldn't cut his ties with the gay community, a condition that Mary had established as an indicator of Joe's commitment to rebuilding their relationship. She found it challenging to maintain a spirit of forgiveness in the face of perceived continuing betrayal. Joe and Mary repeated a cycle of discovery of relapse, angry confrontation, tearful apology and cautious forgiveness until they decided that they no longer had energy to preserve their marriage. Joe was unwilling to abandon his newfound sense of a gay self, and Mary was not willing to live with someone who was not able to be faithful to her in thought, word and deed.

Robert and Jill Donahue had been married for five years, although they had separated for the past twelve months. Robert felt disrespected by Jill, whom he accused of being selfish and self-centered. Jill felt disregarded by Robert, whom she also accused of being selfish and self-centered. Whenever they got together and began to discuss their issues, Jill delivered derisive lectures on the shortfalls of Robert's character. She could not understand why he didn't follow her admonitions, which she believed would improve his life and help them have a Christian marriage. Robert responded with defensiveness, contempt and ultimately stonewalling. He declared that reasoning with Jill was pointless and that he could not live with a woman who verbally ripped him to shreds every time he didn't give in to her demands. Jill countered that she was tired of his broken promises and found him utterly untrustworthy. They hoped that marriage counseling would help them. They were followers of Jesus who struggled with forgiveness and repentance that could lead to reconciliation. From Jill's perspective Robert continued to put his job before their relationship. From Robert's perspective Jill refused to empathize with the nonnegotiable and unpredictable demands of his work. They each felt betrayed by the other and justified in maintaining their own position and perspective. Any changes that they each made over the course of counseling were dismissed or diminished by the other spouse. They were caught in what marriage researcher John Gottman calls "negative sentiment overdrive," which contributed to emotional flooding during conflict conversations.[1] They too ended counseling when they decided that expecting the other person to change was a hopeless cause.

What you can see in these two situations is the challenge that people experience when they are faced with repenting, forgiving and reconciling. Repentance and forgiveness make reconciliation possible, but not inevitable. Yet without repenting and forgiving, reconciliation is highly improbable, maybe even impossible. Repenting, forgiving and reconciling are not only clinical concerns—they are vital theological truths that are at the heart of our relationship with God and one another. The Smiths and the Donahues had experienced God's forgiveness. Yet neither couple wanted to pay the behavioral and emotional cost needed to reconcile at the time that they sought counseling.

Two couples stand in stark contrast to the Smiths and Donahues.[2] Gabriella and Chad's marriage nearly ended after Chad confessed to his three-year affair with Gabriella's best friend. Gabriella told Chad that she forgave him. She wanted to save their marriage. Yet she clarified that her forgiveness did not mean that she trusted him. Reconciliation proved to be a pain-filled process. Chad was not confident that Gabriella would get over the wound that he had inflicted. A turning point in their postconfession relationship was the day that Gabriella called Chad into their bedroom. She was giving herself to him again, to reclaim him as her husband and to sanctify their marital bed. Why did she make such a bold, audacious and generous gesture? Gabriella said it was because she came to an understanding that on the cross Jesus' death and resurrection covered her sins *and* Chad's sin against her. When she was tempted to think, *Chad, you'll pay for this unbearable hurt!* she remembered that her Lord and Savior, Jesus, had already "been there and done that." Standing firmly on the atonement, Gabriella and Chad slowly rebuilt their marriage. Chad demonstrated consistent changed behavior over time. Gabriella extended gracious forgiveness to him. It took them several years and lots of hard work before they declared that they were fully reconciled to one another.

Melissa confronted Luke about his emotional affair with a co-worker. Luke was puzzled by the intensity of her emotional reaction. From his perspective he had not been unfaithful to his wife because his relationship with the other woman had never crossed a sexual boundary. To him it was strictly a work relationship. From her perspective he had crossed a line when she perceived an emotional intimacy between her husband and the other woman that was rightly hers alone. To her it was a betrayal of their marriage. It took Luke a while to understand exactly how he had violated their marriage covenant. He had remained sexually faithful to Melissa, but what he called a "work relationship" she saw as an emotional attachment that was becoming increasingly exclusive. His deep emotional understanding of Melissa's perspective and his wholehearted commitment to change were key factors in their reconciliation. In addition, Melissa was able to move forward as she associated her suffering with Jesus' suffering on the cross. Melissa understood that Christ's agony represented her pain *and* Luke's betrayal. Jesus' death was for her, the offended one, *and* for him, the offender. This theological insight gave an unprecedented depth of meaning to her sense of abandonment, and it contributed to her ability to forgive Luke.

The latter two couples brought the reality of the cross of Christ into their marital crises in striking ways. Gabriella and Melissa (the presumed innocent parties) embraced a deep theological understanding of the cross of Christ. This theological insight allowed them to take a softer stance toward their partners. It enabled them to tolerate reasonable setbacks. It challenged them to acknowledge and repent for their own contributions to their marital dysfunction. Chad and Luke (the identified wrongdoers) experienced a kind of godly sorrow that led to repentance (2 Cor 7:10). They found great motivation to maintain their patterns of changed behavior in the light of their partners' forgiveness. These two couples leaned into their theology of the cross to support their therapy.

This chapter builds upon previous chapters. You may recall that I presented the Trinity as the theological foundation for a strong therapeutic relationship. Then I explored the contours of personal holiness and its relationship with differentiation of self, especially as that pertains to calling clients to accept personal accountability and responsibility for the impact of their words and actions. Next, I discussed God's justice and Wesley's idea of social holiness to provide the interpretive framework for social justice counseling and advocacy. Now I will explore how our understanding of the death of Christ, the atonement, supports theologically reflective counseling when forgiveness, repentance and reconciliation are therapeutic goals. Different theories of the atonement exist, and each one can make a contribution to our understanding of forgiveness and our work with Christian clients who have experienced interpersonal betrayal.

THEOLOGICAL COMMITMENTS: THE ATONEMENT

In theology-speak when I talk about the meaning of the cross of Christ, I am referring to the *atonement*. *Soteriology* is the proper term for the doctrine of salvation, and the atonement is central to soteriology. If you have an answer to the question, why did Jesus have to die on the cross? then you also have a theology of the atonement. In this section I review different ways that theologians throughout the ages have answered the question of the significance of Jesus' death. Then I will explore how John Wesley worked with these multiple images of the atonement. These theological considerations set the stage for the therapeutic discussions that follow.

Theologian Randy Maddox notes that "in its most general sense, an Atonement is simply an action or gift that helps reconcile parties estranged from one another."[3] More specifically the atonement refers to Christian affirmations about the meaning of Christ's death for us. According Joel B. Green and Mark D. Baker the cross is at the center of God's redemptive plan.[4] They propose that the New Testament is clear that through the death of Jesus at Calvary, we can now be forgiven and reconciled to God. However, they observe that the New Testament does not specify *definitively how* Christ's death brings about our forgiveness and reconciliation with God. To say it differently, the biblical writers were more concerned with affirming *that* the cross confirmed Jesus' messiahship than they were with discussing *how* his life, death and resurrection brought salvation to the world. Green and Baker observe that New Testament authors borrowed at least five images from the public life of the Mediterranean world to represent the salvific effect of Christ's death:

- court of law—with language about justification
- world of commerce—using the image of redemption
- personal relationships—in discussions about reconciliation
- temple worship—referring to Christ as the sacrificial lamb
- battleground—denoting Christ's triumph over evil

Green and Baker believe that the saving significance of Jesus' death defies the ability of any one metaphor to capture fully its depth and complexity.

Over the course of time theologians developed four classic theories of the atonement: Christ the Conqueror model (Christus Victor*)*, the satisfaction model, the moral influence model, and the penal substitution model.[5] Each theory not only reflected a truth about the meaning of the death of Christ, it also presented that truth by using metaphors or images that were embedded in the theologian's time and culture. As I summarize each atonement theory, think about which represents what you believe about how Jesus' death brings about our reconciliation with God. Also consider what strengths and problems each view might present when applied to different theologically reflective counseling contexts.

Christus Victor. The metaphor of Christus Victor (Christ the Conqueror) has been around since the second century. If you were alive at that time you believed that earthly conflicts were intertwined with conflicts between nonearthly spiritual powers. In the Christus Victor model of the atonement, Christ's death signifies God's triumph over sin, the devil and all spiritual powers of evil. Between the second and fourth centuries theologians developed two variations of Christus Victor. In the late second century, Irenaeus (c. 130-c. 202) was battling the Gnostic notion that matter was evil and that one could overcome one's enslavement to an evil, physical body through "special knowledge." Irenaeus argued that special knowledge would not gain us victory over sin. Christ was victorious over sin when he died on the cross, and he represents us in his victory. Only faith in Jesus Christ's victory over sin can help us also gain this victory. Gregory of Nyssa (c. 335-c. 395) adapted Christus Victor to the fourth-century world. During this time period people would pay a ransom to free a kidnapped family member or to buy freedom for a slave. Gregory of Nyssa proposed that Jesus' death was a ransom paid to the devil to free humanity. The devil took Jesus and set humanity free. However God outwitted the devil through the resurrection. The devil accepted the ransom payment, but because Jesus was God in human guise, the devil could not keep him. In the twenty-first century, theologian N. T. Wright uses imagery of victory when he writes about Jesus as God's way of dealing with evil and God's intention to set the world to rights.[6] Wright observes that

> the call of the gospel is for the church to *implement* the victory of God in the world *through suffering love.* The cross is not just an example to be followed; it is an achievement to be worked out, put into practice. But it is an example nonetheless, because it is the exemplar . . . for what God now wants to do by his Spirit in the world, through his people. It is the start of the process of redemption, in which suffering and martyrdom are the paradoxical means by which victory is won.[7]

Many clients find it comforting to trust in the cross of Christ to gain victory over the pain they endured when they were betrayed. Others may want to conquer the one who wounded them, just as Christ vanquished the devil. This sentiment is a misapplication of Christus Victor. Regarding the concept of ransom introduced by Gregory of Nyssa, clients may anticipate payment from their offenders as a pathway to emotional freedom. Yet if one looks closely at the ransom theory, it was God, the divine injured party, who paid the ransom. This might be a hard pill for clients to swallow.

Satisfaction model. Developed by Anselm of Canterbury (1033-1109) in his book *Cur Deus Homo* (*Why Did God Become Human?*), the satisfaction model proposes a substitution metaphor in which the death of Christ satisfies the debt that humanity owes to God. If this brings to mind the image of an insulted knight claiming (with a British accent, of course), "I demand satisfaction, sir!" you would not be far off the mark. Anselm's context was one of medieval kings, lords and vassals. If a vassal *dishonored* his lord, then something had to be done by someone to satisfy the offended patron's honor. The degree of satisfaction required was associated with the extent of the dishonor that the lord experienced. When Anselm applied his cultural context as a way to understand the atonement, he reasoned that humanity sinned through acts of disobedience and disloyalty. In this way humanity dishonored God. God's honor demands satisfaction. Anselm proposed that God *cannot* forgive without satisfaction being paid. However, only a human being *without* sin (i.e., had not contributed to dishonoring God) could do something that would satisfy God's honor. Jesus, as true God and sinless human, was the only person who could pay humanity's debt of dishonor to God. Christ's faithful life and obedient death on the cross was the avenue by which God's honor was restored. Jesus represents the debtor and has paid the ultimate cost to restore honor to the creditor. Jesus also represents the creditor in that as God, Jesus experienced dishonor. Jesus absorbs the dishonor into Godself, to restore God's honor.

Many parts of the world operate out of a system of honor and shame. Therefore, while this approach to the atonement sounds strange to some North American ears, counselors may find it useful when working with clients from cultural groups that are founded on honor and shame. Baker and Green report on how a contemporary understanding of honor and shame in Japanese culture became a helpful lens through which the saving significance of Jesus' death was interpreted for the Japanese church as good news.[8]

Moral influence model. The moral influence view of the atonement is associated with Peter Abelard (1079-1142). Contra Gregory of Nyssa, Abelard resisted the idea of a payment made to the devil to achieve God's forgiveness. Contra Anselm, Abelard argued that God was free to forgive humanity if God wanted to do so. Abelard proposed that fear of an angry God prevented humanity from asking for God's forgiveness. He theorized that Jesus' life and death was an audacious, bold demonstration of God's love for sinners. Christ's sinless life logically resulted in his death because it challenged the social standards of Jesus' day. Abelard concluded that Jesus' example should motivate us to repent and love God in return. Abelard saw the salvific effects of the cross as a change that occurs within humans who put their faith in Christ, allowing them to love God more fully and follow more closely after him.

Scripture affirms that "we love because he first loved us" (1 Jn 4:19), and fear of reprisal can keep repentant wrongdoers from approaching the ones they injured to seek forgiveness. Abelard's contention is that the love of God draws out our repentance, and that love is offered without a guarantee that every person will respond with a repentant heart. For injured parties, Christ's sacrificial love can be the prototype for how they might respond to wrongdoers. For wrongdoers, God's forgiveness of their offensive action can motivate them to seek forgiveness. On the other hand, loving forgiveness should not lead to reconciliation if the relationship is not restored to a just and safe foundation. Nor should trespassers take the offered forgiveness for granted and abandon their efforts to demonstrate changed behavior.

Penal substitution model. Christians in the United States are most familiar with the penal substitution model of the atonement. It maintains the concept of satisfaction but shifts the framing metaphor. Instead of satisfaction being paid within a feudal system of honor and shame, now a criminal law court requires satisfaction. Jesus' death does not repay a debt of honor. Instead, he receives the punishment from a wrathful God that is rightfully due to sinful humanity. In this view

God the Father expends humanity's punishment on God the Son. In the death of Christ God's wrath is appeased and God's holiness is maintained. Our pathway to God was earned when Jesus died.

Because penal substitution is the predominate atonement metaphor in the United States, counselors are most likely to hear it echoed in Christian clients' conversations about forgiving, repenting and reconciling. Some wrongdoers will propose that in the heavenly law court, sinners have been declared "not guilty" because of Christ's cross. They will claim that declaration of innocence and may subsequently demand that injured parties forgive them. Others will more accurately see that through the cross of Christ the guilty have been *pardoned*, not acquitted. *Pardon* maintains the idea that sinners really did sin, but they were pardoned nonetheless. With this perspective they were not tried and found innocent. The status of the offender is not romanticized. Pardoned and repentant wrongdoers may take comfort in the fact that God has forgiven them. Strengthened by God's forgiveness, they dedicate themselves to living into that state of God-forgiveness by "sinning no more."

Injured parties may affirm that Christ's payment has quenched their thirst for justice. Christ too was sinned against (as they have been) and offered forgiveness even as he was experiencing the pain of the crucifixion. Conversely, those who have been sinned against may resist seeing themselves as someone for whom Christ died. Specifically, they may deny that they did anything to contribute to the relationship pain that they now experience. In some cases this would be true (i.e., they did not contribute to the relationship pain). However in other situations the named injured party may also have sinned against the one that they have labeled as the trespasser, and therefore they cannot claim the spiritual high ground of innocence.

As a Christian who counsels, which atonement metaphor resonates with you? How does your view of the atonement shape you and the way you think about forgiveness, repentance and reconciliation? How does it affect the way you work with clients? I am not arguing for one theory of the atonement against another. My hope is that these thoughts will whet your appetite to study atonement theology more deeply (see chap.

6 endnotes for suggested readings) and to become more keenly aware of how culture contributes to the metaphors we use to try to make sense of the cross. Of course, it may be enough for us to follow the biblical narrative, to be caught up in the story of God, and to apply this narrative to our own lives without asking questions for which Scripture may offer multiple streams of response. As you ponder this, perhaps seeing how John Wesley understood the atonement might shed some light on your own process and formation.

John Wesley did not bother to summarize his understanding of the atonement in a stand-alone document. Instead, contemporary Wesley scholars infer his views on the atonement through Wesley's responses to various "practical-theological contexts" in which theological considerations of the atonement played a role. This is quite similar to how theologically reflective practitioners might integrate conversations about the atonement in counseling. Wesley started with his congregants' or correspondents' context. He embedded thoughts about the atonement and its effects on our relationship with God and others within his responses to them. Wesley's theology of the atonement is linked to his understanding of salvation. Wesley taught that through the cross of Christ people were not only forgiven of their sins, they also received *new life*. They were not only justified, they were also sanctified. As Wesleyan scholar Henry H. Knight III observes, through salvation "the image of God in us is fully recovered and our hearts and lives are filled with love for God and neighbor."[9] We are reconciled to God and have the capacity to be reconciled with one another. Wesley's understanding of the atonement held in tension the judgment of God and the love of God—the objective, forensic effect of the cross and the subjective experience of a changed human heart. God's grace tied it all together. God's initiating grace provided the way and means for our forgiveness and reconciliation with God, and God's saving grace enabled people to receive and respond to God's offer of forgiveness. Sustaining grace, imparted to the believer through the Holy Spirit, increases our capacity to love God more deeply and to live into the reality of this love in our relationships with one another.

God's holy love was central to Wesley's understanding of the atonement. Consistent with his Anglican heritage, Wesley taught that Christ's death was sacrificial (worship metaphor) *and* substitutionary (forensic/legal metaphor). A God of *holy* love could not simply turn a blind eye to humanity's breaking of divine law. We were guilty as charged. Because of God's holy *love*, Christ came to atone for our guilt. Christ, as the sacrificial Lamb of God, fulfills and satisfies the just penalty for our sins. This is the Godward part of the equation. God's grace provides the way and means for sinful human beings to experience forgiveness and reconciliation with God. Wesley understood Christ's death primarily in terms of its ability to deal with the guilt of sin, that is, to atone for human sin. In Christ the issue of sinful guilt was completely addressed. God can mercifully forgive us and sustain his righteous justice. Wesley believed that Christ's atoning work is offered to all people (it is not limited to "the elect") and that individuals could choose to accept or reject God's invitation of forgiveness (it is not irresistible). This is one way in which Wesley differed from the Calvinist theology of his day.[10]

Wesley not only described the objective effects of the atonement (how Christ's death deals with the guilt of sin), he also explained the subjective effects; that is, how Christ's death helps us to live like God's resurrection people. To achieve this end Wesley borrowed a page from Abelard's moral influence theory. Maddox explains, "Christ's voluntary sacrifice was put forward by God as an exhibition of Divine forgiving love" as a way to overcome humanity's fear of an angry God, and so to empower us through the Holy Spirit to receive God's love so that we are able to love others.[11] Maddox emphasizes that this aspect of Wesley's atonement theology shows that "the Cross is not so much a sacrifice made *to* an offending Judge to obtain our acquittal, as [it is] the basis and offer of forgiveness *from* a loving God to us!"[12] Through the ministry of the Holy Spirit, we are enabled to respond to God's love and to live responsible lives that align our lives with the heart of God.

How can we sum this up? One way is to observe that Wesley integrated a *juridical* emphasis, which stresses the guilt of sin and our inability to atone for ourselves, with a *therapeutic* view, which emphasizes the extent to which salvation can heal humanity's sin-diseased nature, or in the words of Maddox, "One is tempted to describe this as a Penalty Satisfaction *explanation* of the atonement which has a Moral Influence *purpose*, and a Ransom *effect*."[13] In plainer English, Christ died "for us," taking the penalty that was rightfully ours on himself (*explanation*) to show us the extent to which the love of God will go to forgive us so that we might be reconciled to God (*purpose*), and so that we can be free from the guilt of sin (*effect*). Reconciled to God and freed from the guilt of sin, we can orient our lives (as individuals and as members together of the community of believers) more fully to the life of God.

ATONEMENT AND OUR FORGIVENESS OF ONE ANOTHER

A theologically reflective counselor will listen for how clients imply a theory of the atonement framework to their wounded relationships. Counselors may also use atonement imagery to open a door to repenting, forgiving and reconciling. Just as John Wesley employed multiple metaphors to explain the atoning effects of Christ's life, death and resurrection, so too will clients and counselors draw upon diverse images to help clients apply the atonement in their interpersonal relationships.

Remember Gabriella and Chad from earlier in this chapter? Forgiving, repenting and reconciling were major theological concerns for them. When Chad confirmed Gabriella's suspicions about his infidelity, reconciliation was their first priority. They were not sure *how* they would do this, or even *if* they could do this, but they were sure that *they would work diligently toward this end*. This is the first theological implication of their view of the atonement. The atonement not only achieves our forgiveness of sin, it makes possible our reconciliation with God and one another. Reconciliation was the ultimate goal claimed by Gabriella and Chad. Just as we are without excuse before God for the sins we commit against God, Chad knew that he was without excuse before Gabriella for his sin of infidelity. His humble and brokenhearted confession, and his subsequent lived-out commitment to changed behavior, not only established the sincerity of his repentance but it also confirmed his intention to live differently, which he did. Chad experienced freedom from the guilt of his sin (this did not happen overnight). If you were to speak to Chad today, he would surely express deep remorse and regret for the pain that he inflicted on his wife and family. He would also express deep gratitude to God for Gabriella's willingness to forgive him and to give him an opportunity to demonstrate this gratitude through his changed behavior (i.e., new life).

Gabriella's primary understanding of the atonement was *penal substitution*—Christ paid the price for our sins. Gabriella was also "paying a price" for Chad's sin in the form of the emotional turmoil she experienced and the changes in their life and lifestyle that resulted from his infidelity. She could have been bitter about these changes, which she neither deserved nor asked for. She was able to embrace them with less resentment, however, because she saw that Christ's cross already *had paid* the debt for Chad's sin against her. Gabriella also had strands of Christus Victor threaded through her understanding of the atonement. In her heart Chad was not her enemy. Satan was. She claimed Christ's victory over Satan as her own victory over the effects of Chad's affair. She was fighting for her marriage. She believed that through Christ's victory over Satan, she and Chad would be victorious too.

Gabriella's bold welcome to Chad that I described earlier in this chapter was an enactment of Christ's sacrificial love for sinners. Using the metaphor of an embrace, theologian Miroslav Volf describes how the triune God makes space for his enemies through the cross. First, God opens wide his arms for us. The image of Jesus nailed to the cross becomes a powerful visual of God's "open arms of embrace." This is an invitation to us to come to Him. Next, God waits for us to respond. Our response is repentance. When we have drawn near to God through repentance, God gently wraps his arms around us, completing the embrace. In this way God receives us into the communion of divine life. Then, God's arms open again. The reopening of God's arms prevents the divine hug from become an oppressive and dominating choke hold. Christians are to imitate this kind of self-giving love of the Trinity in their relationships.[14]

The theological world of atonement maps onto therapeutic interest in forgiveness, repentance (a.k.a. apology) and reconciliation. Regarding forgiveness, research into the psychological study of forgiveness has exploded during the last few decades. In contrast, research into psychological apology is the closest thing you will find to the Christian ideal of repentance. Repentance is still so strongly associated with religious overtones that it has yet to make it into main stream psychological vocabulary. Many forgiveness researchers will get nervous when the construct of reconciliation is introduced along with forgiving and repenting. In the therapeutic world a clean boundary exists between forgiving and reconciling.[15] Forgiving is something that happens within the skin of the injured party. As soon as we bring any interaction between injured party and wrongdoer into the picture, then we have left the realm of forgiving and entered the arena of reconciliation.

Forgiveness. *Forgiveness* can be defined as an emotional replacement process, where one replaces negative emotions such as rage, bitterness and grudge-bearing with positive emotions such as love, mercy and compassion. Everett Worthington Jr. identifies two kinds of forgiveness: decisional forgiveness and emotional forgiveness. Decisional forgiveness is "controlling our behavioral intentions."[16] Here we make a conscious choice to act *as if* we feel forgiveness toward the person who hurt us. Decisional forgiveness is important. It is a turning away from lobbing emotional grenades into our relationship by extending a cease fire, if not calling a truce. Many Christian clients will begin with decisional forgiveness because they desire to be obedient to the biblical command to forgive one another (Mt 18:35; Eph 4:32). In contrast, emotional forgiveness "is experiencing emotional replacement of negative, unforgiving emotions with positive, other-oriented emotions."[17] Emotional forgiveness is what we long for—to no longer feel the distressing pain of anger, rage or bitterness. Worthington notes that decisional and emotional forgiveness are two different types of forgiveness. Worthington rightly observes, "God *requires* decisional forgiveness of us; God *desires* emotional forgiveness."[18]

Emotional forgiveness takes clients to a deeper level of healing. Several researchers have explored pathways to emotional forgiveness. Differentiation of self (see chap. 4) has been positively associated with forgiveness in terms of one's capacity for managing negative emotional reactivity and restraining one's self from hostile thoughts, feelings or actions toward offenders. The greater one's capacity for differentiation, the greater the likelihood that one will achieve neutrality when forgiving another person.[19] The emotional regulatory benefits of differentiation of self support enacting the behavioral aspects of forgiveness as described in Ephesians 4:25-32. In the following, I have noted central aspects of differentiation of self (i.e., "I" position, emotional reactivity, cutoff, emotional fusion, self-soothing, self-responsibility) in brackets throughout this passage.

> So then, putting away falsehood, let all of us speak the truth to our neighbors, for we are members of one another ["I" position]. Be angry but do not sin; do not let the sun go down on your anger, and do not make room for the devil [managing emotional reactivity]. Thieves must give up stealing; rather let them labor and work honestly with their own hands, so as to have something to share with the needy [self-responsibility]. Let no evil talk come out of your mouths [hostile anger can be a way of emotional distance *or* emotional fusion; self-soothing], but only what is useful for building up, as there is need, so that your words may give grace to those who hear ["I" position and managing emotional reactivity]. And do not grieve the Holy Spirit of God, with which you were marked with a seal for the day of redemption. Put away from you all bitterness and wrath and anger and wrangling and slander, together with all malice [self-soothing; managing emotional reactivity], and be kind to one another, tenderhearted, forgiving one another, as God in Christ has forgiven you ["I" position, self-responsibility].

Counselors working from a Bowenian perspective can help clients move closer to forgiving another person by helping them to increase their capacity for self-differentiation in ways quite similar to that described by the Scripture verses above.

Worthington has developed an empirically validated approach to forgiveness counseling: REACHing for forgiveness.[20] REACH is an acrostic for how to forgive another person.

- *Recall* the hurt. In the REACH model one recalls the wounding event truthfully and as objectively as possible, taking extra care not to vilify the offender by ignoring circumstances that may shed light on the offender's actions or to "saint"-ify the self by minimizing, ignoring or excusing one's own contribution to the conflict.

- *Empathize* with the offender. This is a particularly challenging step as it asks the injured party to walk a mile in the offender's shoes, to view the event from the wrongdoer's perspective.

- Give the *Altruistic Gift* of forgiveness. Just as God's forgiveness of us is sheer gift by the grace of God, so too is our forgiveness of the ones who hurt us.

- Publically *Commit* to forgiveness. This does not mean to post something on Facebook or to make an announcement from the church pulpit. It does mean find a friend, mentor or prayer partner who knows that you have forgiven another and who can support you in this process.

- *Hold* onto forgiveness. Periodically you will doubt that you have forgiven the one who hurt you. Find ways to remind yourself of your choice and commitment to forgive and REACH for forgiveness as often as you need to.

Maria, age twenty-five, sought counseling for depression and anxiety issues. She had been sexually assaulted by a stranger when she was nine years old, and the memories of this event still haunt her. An important part of Maria's work was to confront the violation that she experienced as a child and to forgive the perpetrator. The REACH model was instrumental in Maria's forgiveness work.

Repentance. Theologically "to repent" is to experience a complete life reorientation.[21] It is a redirection of one's entire being toward God that results in a Holy Spirit-empowered capacity to conform one's life to mirror the heart of God. It is *way more* than saying "I'm sorry, God," although that would be a good start (especially if you mean it). Interpersonally, repentance refers to a decisive *turning away* from thoughts, words and deeds that have betrayed love and trust in a relationship, and a wholehearted *turning toward* attitudes that can restore love and trust to the damaged relationship. Repentance results in a transformation of the self, and by extension, a transformation in how you view the one you hurt.

Repentance is something that happens within a transgressor's heart through the internal process of *awareness*, and it is something that is transacted between transgressors and the ones they have hurt through the interactive process of *accountability*. Awareness involves a change in perception—about self, the other and the harmful event. It is akin to the prodigal son's coming to his senses (Lk 15:17). Awareness is developed through humility and empathy. These moral emotions have been associated with granting forgiveness, and I believe that they play an important role in seeking forgiveness too.[22] Through humility wrongdoers develop a more accurate picture of themselves as a person capable of inflicting pain on another. The actions that they may have previously defended as acceptable responses are no longer held in such high esteem. They see themselves as without excuse, even if they may have had a reasonable explanation for why they did what they did. Empathy is like a huge "aha" about the injured party. Through empathy, wrongdoers come to understand the injured party's version of what happened and credit the injured party's thoughts, feelings and interpretation about the transgression.

In contrast to awareness, accountability means accepting responsibility for the impact of offending actions and seeking to repair the damage if possible. This is similar to the prodigal son's rising, going home and confessing to his father (see Lk 15:20-21). Accountability includes confession and rebuilding trustworthiness, processes that happen between injured parties and wrongdoers. Authentic apology is the hallmark of confession. It is the outpouring of a broken and contrite heart. Offenders take full responsibility for the impact of their actions without offering excuses or justifications. On the other hand rebuilding trustworthiness involves reliable efforts on the offender's part to demonstrate consistent changed behavior over time. This is more than restitution. One can replace a broken item, but that doesn't mean that one has repaired broken trust.

Differentiation of self can help wrongdoers sustain a repentant spirit. For many of us it will take courage to take an "I" position of repentance, which includes admitting the error of one's way and acknowledging how one has wounded another. Instead of distancing from the relationship through cutoff, one remains emotionally connected, enduring the wounded partner's distrust in the early stages of rebuilding. Instead of fusing with the injured party by mindlessly catering to unreasonable demands, repentant transgressors act in ways that are full of integrity. At times wounded individuals may lash out in anger. During these exchanges, self-soothing and managing one's emotional reactivity will help repentant transgressors to stay engaged rather than avoid their partner or retaliate in kind. Finally self-responsibility maintains transgressors' efforts to own their part of undermining trust and fairness in the relationship.

Injured parties watch actions of wrongdoers very closely. Will they be faithful to keep new promises—or not? Until transgressors have established a track record of consistent changed behavior over time, injured parties may be hesitant to invest in the relationship. They are also likely to magnify the importance of small infractions of trust, which might have been dismissed prior to the offense. Moreover, counselors will need to guard against clients' framing the atonement as a call to endure dangerous relationship dynamics. On the cross Christ represents victimizers and victims, but the cross does not call men or women to be victimized by people who had pledged to love them. This is a misapplication of the atonement.

Samuel, age eighteen, was enjoying the freedom of his freshman year at school. Unfortunately, his pleasure came at the expense of his academic performance. He lost his scholarship at the end of that academic year. His parents were deeply wounded by Samuel's action. They had sacrificed much so he could attend the college of his choice. In a moment of insight, Samuel saw how he had affected his parents and finally came to realize the extent to which they had gone to provide him with this educational opportunity. He apologized to them with sincerity. He enrolled in a local community college for his sophomore year, paying for his own tuition and books.

Reconciliation. If counselors have the benefit of working with injured parties and wrongdoers, then it is possible (although not inevitable) that reconciliation can become a therapeutic goal. Reconciliation is challenging under the best of circumstances. It requires that wrongdoers come under the "trust microscope" and remain committed to promises of changed behavior. It requires willingness to risk loving and trusting again on the part of injured parties. Many clients will decide that they are too hurt to reconcile. At other times an injured party may long to reconcile but the offender is not interested in being held accountable. Many clients find it easier to let the relationship die than to work at reconciling, especially when there are no legal ties binding the two together. What contributes to successful reconciliation? As you have already guessed, forgiveness and repentance are two keys. Reconciling individuals will also need a support system to help them during rocky times. Supporters can be prayer partners, friends, pastors and counselors. Reconciling takes a determined kind of commitment—one willing to endure short-term pain for the longer-term gain of a "brother or sister" or husband or wife. This kind of commitment is not set aside when the relationship faces early setbacks. It continues to persevere as long as evidence of changed behavior continues to exist. I believe that reconciliation is the ideal and ultimate goal when theologically reflective counselors work with clients.[23] Christ died so that we might be *reconciled* to God. The atonement opens the door for us to receive God's great gift of forgiveness and reconciliation with God. As forgiven Christ-ones, and now empowered by the Holy Spirit, we are Spirit-enabled to live holy lives of forgiving, repenting and reconciling as members of God's family.

THE THEOLOGICALLY REFLECTIVE PRACTITIONER AND FORGIVENESS COUNSELING

It is highly unlikely that you will engage a client in extended conversation about the atonement. On the other hand, it is most certain that you will discuss forgiveness, repentance/apology or reconciliation with clients. Here is where you will hear echoes of Christian clients' atonement theology. An interesting phenomenon arises when Christian clients present issues that challenge their capacity to align their life with what they profess. To what extent does the cross of Christ become formative? Following the way of the cross through forgiving, repenting and reconciling is easier said than done. Forgiving, repenting and reconciling are most readily accomplished when the issues are small, mundane and quickly repairable, or when the dyad can draw upon a solid foundation of friendship, love, respect and mutual trust to help them heal from more problematic betrayals.[24] The relationship challenges that clients face to which atonement theology may be essential are the same challenges that make living into the atonement most difficult. We are eternally grateful that Christ died for us, absorbing the pain that allows us to be reconciled to God. We are ever so hesitant when we realize that being "like Jesus" in this way means that we too will bear pain when we forgive.

Attending to theological echoes. Belinda is an effervescent young adult. I had seen Belinda and her parents a few years ago when they went through a particularly rocky place in their relationship. That season of counseling ended successfully. Belinda, now a junior in college, returned for counseling with a deep sense of having betrayed her parents' trust and with a major decision to make. For a period of time she had grown tired of living like a "good Christian." One night she got drunk, had sex and got pregnant. Belinda was now faced with telling her parents about her pregnancy and deciding whether she was going to put her baby up for adoption.

Belinda feels a deep sense of guilt for having violated her own moral and spiritual values. She believes she has disappointed her Lord and her parents. The theological world that resonates with themes of forgiveness, repentance and reconciliation is that of the *fugitive.* You may remember that the theological world of the fugitive is one of powerlessness. They feel condemned and fearful, convinced that they have fallen short. They are powerless to do anything to effect their felt state of being. They are burdened by a deep sense of guilt. The *obsessio* of the fugitive is the power of sin to shape one's will. The *epiphania* is the realization that the human condition is one of *brokenness.* Resolution is found in God's forgiveness. Fugitives' response to God's forgiveness (i.e., repentance) manifests their awareness that they trust God to have forgiven them. The rhythm of this world is movement between condemnation and forgiveness. The cross of Christ takes away their guilt. They can experience God's love as that kind of love which offers forgiveness to one who does not deserve it, and through this love of God they are freed from their guilt and are able to please God as they live a new life. This was indeed true for Belinda.

Because I had worked with Belinda before, I had some idea of the theological commitments that shaped the relationships in this family. Belinda's parents took solace in their role as a "good church family." Both parents were mature believers who had weathered their own emotional storms over the course of their marriage. They knew the power of God's forgiveness in their own hearts, and they sought to model Christlikeness in their parenting. Belinda had been raised in a church that affirmed the authority of the Bible and helped its members to mature through small group interaction, discipleship opportunities and mission trips. If Belinda chooses to raise her baby, she will find a support network in her family's church. If she decides for adoption, she can turn to her church friends to help her release her child into the care of another couple.

Addressing salient theological themes. Belinda takes full responsibility for her behavior. She humbly offered a confession to her parents in which she takes ownership of her actions. She affirms that her pregnancy was not the result of a date rape. She describes the sexual encounter with the father of her baby as a "one-night stand." She does not want to marry the father of her child because she does not love him. Belinda identifies the issues that will shape our early work together. She asks God and her parents for forgiveness. She is working on repentance issues. Now that she has experienced sinning in a way that resulted in a permanent relationship consequence (pregnancy), she comes to God emotionally ready to grasp a deeper understanding of God's forgiveness. She is also wrestling with self-forgiveness.[25] Research found that anxiety, shame and anger are associated with self-forgiveness,[26] and these emotions permeated Belinda's life at the beginning of counseling. Justice concerns are present in this case. Perhaps these are not necessarily the social justice concerns from chapter five, but there are nevertheless justice and fairness dynamics within this family. What does a just solution look like for this infant? Is it fair to ask Belinda's parents to support her financially and with childcare so that she can complete her college education? Will they do so? What responsibility does the baby's father carry? A paternity suit will involve the court system if he contests Belinda's claim of paternity.

Multiple layers of forgiveness, repentance and reconciliation are present. Belinda is dealing with self-forgiveness, repentance, asking forgiveness of her parents and seeking to reconcile with them. Her parents face the challenge of forgiving Belinda, reconciling with her and either welcoming this new life into their family or releasing this infant into the care of others. This family's Christian commitments will aid them in these processes. It will be important to understand how the family thinks about the cross of Christ and forgiveness. Does forgiveness mean "forgive and forget"? A victory over sin? Satisfying the parents' embarrassment that their daughter is pregnant without the benefit of a marital bond? What demonstrations of trustworthiness will Belinda's parents need to see, assuming that they forgive her and then also agree to be an integral part of her parenting support system if she keeps her baby?

Aligning areas of life to be more theologically congruent. Clinically Belinda will need coaching in how to offer a sincere confession and will need all of her resolve to comply with reasonable and appropriate stipulations that her parents may insist on as a sign of her contrition. These reparative behaviors will help her to forgive herself.[27] The family will need to discuss what a just and fair resolution looks like and what interactions will help close any *injustice gap* that they experience within the immediate context of their family. Christian psychologist Everett Worthington defines the injustice gap as

> the ongoing tally we make, rationally or intuitively, that informs us how fair or unfair the outcomes surrounding a transgression are. The gap is the difference between my desired ideal solution . . . and the current status as I now see it. . . . We act based on our current injustice gap. . . . The injustice gap drives people's motivation to respond with justice or forgiveness. [28]

Increasing Belinda's awareness of the meaning of the cross of Christ as she applies it to her specific situation can support her resolve to live a new kind of life and to let God's forgiveness take her guilt away. Because the members of this family had experienced God's forgiveness in their lives, they may draw strength from that to extend forgiveness to one another, especially in light of Belinda's confession and repentance. In Belinda's case, her parents may offer her the gift of forgiveness, but this does not automatically make for easy decision making. Belinda's actions have consequences for the entire family system. Therefore, this family will need to be able to take clear "I" positions on what each one desires, hopes and wants, including what each is willing or not willing to do in relationship to Belinda's pregnancy. Belinda will need to have strength to tolerate parental disappointment, disapproval, anger and resentment as they work through their forgiveness toward reconciliation. This trio will also need to be clear on who will be responsible for what in the light of decisions to adopt out or to keep the baby.

Attaining a deepening Christian character. Belinda's broken and contrite heart and her parent's willingness to forgive her contributed to a *relatively* smooth reconciliation. But their real work was just beginning. *As a family* they decided against adoption. Belinda's parents committed to remodeling their home to provide a suite for Belinda and her baby, affording each subsystem some privacy. Together they worked out a plan so that Belinda could complete her college undergraduate degree.

I have a postscript to this clinical vignette. A few years later Belinda's name was once again on my case load. By this time she had transitioned from a single parent to a married woman with two children. She had grown into a mature Christian woman, wife and mother. She and her husband were coming in for a marital wellness check up.

CONCLUSION

Authors have the luxury of selecting the clinical examples that they employ. This particular example has a happy ending. Not all clients who cope with repenting, forgiving or reconciling will achieve the degree of relationship renewal that this case family did. My own clinical work testifies to the challenges that counselors face when they seek to help clients forgive and repent. For many the injustice gap is too wide and the repair efforts too weak. In such cases clients may not name reconciliation as a clinical goal, and counselors will need to adjust accordingly.

Theologically reflective counseling in contexts of forgiveness, repentance and reconciliation involves developing a strong working alliance with clients (chap. 3), calling clients to personal responsibility (chap. 4), attending to issues of injustice in relationships (chap. 5), and supporting clients as they wrestle with forgiving, repenting and reconciling. As already noted in this chapter, many relationships end prior to reconciliation. Clients then grieve the lost relationship, commending the other into the hands of God. In chapter seven I will explore how eschatological perspectives can help these same clients develop hope for futures that otherwise may appear hopeless.

7

Seeing Now in
Light of the Not Yet

ESCHATOLOGY AND
THEOLOGICALLY REFLECTIVE COUNSELING

✍

Away with our sorrow and fear!
We soon shall recover our home,
The city of saints shall appear,
The day of eternity come:
From earth we shall quickly remove,
And mount to our native abode,
The house of our Father above,
The palace of angels and God.

Our mourning is all at an end,
When, raised by the life-giving Word,
We see the new city descend,
Adorned as a bride for her Lord;
The city so holy and clean,
No sorrow can breathe in the air;
No gloom of affliction or sin,
No shadow of evil is there.

CHARLES WESLEY,
"Away with Our Sorrow and Fear"

He spoke of living in abject poverty in a wilderness area. Church members would bring food to his family's home when the hunting was plentiful. He could not recall the number of times that his father beat him while his mother remained a passive observer. Every Sunday he was expected to attend church and to do his part to portray a happy, holy family because his father was the pastor.

She had faith that God would heal her cancer. She had much to live for. She had a husband that she adored and two of the sweetest children in the world. Her Bible study group prayed for a miracle. Soon this group was praying for comfort and strength for those who mourned her untimely death. Her widowed husband struggled to make sense of it all.

He couldn't understand why he had been fired. He had been a charge nurse with a history of excellent performance reviews. When a new administration took over the hospital he worked in, he believed the management created black marks on his record to justify their action. He knew that God would take care of him, but he felt depressed and anxious nonetheless.

Suffering is a universal experience. Like beauty, suffering is in the eye of the beholder.[1] What brings intense sadness, loss and desperation to one individual is experienced as a mere ripple in water to another. A dreadful event may culminate in a diagnosis of posttraumatic stress disorder for some, but not for others. Ronnie Janoff-Bulman proposes that when such events shatter the tacit assumptions on which we have built our lives, our degree of recovery rests on the extent to which we can rebuild these shattered assumptions.[2] While Janoff-Bulman's work refers to general worldview assumptions, such as the self is worthy, the world is beneficent, and the world is meaningful, followers of Christ line these assumptions with theological meaning. The assumption of the self as worthy is transformed into "I am a child of God and a person of worth because I am created in the image of God." The assumptions of a good and meaningful world are converted to reflect Romans 8:28, 38-39: "We know that all things work together for good for those who love God, who are called according to his purpose. . . . For I am convinced that neither death, nor life, nor angels, nor rulers, nor things present, nor things to come, nor powers, nor height, nor depth, nor anything else in all creation, will be able to separate us from the love of God in Christ Jesus our Lord."

The degree to which we have taken these truths deep into the marrow of our bones isn't evident until we face circumstances that we perceive to be unbearable. We may experience sacred loss (under the "best" of troublesome circumstances) or desecration (under the worst case scenario) during times of crisis or trauma. With sacred loss, we experience a *benign* passing away of something that we had connected with God. Something is missing, has disappeared or is now absent from our lives. Such may be your experience if you move to a new city, leaving behind a church home that you cherished. Conversely, we experience desecration as a *willful violation* of something directly connected to God. Something is not just missing. It has been ruined, dishonored, torn out, attacked or intentionally harmed. Research studies have associated experiences of sacred loss with intrusive thoughts and depression, while perceptions of desecration are even more strongly associated with intrusive thoughts and anger.[3] During times of trials, tribulation, tragedy and trauma, clients struggle to make sense of sacred loss and desecration. An explanation may be close at hand for some people. When a loved one dies after a battle with a debilitating illness, Christian families may say something like this: "Grandpa is no longer suffering. He is better off now because he is with Jesus." This would be typical for sacred losses. But desecrations baffle us. No explanation makes enough sense to account for the willful hurt of child sexual abuse or the destruction wrought by genocide. Even forgiveness seems impossible.[4]

Perhaps no other area of counseling reveals the robustness (or paucity) of a therapist's theology quite like crisis or trauma counseling. *Why* was my child murdered? *Why* did God spare that block of houses during the tornado but not this block, and more specifically, not *my block*? Psychological explanations go only so far. Ultimately, answers to the *why* questions of life fall within the purview of theology. What theological resources may therapists draw on to make sense of clients' pain for themselves—and to assist clients in a theological meaning-making process? Is the theology of the counselor thick enough?

The biblical narrative is replete with men and women of God who experienced trials, tribulation, tragedy and trauma. Adam and Eve experienced the heartbreak of fratricide (Gen 4). Esau was betrayed by his twin brother with the help of their mother (Gen 25:19–28:9). Joseph, son of Jacob, was sold into slavery by his brothers, framed by Potiphar's wife and left to languish in Pharaoh's prison for a crime he did not commit (Gen 37–41). Following the exodus and the establishment of the kingdom of Israel, God's people experienced the division of the united kingdom into two parts: Israel, the descendents of the sons of Jacob who settled the land to the north of Jerusalem, and the territory occupied by the offspring of Judah and Benjamin (Jerusalem and the surrounding area). Foreign powers invaded and destroyed the northern nation of Israel. Some time later the southern nation of Judah also experienced invasion and the majority of the populace was deported to live in exile in the homeland of their conquerors. When the descendents of those taken in captivity were finally allowed to return to their homeland, they faced the challenge of rebuilding their religious and civil society (symbolized in the restoration of the temple and temple worship) and in the reconstruction of Jerusalem, a city that had been left in ruins (Ezra, Nehemiah). The story doesn't get prettier in the New Testament. One look at the life of Jesus Christ reveals that suffering frequently accompanies those who follow the Son of God (Phil 3:10). The apostle Paul summarizes his experiences in 2 Corinthians 11:24-28:

> Five times I have received from the Jews the forty lashes minus one. Three times I was beaten with rods. Once I received a stoning. Three times I was shipwrecked; for a night and a day I was adrift at sea; on frequent journeys, in danger from rivers, danger from bandits, danger from my own people, danger from Gentiles, danger in the city, danger in the wilderness, danger at sea, danger from false brothers and sisters; in toil and hardship, through many a sleepless night, hungry and thirsty, often without food, cold and naked. And, besides other things, I am under daily pressure because of my anxiety for all the churches.

What resources might theology provide for theologically reflective practitioners as they help clients bear the emotional burdens of trauma and tragedy? The apostle Paul's recommendation is to see today's "temporary" troubles in light of God's eternal tomorrow. Paul reports that he has been "afflicted in every way, but not crushed; perplexed, but not driven to despair; persecuted, but not forsaken; struck down, but not destroyed" (2 Cor 4:8-9). Then Paul concludes:

> So we do not lose heart. Even though our outer nature is wasting away, our inner nature is being renewed day by day. For this slight momentary affliction is preparing us for an eternal weight of glory beyond all measure, because we look not at what can be seen but at what cannot be seen; for what can be seen is temporary, but what cannot be seen is eternal. (2 Cor 4:16-18)

In theological terms, Paul has adopted an *eschatological perspective*. Technically, eschatology is the study of "last things"—the end of this world and the beginning of God's fully realized kingdom. This Christian doctrine of the future centers on Jesus Christ as the crucified Lamb of God, the resurrected Lord and the victorious Lion of Judah who comes to judge this world and finally sets things to rights. The *eschaton* is "the final revelation of God in history through the coming of Christ."[5] According to New Testament scholar Joel B. Green, "eschatology is a cornerstone of the Christian imagination—a lens through which to view day-to-day life and the whole of time, . . . comprised of beliefs and values to which the Christian community, individually and collectively, is deeply attached, . . . whose terms give rise to certain behaviors."[6] Eschatology helps us makes sense of today in light of what God's ultimate plan is for God's eternal tomorrow.

An eschatological perspective provides the widest angle lens through which to view pain and suffering. An eschatological view of life is like reading a mystery from front to back to front. I am a huge fan of mystery and suspense novels. But I am also a tension wimp. I hate getting attached to a major character only to discover that he or she has been killed off. Therefore I read the beginning of the novel to get the gist of the story. Then I skim enough of the end of the novel to know who lives and who dies. Then I go back to the beginning and pick up where I had left off. Knowing how the story ends provides an interpretive lens for me. When my favorite character gets into a mess, I reassure myself that he or she will live to investigate another day. Eschatology is like that—only more so! Our understanding of the "end" of God's story provides a framework for the decisions we make today and it offers hope to sustain us through suffering *in light of God's tomorrow.*

My focus on eschatology is not an attempt to weigh in on end times issues such as the millennium, the tribulation and the rapture. Nor is it to speculate on the day and time of Christ's return. My intent in this chapter is to consider how viewing today's afflictions in light of Christ's coming kingdom contributes to theologically reflective counseling so that with Paul we can "consider that the sufferings of this present time are not worth comparing with the glory about to be revealed to us" (Rom 8:18). Toward that end I first review theological perspectives associated with eschatology and then explore therapeutic perspectives that guide clinicians' work. Finally, I will apply these thoughts to a case study using our model of theologically reflective counseling.

THEOLOGICAL CONSIDERATION: ESCHATOLOGICAL HORIZONS

Eschatology is an area of theology with many viewpoints about what will happen on planet earth prior to the final state of eternal bliss. As I mentioned before, it is not my intent to discuss perspectives on the tribulation, the rapture of believers, the millennium or the like. N. T. Wright notes in *Surprised by Hope* that

> there is very little in the Bible about "going to heaven when you die" and not a lot about a postmortem hell either. . . . "God's Kingdom" in the preaching of Jesus refers not to postmortem destiny, not to escape from this world into another one, but to God's sovereign rule coming "on earth as it is in heaven." . . . Heaven in the Bible is not a future destiny but the other, hidden, dimension of our ordinary life—God's dimension, if you like. God made heaven and earth; at the last he will remake both and join them together forever.[7]

While end time events and timelines may hold interests for some counselors and may contribute to healing for some clients (e.g., at times particular clients may find the image of their offenders burning in hell for eternity to be quite comforting), I believe that other factors associated with the eschaton offer greater clinical help. Specifically, I am interested in the question of how counselors' theological perspectives of the then-and-there can be a source of hope for clients who are in the midst of a here-and-now that is laced with pain and suffering.

In this section I want to look at the thinking of three theologians: eighteenth-century John Wesley and twenty-first-century theologians N. T. Wright and Miroslav Volf. My excursion into the eschatological thought of these three scholars scratches the surface of their thinking, yet it will provide a sufficient foundation for our subsequent discussion on theologically reflective counseling. Wesley gives us a picture of heaven that is held by many evangelical or theologically orthodox Christians. Wright and Volf will help us think about how we live with today's pain in light of God's future reign. They will also be our guide in some theological explorations into what will happen then-and-there with the pain that we experience here-and-now. In sum, these theologians will help us attend to the question of how eschatological perspectives can assist clients to find hope and make meaning out of trials, tribulation, tragedies and traumas.

John Wesley. Wesley links our eternal future with our present salvation. The life of holy love that believers live today is a marker. It signifies that God's *eternal* life of holy love has begun in believers in the here-and-now. This present life is a preparation and preamble for the fuller experience of seeing God face to face upon death. As church historian Ken Collins notes, salvation "is the bridge, the way, that will transport the redeemed to eternity."[8] Wesley maintained that God's grace through the Holy Spirit empowered and enabled believers to live lives marked by holy love. This includes responding to life's hardships in ways consistent with God's holy love, trusting God to provide sufficient strength and help in their time of need. Wesley preached that when one died the immortal soul would shuck its physical body. Wesley believed in a dualistic view of humanity: an immaterial, immortal soul requires a physical body in this life, and it would leave the body behind upon death. Believers would come face to face with God, who would ultimately judge them and also welcome them into heaven because of God's own grace, which sustained them in this life and the life to come.[9]

Ken Collins highlights one aspect of John Wesley's teachings related to eschatology: the new creation. Collins notes that Wesley devoted a considerable portion of his writings to this topic. Wesley advocated the establishment of a new heaven and a new earth, as promised in the book of Revelation, where the elements of this world (wind, fire, rain, etc.) will no longer bring destruction through natural disasters, and where God's children will no longer suffer. Collins summarizes Wesley's position as follows:

> In a real sense, then, Wesley's doctrine of the new creation, of a newly fashioned physical world in which the righteous dwell, spills into question of theodicy. In other words, the whole problem of natural evil in the form of floods, earthquakes, and so on, receives a definitive answer only in the coming new creation. Here natural evil will finally be a thing of the past, as will sorrow, pain, and death. Thus, grace will triumph where sin once ruled; life will be victorious where death once held sway.[10]

Given that many of Wesley's congregants lived hard lives on the margins of society, Wesley's theological position would bring comfort to them. Their challenge was to embody holy love for God and neighbor in the midst of trying circumstances because that would be preparation for their eternal life. The idea of an immortal soul shedding its encumbering mortal flesh and finding holiness and happiness in heavenly bliss is reflected in many spirituals, hymns and praise songs—then and now. Many who suffer this side of eternity find solace and strength in this imagery and promise.

N. T. Wright. N. T. Wright broadens our understanding of eschatology itself. In *Surprised by Hope* Wright clarifies:

> Eschatology . . . refers to the strongly held belief of most first-century Jews, and virtually all early Christians, that history was going some-

where under the guidance of God and that where it was going was toward God's new world of justice, healing, and hope. The transition from the present world to the new one would be a matter not of destruction of the present space-time universe but of its radical healing. . . . Eschatology [does not] simply mean the second coming [of Jesus Christ], still less a particular theory about it; [it means], rather, the entire sense of God's future for the world and the belief that the future has already begun to come forward to meet us in the present.[11]

Wright proposes that the entire biblical narrative is the unfolding story of God's plan for putting the world to rights—where ultimately death will be defeated, decay will cease and God's people will be transformed. This mirrors the eschatology picture painted by John Wesley. What Wright clarifies, at least for me, is an emphasis on "collaborative eschatology."[12] By this Wright refers to the privilege and responsibility that falls to Jesus' followers, as empowered by the Holy Spirit, to begin transforming the present in light of God's ultimate future.

Wright proposes that the biblical narrative does not answer the human question of *why* evil exists in the world. It reveals what God is doing about it instead.[13] In an amazing act of grace, God chose to work through Abraham and then the children of Israel to establish communities of holy and just living. These chosen instruments failed, being overcome by the sin that they were meant to defeat. Ultimately, God sent Jesus Christ, the true and faithful human, who fulfilled God's mission. On the cross Jesus "absorbed" the worst that evil could dish out, and he destroyed death itself. The bodily resurrection of Jesus was a confirmation of Christ's victory over evil and death. Jesus is God's answer to the problem of evil. Jesus inaugurated God's just and righteous kingdom as "God's future-arrived-in-the-present."[14] Now through the Holy Spirit, followers of Jesus are empowered to transform the present in light of God's future.

What does Wright's perspective on eschatology have to do with theologically reflective counseling? First, I propose that as Christian counselors employ their skills by calling clients to responsible, holy living (chap. 4), by joining clients in the struggle to transform unjust familial or societal structures (chap. 5), and by helping clients to find release from the wounds that they receive through forgiveness, repentance and even reconciliation (chap. 6), they are partners in "collaborative eschatology," helping to bring about God's already-but-not-yet kingdom on earth as it is in heaven. In addition, clients who currently struggle with trials, tribulation, tragedies and traumas, for which there is no immediate relief in sight or for whom the aftermath will leave them permanently changed (i.e., physically disabled, death of loved one, etc.) may find strength to persevere, meaning for today and hope for tomorrow by seeing their difficulty within the horizon of God's ultimate intent to set the world to rights. Pain tends to obscure one's ability to foresee a future where pain does not exist. Wright's vision of the eschaton may offer a perspective that brings hope when clients feel that all they have left is hope against hope.

Miroslav Volf. Theologian Miroslav Volf understands firsthand the pain associated with suffering and the challenges that presents to Christians who seek to align their lives with God's kingdom purposes. In his book *The End of Memory* Volf tackles the question of how Christians should remember wrongs suffered. Volf's context for his theological reflection on memory is his experience of trauma. Volf begins by stating a truth about memories; that is, we do not live with the facts of our lives. Instead, we live with the stories that we tell ourselves about the facts of our lives. Self and memory stand in dynamic relationship to one another—we shape the memories that shape us. Volf observes,

> If salvation lies in the memories of wrongs suffered, it must lie more in what we do with those memories than in the memories themselves. And what we do with our memories will depend on how we see ourselves in the present and how we project ourselves into the future.[15]

Janoff-Bulman asserts in *Shattered Assumptions* that personal healing occurs when traumatic memories are integrated into a larger pattern of meaning and woven into the fabric of one's life. Volf proposes that "the means of healing of personal memory is the *interpretive* work a person does *with* memory."[16] The skill that Christians must develop is that of *remembering well*. Volf explains that "redemption of the past is nestled in the broader story of God's restoration of our broken world to wholeness—including past, present, and future."[17] Can we integrate the memory of our trouble into God's larger narrative of redemption rather than be left with only *our own* history to frame the memory? God's redemptive narrative includes what God has done in the past, how God relates to our present and, most salient to this chapter, what God intends to do as God's future activity relates to our experience of trauma and tragedy.

Five movements in God's redemptive narrative make remembering well possible. First, the love shared among members of the Trinity spilled over into the creation of humanity and the world. Second, humanity was created not for self-centered pursuits but to live with God and one another in a world of justice and in love. Third, humanity made a mess of God's good world. But, in Christ, God entered human history, and through Christ's death on the cross we are reconciled to God and to one another. We are not left to clean up our mess on our own. Volf's account of the first three movements in the Christian story echo themes that were developed earlier in this book. The final two movements find a home in this chapter. Fourth, at the end of time we will be transformed so that we may enjoy God and each other in Christ for all eternity. Fifth, and most germane to our present discussion, the irreversibility of time does not mean that suffering will have the final word. God will expose the truth about wrongs, condemn evil deeds and redeem both repentant perpetrators and their victims, thus reconciling all things.

While the main thrust of Volf's *End of Memory* is a challenge to believers to (1) remember rightly, (2) remember so as to heal, and (3) to let truths of the exodus and the Passion provide interpretive frames for one's painful memory, it is the final portion of his work that I wish highlight, where Volf engages in what I will call "theologically reflective imagination." Volf opens *The End of Memory* with a vivid account of his painful memories of being interrogated by "Captain G." in Yugoslavia. Volf asks his readers to think about *how* in this life we are to remember those who have wronged us severely and unjustly. The final section of Volf's book turns to a different question: What will happen to our memory of those painful experiences at the end of time?

Until this point Volf has presented ways in which victims of horrendous evil ought to remember—remember rightly, remember so as to
heal, and remembrance of wrongs that are embedded within the larger
narratives of (1) the liberating and redemptive exodus of the Israelites
from Egyptian slavery, and (2) the passion of Jesus Christ, which lib-
erates and redeems all humanity from the slavery of sin through forgiveness and reconciles us to God and potentially to one another. But
what will happen to those memories of wrongs suffered when we no
longer "see in a mirror, dimly" (1 Cor 13:12)—when injustice has been
named, when God's justice has been brought to bear upon those situations and when God's world of perfect love has fully come into being?

Volf suggests that when God makes all things new in the new heaven
and the new earth, victims will no longer need to remember the evils
that have befallen them. He calls this the "non-remembrance of wrongs
suffered." It is not as if we will have forgotten the woes that have befallen us. Instead Volf suggests we will be so caught up in God and in
God's world of *perfect love* that God's love will flow into us. Therefore
there will be no *need* for remembering wrongs suffered. We will experience a "not-coming-to-mind of sufferings." We will have been transformed into the likeness of Jesus Christ so that even our memories will
have been transformed. If our wrongdoers also happen to be repentant
members of God's family, they too will have been transformed through
the cross of Christ and the power of the Holy Spirit. Volf writes:

> Being in God frees our lives from the tyranny the unalterable past exer-
> cises with the iron fist of time's irreversibility. God does not take away
> our past; God gives it back to us—fragments gathered, stories recon-
> figured, selves truly redeemed, people forever reconciled.[18]

How can we gather together these theological threads for the benefit
of theologically reflective counseling? When clients experience crisis
and trauma, the human impulse is to wring some meaning from those
events. For many types of painful experiences, meaning-making may
come easily, but in cases of horrendous evil and unjust suffering, I
suggest that ultimate meaning comes through the lens of eschatology.
Whether the one who suffers concludes "I can trust in God's unfailing

love to eventually make something good come out of this tragedy," or "I can depend on God's unfailing justice to prevail—maybe not in my lifetime—but at some time of God's choosing," or "One day I will be 'changed from glory into glory,' and then I will see Jesus, and nothing else will matter," the sufferers call on their beliefs about the things that are to come to help make sense of the things they must bear today.

THERAPEUTIC COMMITMENTS:
CRISIS AND TRAUMA COUNSELING

Up until this point I have referred to crisis and trauma as if they were a unit. In some cases they are intimately linked, while in other situations they are distinct entities. Traumatic events include aspects of crises, but not all crises evolve into traumas. Technically crisis counseling is short-term, situation-specific and usually focuses on problem solving. The crisis event that creates the client's presenting problem is often (although not always) readily identifiable, such as the aftermath of natural disaster, escalation of family problem to noteworthy proportions and the like. The hallmark of a crisis is that clients' normal coping skills have been maxed out. Clients are in uncharted emotional territory and in a state of disequilibrium. Diagnoses of adjustment disorders or even acute stress disorders are likely. Counselors assess the degree to which clients have adequate coping skills and social support. They also assist clients to develop adequate perceptions about the crisis. The goal of crisis counseling is to ensure client safety, help the client secure assistance through appropriate referral networks, and assist the client in emotional and behavioral regulation until the client returns to a state of equilibrium.[19]

In contrast, trauma counseling is longer-termed and more focused on helping the client to manage debilitating emotional and psychological symptoms that develop following a traumatic event. Trauma counseling can include the problem-solving aspects of crisis counseling noted previously. But the return to a state of equilibrium is more challenging because of the intense nature of anxiety and stress that follows traumatic events, and because of the powerful nature of intrusive symptoms (emotional dysregulation, flashbacks, etc.). Diagnoses of anxiety disorders, such as posttraumatic stress disorder, are likely. As noted earlier trauma can rip apart clients' assumptive worldviews. Trauma counseling includes helping clients to rebuild their assumptive worlds in ways that contribute to healing and openness to the future. Counselors will need to attend to the specific aspects of crisis and trauma counseling that are called for by clients' presenting problem even as they consider the place of theological reflection in the client's treatment.[20]

As clients share their stories of suffering, theologically reflective counselors can consider the source of pain that this implied by clients' narratives. While some clients will attribute pain to either God or the Satan, I propose that a more nuanced view of human suffering is supported by Scripture. Each source of pain carries with it a different avenue of relief, which can be of great help to counselors in treatment planning. Four sources of pain include (1) pain that results from our own sinfulness, (2) pain that we experience because we have been sinned against, (3) pain that is the result of living in a world affected by the Fall, and (4) pain that we experience for the sake of the gospel. These are not mutually exclusive categories. For example, being sinned against and responding to that hurt in sinful ways are frequent partners, as is suffering for the sake of the gospel and being sinned against. Nevertheless, counselors and clients may find it helpful to explore these different sources of pain and suffering as part of crisis or trauma counseling.

Pain from our own sinfulness. The biblical narrative is long on examples of people who suffer as a consequence of their own sinfulness. Adam and Eve are evicted from the Garden of Eden and now experience alienation from God and one another, hardship in their relationship to creation (work is now toilsome) and a power struggle in their relationship with one another. Cain is banished because he murdered his brother Abel. God's people are exiled because they forgot their covenant relationship with the one true God. God does not release us from the natural consequences of our sin. However we can be forgiven by God and often by others through confession and repentance, and we can find strength to live with the consequences of our own sinfulness.

Marvin is a sixty-five-year-old who sought counseling to help him repair his damaged relationship with his adult children. He had become a Christian at age sixty. His wife had divorced him and remarried. His two adult children had taken their mother's side in the divorce process and had cut ties with their father. He had recently received a diagnosis of prostate cancer.[21] As he faced this diagnosis, he reviewed his life and decided that he would use whatever time he had remaining to try to repair the damage his selfish lifestyle had created. Marvin was suffering from consequences of his own sinful behavior. Counseling included work on repentance and his tentative steps to reconnect with his adult children.[22] Unfortunately, they rejected his initiative. Marvin held onto the hope that in the eschaton Marvin and his former family would be reconciled in and through Jesus Christ even if his adult children rejected him now. He counted on a transformation that would happen in his heart and their hearts at that future time that would destroy the barriers that presently divided them.

Pain from being sinned against. The circumstances that call us to forgive are the same situations that can create tremendous pain in our lives. Sin is never a private affair. It always carries *relational* consequences. Our reactions to the wrongs that have been perpetrated against us are regularly the meat of many counseling sessions. Humanity is capable of horrendous evil. Coping with the aftermath of genocide, torture, human trafficking, child sexual abuse and the like taxes clients' coping skills and press counselors' clinical skills to their limits. To what degree can clients forgive their perpetrators (see chap. 6)? To what extent are clients capable of living rightly as they cope with the consequences of being sinned against? How might an eschatological horizon help victims to move forward when no justice on earth can ever compensate for the pain they endured?[23]

Eve, now age thirty, had been sexually abused by her stepfather from eight to sixteen. She clearly remembers her confusion and fear. She was promiscuous in her young adulthood and regularly used marijuana to self-medicate. She became a Christian at age twenty-five. She sought counseling to help her deal with intimacy issues, depression, anxiety and a negative self-image. Eve suffers because she was "sinned against." Her therapeutic work includes forgiveness of her perpetrator without reconciliation, forgiveness of herself and cognitive-behavioral interventions to help her manage her depression and anxiety.[24] She firmly believes that either in this life or the next Jesus will redeem her pain because Christ has been a victim of abuse too.

Pain from living in a fallen physical world. Whether or not the insurance companies have it right by calling natural disasters "acts of God," the reality is that we live in a world where hurricanes, tornadoes, tsunamis and earthquakes happen. Many families are devastated by these events and experience prolonged disruption. In addition to natural disasters, our physical bodies suffer the effects of the Fall. Clients will present various theological interpretations of such natural disasters. These perspectives can including blaming the event on Satan, attributing the destruction as God's way to punish sin or to teach a spiritual lesson, or, for the brave at heart, living with the ambiguity of not knowing why this happened (theologically speaking), but trusting in God's faithfulness to see one through.

When Hurricane Katrina hit the Gulf Shore states of Louisiana, Mississippi and Alabama, many people were traumatized. Based on his experience of living through Hurricane Katrina and working with clergy whose congregations were affected by it, Dr. Jamie Aten developed a program that fosters collaboration between the mental health community and local churches in the disaster areas. In his research he observed common religious and spiritual responses to disasters. Some survivors reexamined their belief in and relationship with God. He found that religious and spiritual coping had a buffering effect and added a layer of protection compared to those who did not access religious or spiritual coping strategies.[25] Dr. Aten encourages mental health professionals to develop collaborative relationships with members of the clergy in areas prone to natural disasters.

Pain from suffering for the sake of the gospel. The book of 1 Peter is written to Christians who were suffering *because* they were Christians and their lifestyle was an implicit challenge to the societies they lived in; that is, they suffered for the sake of the gospel.[26] The message of 1 Peter is that perseverance will sustain you through times of persecution.

While this category is linked to the second, suffering because of others' sinfulness, it is also distinct because one's identity as a *follower of Jesus* is the cause of one's suffering.

One of my most memorable cases was work with the ten-year-old daughter of a missionary family. The family's home had been invaded by a group of drunk, young men. This young girl and her mother were raped. Her brother and father were physically assaulted. The family was targeted because they were preaching the gospel of Jesus Christ. The family had come home to the United States to seek Christian mental health counseling. Coming to grips with the reality of evil and sin *while* her family was representing Jesus Christ contributed to this family's recovery.

Counseling in contexts of crisis and trauma includes coming alongside clients as they cope with their perceptions about what has happened to them. For Christian clients this includes coming to terms with where in the world God was and what did he think he was doing by letting this troublesome event befall them. To some extent clients may echo sentiments voiced by the children of Israel who exclaimed "My way is hidden from the LORD, and my right is disregarded by my God" (Is 40:27). Clients' immediate answers to these questions are associated with their understanding of who God is and what God "owes" them. Too often in Western Christianity we assume that God owes us a comfortable life, and that if we are truly following God that no bad thing will happen to us and that we will not suffer.[27] Crisis and trauma tends to expose the thinness of clients' (and counselors') theology because these assumptions are smashed to smithereens. Clients are subsequently angry with God—and even *that* becomes problematic if their theology disallows this kind of emotional response. Julie Exline and Joshua Grubbs reported that when survey participants found a receptive response in the face of the participants' disclosure of anger with God, then these participants experienced greater spiritual engagement. In contrast, anger at God, more rebellion and rejecting God transpired for those participants whose disclosure to another was not supported.[28]

The level of counselors' theological maturity makes theologically reflective counseling challenging during times of crisis and trauma. Does a Christian counselor feel obligated to defend God when clients shake their fist at God and then reject God because God has not lived up to their expectations of how God should intervene? Is the Christian counselor tempted to lapse into a theological minilecture when clients ask why God allowed this tragedy to happen or when they question where God was during the traumatic event that has turned their life upside down? I suggest that neither of these knee-jerk responses is particularly helpful to clients, even if they may make counselors feel more secure. When there is no answer in sight (which is more often the case in trauma therapy), Christian counselors may best work with their clients by offering to them the gift of a nonanxious presence.[29]

I recall my first encounter with theological helplessness. I was working as a Director of Christian Education in a local church. One of our families was grieving the sudden death of their infant son from a wasting disease. I had grown up in the church and had survived my own life tragedies with my faith intact. I had attended a Christian graduate school. But none of that prepared me for the emotional and theological wallop that I experienced during the weeks this family suffered. Fortunately, I was working under the supervision of a senior pastor whose faith was more mature than mine. With his guidance I managed my theological panic, grew in my understanding of the God of crisis and trauma, and successfully came along side this family as they grieved their loss.

Collaborating with clients in terms of theological reflection during crisis or trauma counseling requires discernment. Timing is everything! If counselors launch into theological discourse prematurely or if they default to defending God in the face of clients' anger at God, then clients may experience counselors as insensitive at best and perhaps even incompetent! These actions are more likely to disrupt or even destroy the therapeutic alliance than contribute to it. Counselors need to engage in their own emotional self-regulation when their anxiety about the state of their clients' souls threatens to disrupt ethical clinical practice. If counselors have a big enough view of God, then counselors can rest in the Holy Spirit to attend to the clients' theological and spiritual needs. Our job as Christian counselors who work with Christian clients experiencing crisis and trauma is "to prepare the way for the LORD" in the midst of the clients' emotional desert by using our clinical skills to raise up every valley of depression, to make low every mountain of anxiety and to make level the roughed-up places in the clients' relationships (Is 40:3-4). Sometimes this means getting out of the way of the Spirit's work; at other times it means becoming an active participant with what God is doing in clients' lives.

THEOLOGICALLY REFLECTIVE COUNSELING IN ACTION

Victoria and her fiancé were anticipating their wedding that was less than four months away. She and David had met at church, had dated for about a year and now were looking forward to a lifetime of serving God as a couple. God was in his heaven and all was right with their world. And in a moment that changed. An impatient driver cut in front of a car that was traveling on the other side of the highway, causing that driver to swerve into the lane in which Victoria and her fiancé were traveling, T-boning the driver's side of Victoria's fiancé's car. The next thing that Victoria remembers was someone telling her that help was on the way. She and her fiancé were taken to a nearby medical trauma center. Victoria was placed in trauma ICU. Her fiancé died from his injuries a few hours following the crash. Victoria's friends and family kept a vigil in the ICU waiting area. Her family was warned to not tell Victoria that David had died until her medical condition was more stable. Her recovery in ICU was slow but steady. Eventually she gained enough awareness to ask about David's well-being. Only then did she learn about his death.

Attending to theological echoes. I met with Victoria several months after the accident. Victoria had been released from the hospital and was now receiving outpatient physical therapy. While the doctors anticipated that she would soon be restored to physical health, she was only now beginning to deal with the emotional aftershock of the accident. Victoria was a mature believer, yet this experience rocked her spiritual world. She listed her grievances against God. Why had God let this accident happen to begin with? Why had he taken David and let her live? Where was he when this was going on? To add insult to injury, David's funeral had been held while Victoria had been in ICU. She grieved that she had not had a chance to experience the support of family and friends on the occasion of his burial. And the video recording equipment at the funeral home had not been working on the day of David's funeral so she didn't even have *that*. At the time of the accident, she and David were in the process of moving her belongings into the home they would share after their wedding. Her rental lease expired while she was hospitalized. Friends finished moving her out of her apartment. She discovered that items that her friends had donated to Goodwill were in reality treasured mementos of her relationship with David. Victoria said, "I can deal with my physical injuries. They are nothing in comparison to losing David and our dreams for our life together."

How might an eschatological horizon assist Victoria in coming to terms with the emotional aftermath of this horrible accident? Because Victoria presented her counseling concerns with theological highlights, we collaborated to name the following as one of her counseling goals: What sense was she going to make of God in light of this tragedy?

Addressing salient theological themes. Victoria had sustained sacred loss and desecration. Injury to her dominant hand meant that she now struggled to play the piano. Victoria regularly used music as part of her devotional life, and she had temporarily lost the fluidity of moving from Scripture reading to "Scripture playing." Her greatest struggle was making sense of David's untimely death. This was not a sacred loss. This was a desecration. Because the driver who caused the chain of events that resulted in the accident was still unknown and at large, Victoria sometimes had fantasies of what she might say and do if she ever got her hands on that driver. She knew that she would eventually forgive, but she struggled to do so. Her understanding of God as good and just had been shaken too. Why would he let this happen to them? Victoria had been a follower of Jesus long enough that she had faith that the Holy Spirit would sustain her throughout her recovery. This was one source of hope that she carried. Yet she was honest enough with herself to experience spiritual disillusionment and to give voice to her anger with God.

At that moment Victoria occupied the theological world of the flat-tened. She felt like a victim in some cosmic drama. The *obsessio* of the flattened is suffering; the *epiphania* is endurance. The death of David was totally meaningless, and she was often flooded by feelings of rage against the unidentified driver who had so grievously wronged her. In addition to this she was overwhelmed by sadness and loss. She was keenly aware of her suffering—physical, emotional, relational and spir-itual. She longed for intimacy with Christ as God's suffering servant (Is 53). In the crucified Jesus she found one who could identify with her many levels of loss. Jesus was the one who bore her grief and sorrow, who suffered when she did. In the resurrected Christ she found one who offered her *hope:* hope that someday all wrongs would be righted and all tears would be dried.

Aligning areas of life to be more theologically congruent. Victoria's willingness to place her sorrow and loss within God's eschatological horizon was a turning point in her capacity to make sense out of a senseless accident, and it contributed to her ability to live with ambi-guity. On one hand she firmly believed that God was good (in spite of David's death) and that God's power would redeem this dreadful situ-ation (in spite of the fact that she could not imagine how that would happen). She used the REACH model (chap. 6) to forgive the unknown driver who had been the catalyst for the accident. While Victoria prayed that this person would somehow be brought to justice, she also was eventually content to cast this care on God (1 Pet 5:7).

Perhaps you have already noted the environmental variables at work in Victoria's case. On the microsystem level Victoria experienced Da-vid's death and the loss of the dreams associated with their future life together. She found comfort, support and strength from her family and friends, who surrounded her in Christian love. On the mesolevel Vic-toria worked with the medical community to regain her physical health and with her church community to strengthen her spiritual health. She eventually returned to her graduate studies and completed her degree in mental health counseling. Victoria cooperated with law enforcement to provide whatever information she could that might lead to the appre-hension of the person who caused the accident. My role was to support her in the decisions she made regarding her relationships with these environmental factors and to empower her voice medically and legally (chap. 5). She believed that God's justice is good and that eventually this wrong would be righted.

Much of Victoria's therapy followed best practices for crisis counseling. Fortunately, her innate resiliency contributed to her treatment outcome. A proportion of many sessions centered on theological concerns. She used the Psalms as a model for voicing her anger to God, in a sense taking an "I" position with her heavenly Father. She meditated on the life of Christ and allowed the Holy Spirit to increase her awareness of God's peace within her. This dispelled her fear about her immediate future as her sense of hopefulness, founded upon God's eschatological promises, increased. She wanted to act like a kingdom person even in the midst of her sufferings.

Attaining a deepening Christian character. In a very real sense Victoria participated in "collaborative eschatology." She knew that today's tragedy was not the end of her story, nor did it define who God was, nor did it determine the degree to which God loved her. Without getting caught up in end times details, Victoria took comfort in the thought that at some future point Christ would return and make all things new. This was the horizon within which she saw the accident. She accepted that her immediate future was not going to be the one that she had thought she would live. Nevertheless, she had hope in God's faithfulness to restore to her that which she had lost. And she trusted him enough to not dictate to God the shape that this restoration would take. She left that in the hands of a loving and faithful God.

CONCLUSION

An eschatological horizon helps us all to live with the evil that befalls us. While it would be nice to know why God allows trials and tribulations to come into our lives, it is not necessary. What is necessary, however, is to see that God's kingdom will come, that God's will will be done on earth as it is in heaven. We want to be a part of *that* in our role as theologically reflective counselors.

Postscript

There's a wideness in God's mercy,
Like the wideness of the sea;
There's a kindness in his justice,
Which is more than liberty.

There is welcome for the sinner
And more graces for the good;
There is mercy with the Savior;
There is healing in his blood.

For the love of God is broader
Than the measure of [our] mind;
And the heart of the Eternal
Is most wonderfully kind.

If our love were but more simple,
We should take him at his word;
And our lives would be all sunshine
In the sweetness of our Lord.

FREDERICK FABER,
"There's a Wideness in God's Mercy"

TOMORROW IS THE FIRST DAY OF A NEW ACADEMIC YEAR. I have prepared my syllabi and lectures. I am ready to greet my counseling students. Or am I? Theologically reflective counseling is in part *information*. In this book I have proposed that theologically reflective practitioners possess a good measure of theological information. How would you bring the theological thinking that is at the core of your being into conversation with the counseling concerns that I have identified in the preceding chapters? What insights could your theological convictions contribute to clients' well-being when clients have given consent to include theological conversation as part of their treatment? You may consider asking your pastor for a reading list of theology books that might assist you in widening your theological knowledge base. If you participate in a consultation or peer supervision group with other Christian counselors, you could suggest that this group add a component of theological reflection to case consultation. Merely raising the question about what theological themes may be present in clients' cases begins the discussion. Your group can start with the themes that I have highlighted in this book, and then you can add to them. Your group could also develop its own theological reading list. You can invite area clergy to participate in some of your discussions to help you deepen your own theological reflection and build a collaborative network.

Theologically reflective counseling is also about *Christian spiritual formation*. Theological musing can result in a conversion of your imagination so that the categories and stories which shape your life now resound with those found in Scripture. The apostle Paul put it like this in Romans 12:2: "Do not be conformed to this world, but be transformed by the renewing of your minds, so that you may discern what is the will of God—what is good and acceptable and perfect." Theological formation in this sense takes a lifetime. John Coe and Todd Hall present a strong argument for the centrality of the spiritual formation of the therapist in their presentation of transformational psychology.[1] Do not be surprised if your Christian clients contribute as much to your formation as you may to theirs, and I doubt that God's use of our clients in our spiritual formation is limited to those clients who are overtly Christian.

What this all comes down to is that theologically reflective counseling is by and large an invitation to *participation*—in the life of God and in the life of God's people at a time when particular individuals, families or groups need someone with your special skill set to come along side of them at a time of affliction (cf. 2 Cor 1:3-7). My professional life verse is Isaiah 50:4:

> The Sovereign LORD has given me a well-instructed tongue,
>   to know the word that sustains the weary.
> He wakens me morning by morning,
>   wakens my ear to listen like one being instructed. (NIV)

In this verse I hear God calling me to continue to be a student of God's Word and the writings about God's word (theology). This is not for my own benefit but for the benefit of others (i.e., the weary).

Models of theological reflection, such as the one that I offered to you, are helpful heuristics in our work as specialists in applied sanctification. Other models of integration have been developed by noteworthy Christian mental health professionals, and one of them may be a better fit for you.[2] I encourage you to check them out. With a firm understanding of our theological, therapeutic and ethical commitments, we can welcome all of our clients into the healing space of our offices. When clients tell us their stories, we are standing on sacred ground. We join them on their journey. Models are nice, but what is ultimately necessary for theologically reflective counseling are therapists secure in the love of the Father, whose hearts echo the heart of the Son for the wounded individuals, families and groups of this world, and who are committed to becoming open channels through which the Holy Spirit may work. May that be true for you and for me.

Notes

𝕯

Preface
[1]If you are interested in the various contours of Christian counseling, I refer you to Mark R. McMinn, Ryan C. Staley, Kurt C. Webb and Winston Seegobin, "Just What Is Christian Counseling Anyway?" *Professional Psychology: Research and Practice*, September 6, 2010, doi:10.1037/a0018584.

Chapter 1: Is All This Fuss About Theology Really Necessary?
[1]LeRon Shults and Steven Sandage present a model of spiritual transformation that explores the dynamics of spiritual seeking and dwelling. Life crises, such as the kind that many clients experience, eject them out of spiritual comfort/safety (dwelling) and onto a path of seeking. See F. LeRon Shults and Steven J. Sandage, *Transforming Spirituality: Integrating Theology and Psychology* (Grand Rapids: Baker Academic, 2006), p. 33.

[2]Joel B. Green and Mark D. Baker, *Recovering the Scandal of the Cross: Atonement in New Testament and Contemporary Context* (Downers Grove, Ill.: InterVarsity Press, 2011), p. 88.

[3]Therapeutically, the turn toward relationality is seen in an emphasis on the quality of the counseling relationship as a common factor in successful therapy across diverse therapeutic approaches. (I will say more about this in subsequent chapters.) It is also reflected in therapeutic approaches that emphasize attachment theory such as emotionally focused couples therapy and contemporary psychodynamic therapies. Theologically, you can read more about this in F. LeRon Shults, *Reforming Theological Anthropology: After the Philosophical Turn to Relationality* (Grand Rapids: Eerdmans, 2003); and Stanley J. Grenz, *The Social God and the Relational Self: A Trinitarian Theology of the Imago Dei* (Louisville: Westminster John Knox Press, 2001).

[4]For instance see Daniel J. Siegel, *The Developing Mind* (New York: Guilford Press, 1999); Louis Cozolino, *The Neuroscience of Psychotherapy* (New York: W. W. Norton, 2002), and *The Neuroscience of Human Relationships* (New York: W. W. Norton, 2006); Barbara Bradley Hagerty, *Fingerprints of God: The Search for the Science of Spirituality* (New York: Riverhead Books, 2009); Warren Brown, Nancey Murphy and H. Newton Malony, eds., *Whatever Happened to the Soul? Scientific and Theological Portraits of Human Nature* (Minneapolis: Fortress Press, 1998); Joel B. Green, ed., *What About the Soul? Neuroscience and Christian Anthropology* (Nashville: Abingdon, 2004). See note 3 for additional theological resources.

[5]Stanley J. Grenz, *The Social God and the Relational Self: A Trinitarian Theology of the Imago Dei* (Louisville: Westminster John Knox Press, 2001).

[6]Michael Battle, *Reconciliation: The Ubuntu Theology of Desmond Tutu* (Cleveland: Pilgrim Press, 1997); Gregory Jones, *Embodying Forgiveness* (Grand Rapids:

Eerdmans, 1995); and Miroslav Volf, *Exclusion and Embrace* (Nashville: Abingdon, 1996).

[7]N. T. Wright, *Evil and the Justice of God* (Downers Grove, Ill.: InterVarsity Press, 2009).

[8]Dorothee Sölle, *Suffering* (Philadelphia: Augsburg Fortress, 1975).

[9]Hugh T. Kerr, ed., *Readings in Christian Thought* (Nashville: Abingdon, 1990).

[10]Kenneth J. Collins, *The Theology of John Wesley: Holy Love and the Shape of Grace* (Nashville: Abingdon, 2007).

[11]Warren S. Brown, Sarah D. Marion and Brad D. Strawn, "Human Relationality, Spiritual Formation, and Wesleyan Communities," in *Wesleyan Theology and Social Science: The Dance of Practical Divinity and Discovery* (Newcastle upon Tyne, U.K.: Cambridge Scholars, 2010).

[12]Judith A. Lewis, Michael D. Lewis, Judy A. Daniels and Michael J. D'Andrea, *Community Counseling: A Multicultural-Social Justice Perspective*, 4th ed. (Pacific Grove, Calif.: Brooks/Cole, 2011).

[13]For example, see H. Newton Malony, "John Wesley and Psychology," *Journal of Psychology and Christianity* 18 (1999): 5-18; Brad D. Strawn and Michael G. Leffel, "John Wesley's Orthokardia and Harry Guntrip's 'Heart of the Personal': Convergent Aims an Complementary Practices in Psychotherapy and Spiritual Formation," *Journal of Psychology and Christianity* 20 (2001): 351-59; *Journal of Psychology and Christianity* 24, no. 2 (2004), for a special section dealing with psychology and Wesleyan theology; M. Kathryn Armistead, Brad D. Strawn and Ronald W. Wright, eds., *Wesleyan Theology and Social Science: The Dance of Practical Divinity and Discovery* (Newcastle upon Tyne, U.K.: Cambridge Scholars, 2010). Information about the Society for the Study of Psychology and Wesleyan Theology may be found at the Point Loma Nazarene University website: www.pointloma.edu/experience/academics/centers-institutes/wesleyan-center/society-study-psychology-wesleyan-theology.

[14]Joel B. Green and William H. Willimon, eds., *The Wesley Study Bible (NRSV)* (Nashville: Abingdon, 2009), p. 547.

[15]Collins, *Theology of John Wesley*, p. 2.

[16]Brad D. Strawn, "Restoring Moral Affections of Heart: How Does Psychotherapy Cure?" *Journal of Psychology and Christianity* 23, no. 2 (Summer 2004): 140-48.

[17]Green and Willimon, eds., *The Wesley Study Bible*, p. 860.

[18]For differences between Calvinism and John Wesley, see Robert A. Peterson and Michael D. Williams, *Why I Am Not an Arminian* (Downers Grove, Ill.: InterVarsity Press, 2004), and Jerry L. Walls and Joseph R. Dongell, *Why I Am Not a Calvinist* (Downers Grove, Ill.: InterVarsity Press, 2004).

[19]Douglas H. Sprenkle, Sean D. Davis and Jay L. Lebow, *Common Factors in Couple and Family Therapy* (New York: Guilford, 2009).

[20]This research was supported by a generous grant from the 2007-2008 Mid-Career Faculty Colloquy through the Wabash Center for Teaching and Learning in Theological Education, Crawfordsville, Indiana.

[21]Mark R. McMinn, Gary W. Moon and Angela G. McCormick, "Integration in the Classroom: Ten Teaching Strategies," *Journal of Psychology and Theology* 37, no. 1 (Spring 2009): 39-47; Jennifer S. Ripley, Fernando Garzon, M. Elizabeth Lewis Hall and Michael W. Mangis, "Pilgrims' Progress: Faculty and University Factors

in Graduate Student Integration of Faith and Profession," *Journal of Psychology and Theology* 37, no. 1 (Spring 2009): 5-14.

[22]Randall Lehmann Sorenson, Kimberly R. Derflinger, Rodger K. Bufford and Mark R. McMinn, "National Collaborative Research on How Students Learn Integration: Final Report," *Journal of Psychology and Christianity* 23, no. 4 (Winter 2004): 355-65.

[23]For a discussion on a developmental model of counselor formation see Cal D. Stoltenberg and Ursula Delworth, *Supervising Counselors and Therapists: A Developmental Approach* (San Francisco: Jossey-Bass, 1987). For information on the scope and shape of explicit and implicit integration see Siang-Yang Tan, "Christian Faith in Clinical Practice: Implicit and Explicit Integration," in *Counseling and Psychotherapy: A Christian Perspective* (Grand Rapids: Baker Academic, 2011), pp. 339-62.

[24]M. Elizabeth Lewis Hall, Jennifer S. Ripley, Fernando L. Garzon and Michael W. Mangis, "The Other Side of the Podium: Student Perspective on Learning Integration," *Journal of Psychology and Theology* 37, no. 1 (Spring 2009): 15-27.

[25]Theologically oriented counseling texts tend to be coauthored by a counselor or psychologist and a theologian/philosopher. See, for example, John H. Coe and Todd W. Hall, *Psychology in the Spirit: Contours of a Transformational Psychology* (Downers Grove, Ill.: InterVarsity Press, 2010); F. LeRon Shults and Steven J. Sandage, *Transforming Spirituality: Integrating Theology and Psychology* (Grand Rapids: Baker Academic, 2006). Three exceptions to this include Kent J. Dunnington, *Addiction and Virtue: Beyond the Models of Disease and Choice* (Downers Grove, Ill.: InterVarsity Press, 2011); Mark H. Mann, *Perfecting Grace: Holiness, Human Being, and the Sciences* (New York: T & T Clark, 2006); and David L. Thompson and Gina Thompson Eickoff, *God's Healing for Hurting Families: Biblical Principles for Reconciliation and Recovery* (Indianapolis: Wesleyan Publishing House, 2004).

[26]Professional counseling license regulations are determined by each of the fifty states. At the writing of this book no portability of counselor license exists between states. While some state counselor licensure laws stipulate that applicants must have forty-eight semester hours of counseling course work at the master's level, the majority of state boards required sixty hours of counseling course work.

[27]Christopher R. Grace and Paul L. Poelstra, "Excellence in Pedagogy: Some Obstacles to Integration for the Christian Psychology Professor," *Journal of Psychology and Theology* 23, no. 4 (Winter 1995): 237-43. While theological training is not a particular concern in secular counselor education or in training professional psychologists, readers may be interested in the following studies on religion, spirituality and mental health professionals: Harold D. Delaney, William R. Miller and Ana M. Bisonó, "Religiosity and Spirituality Among Psychologists: A Survey of Clinician Members of the American Psychological Association," *Professional Psychology: Research and Practice* 38, no. 5 (2007): 538-46, doi:10.1037/0735-7028.38.5.538; Mark R. McMinn, William L. Hathaway, Scott W. Woods and Kimberly N. Snow, "What American Psychological Association Leaders Have to Say About *Psychology of Religion and Spirituality*," *Psychology of Religion and Spirituality* 1 (2009): 3-13, doi:10.1037/a0014991; Eugene W. Kelly Jr., "The Role of Religion and Spirituality in Counselor Education: A National Survey," *Counseling and Values* 33, no. 4 (1994): 227-37.

[28]Julie J. Exline, "Stumbling Blocks on the Religious Road: Fractured Relationships, Nagging Vices and the Inner Struggle to Believe," *Psychological Inquiry* 13, no. 3 (2002): 182-89, doi:10.1207/S15327965PLI1303_03; Julie J. Exline, Ann Marie Yali and Marci Lobel, "When God Disappoints: Difficulty Forgiving God and Its Role in Negative Emotions," *Journal of Health Psychology* 4, no. 3 (1999): 365-79, doi:10.1177/135910539900400306.

[29]Stanley J. Grenz and Roger E. Olson, *Who Needs Theology? An Invitation to the Study of God* (Downers Grove, Ill.: InterVarsity Press, 1996), p. 49.

[30]Andrew F. Walls, "Afterword: Christian Mission in a Five-Hundred-Year Context," in *Mission in the Twenty-first Century: Exploring the Five Marks of Global Mission*, ed. Andrew F. Walls and Cathy Ross (Maryknoll, N.Y.: Orbis, 2008), p. 203.

[31]Categories of systematic theology include the study of God, of Christ (Christology), of the Holy Spirit (pneumatology), of the church (ecclesiology), of salvation (soteriology), of the end times (eschatology), etc.

[32]Green and Baker, *Recovering the Scandal of the Cross*, p. 43.

[33]Catherine Stonehouse, *Joining Children on the Spiritual Journey: Nurturing a Life of Faith* (Grand Rapids: Baker Academic, 2007). An emphasis on counselor's own spiritual formation is central in the thinking of John C. Coe and Todd W. Hall in their work *Psychology in the Spirit*.

[34]Ellen L. Marmon, personal communication, August 9, 2011. See also Walter Ong, *Orality and Literacy: The Technologizing of the Word*, 2nd ed. (New York: Routledge, 2002); Ellen L. Marmon, "Women from the Bible, Bihar, and the Bottom: Contextual Discipleship in Process" (unpublished manuscript, 2011).

[35]Carol Tavris and Elliot Aronson, *Mistakes Were Made (but Not by Me): Why We Justify Foolish Beliefs, Bad Decisions, and Hurtful Acts* (Orlando: Harcourt, 2007).

[36]Kenneth J. Collins, "Spirituality and Critical Thinking: Are They Really So Different?" *Evangelical Journal* 16 (1998): 30-43. A similar process is discussed applying differentiation of self to spiritual maturity in Brian D. Majerus and Steven J. Sandage, "Differentiation of Self and Christian Spiritual Maturity: Social Science and Theological Integration," *Journal of Psychology and Theology* 38, no. 1 (2010): 41-51.

[37]For example, see Stanton L. Jones and Richard E. Butman, *Modern Psychotherapies: A Comprehensive Christian Appraisal* (Downers Grove, Ill.: InterVarsity Press, 1991); Siang-Yang Tan, *Counseling and Psychotherapy: A Christian Perspective* (Grand Rapids: Baker Academic, 2011); Mark A. Yarhouse and James N. Sells, *Family Therapies: A Comprehensive Christian Appraisal* (Downers Grove, Ill.: InterVarsity Press, 2008).

[38]A growing literature base has developed on the integration of religion and spirituality into psychotherapy. For example see Jamie D. Aten, Mark R. McMinn and Everett L. Worthington, eds., *Spiritually Oriented Interventions for Counseling and Psychotherapy* (Washington, D.C.: American Psychological Association, 2011); William R Miller, ed., *Integrating spirituality into Treatment: Resources for Practitioners* (Washington, D.C.: American Psychological Association, 1999); and P. Scott Richards and Allen E. Bergin, *A Spiritual Strategy for Counseling and Psychotherapy*, 2nd ed. (Washington, D.C.: American Psychological Association, 2005).

[39]See, for example, George R. Ross, *Evaluating Models of Christian Counseling*

(Eugene, Ore.: Wipf & Stock, 2011); and Eric L. Johnson, ed., *Psychology and Christianity: Five Views*, 2nd ed. (Downers Grove, Ill.: IVP Academic, 2010).

[40]Saing-Yang Tan, "Developing Integration Skills: The Role of Clinical Supervision," *Journal of Psychology and Theology* 37, no. 1 (Spring 2009): 54-61.

[41]The American Association of Christian Counselors offers a certification as a Board Certified Professional Christian Counselor (BCPCC) through their Board of Christian Professional and Pastoral Counselors. For more information see www .bcppc.net/bcpcc.php.

[42]Ronnie Janoff-Bulman, *Shattered Assumptions* (New York: Free Press, 1992).

[43]Grenz and Olson, *Who Needs Theology?* pp. 124-25.

[44]I owe my colleague Steve Stratton a note of deep gratitude for continually highlighting the vital importance of the Christian community in the formation of theologically reflective counselors.

[45]An early version of this model emerged from conversation with Edward Decker Jr., Ph.D., professor of Christian counseling at Oral Roberts University.

[46]Joel B. Green and William H. Willimon, eds., *The Wesley Study Bible, NRSV* (Nashville: Abingdon, 2009), p. 860.

[47]G. Michael Leffel, "Prevenient Grace and the Re-Enchantment of Nature: Toward a Wesleyan Theology of Psychotherapy and Spiritual Formation," *Journal of Psychology and Christianity* 23, no. 2 (Summer 2004): 130-39.

Chapter 2: A Metamodel of Theologically Reflective Counseling

[1]Stanley J. Grenz and Roger E. Olson, *Who Needs Theology? An Invitation to the Study of God* (Downers Grove, Ill.: InterVarsity Press, 1996), p. 49.

[2]For an expanded discussion of therapy as a worldview see Steve Wilkens and Mark L. Sanford, "Salvation by Therapy: Not as Good as It Gets," in *Hidden Worldviews: Eight Cultural Stories That Shape Our Lives* (Downers Grove, Ill.: InterVarsity Press, 2009), pp. 160-82.

[3]Paul Pedersen, "The Multicultural Perspective as a Fourth Force in Counseling," *Journal of Mental Health Counseling* 12, no. 1 (1990): 93-95.

[4]Jamie D. Aten, Mark R. McMinn and Everett Worthington Jr., eds., *Spiritually Oriented Interventions for Counseling and Psychotherapy* (Washington, D.C.: American Psychological Association, 2011); Craig S. Cashwell, *Integrating Spirituality and Religion into Counseling: A Guide to Competent Practice* (Alexandria, Va.: American Counseling Association, 2011); Daya Singh Sandhu, ed., *Spirituality as a Fifth Force in Counseling and Psychology: Implications for Practice, Training, and Research* (Alexandria, Va.: American Counseling Association, in press); and Edward P. Shafranske, *Religion and the Clinical Practice of Psychology* (Washington, D.C.: American Psychological Association, 1996).

[5]For more expanded discussions see Eric L. Johnson and Stanton L. Jones, "A History of Christians in Psychology," in *Psychology and Christianity*, ed. Eric L. Johnson and Stanton L. Jones (Downers Grove, Ill.: InterVarsity Press, 2000), pp. 11-53.

[6]A full discussion of these positions is found in David N. Entwistle, *Integrative Approaches to Psychology and Christianity: An Introduction to Worldview Issues, Philosophical Foundations, and Models of Integration* (Eugene, Ore.: Wipf & Stock, 2004).

[7]For example, Aten, McMinn and Worthington, *Spiritually Oriented Interventions for Counseling and Psychotherapy;* William L. Hathaway, Stacey Y. Scott and Stacey

A. Garver, "Assessing Religious/Spiritual Functioning: A Neglected Domain in Clinical Practice?" *Professional Psychology: Research and Practice* 35, no. 1 (2004): 97-104; P. S. Richards and A. E. Bergin, *A Spiritual Strategy for Counseling and Psychotherapy*, 2nd ed. (Washington, D.C.: American Psychological Association, 2005); Edward P. Shafranske and H. Newton Malony, "Clinical Psychologists' Religious and Spiritual Orientations and Their Practice of Psychotherapy," *Psychotherapy* 27, no. 1 (1990): 72-78; William M. Struther, "Snark or Boojum? Trends in the Integration of Psychology and Christianity," *Journal of Psychology and Christianity* 24, no. 3 (2005): 195-209; J. Scott Young, Marsha Wiggins-Frame and Craig S. Cashwell, "Spirituality and Counselor Competence: A National Survey of American Counseling Association Members," *Journal of Counseling and Development* 85 (Winter 2007): 47-52.

[8]See chap. 1, n. 13 for a sample list.

[9]For schools of therapy example see Marie T. Hoffman, *Toward Mutual Recognition: Relational Psychoanalysis and the Christian Narrative* (New York: Routledge, 2010), for relational psychodynamic; Mark R. McMinn and Clark D. Campbell, *Integrative Psychotherapy: Toward a Comprehensive Christian Approach* (Downers Grove, Ill.: InterVarsity Press, 2007), for relational cognitive-behavioral therapy; James N. Sells and Mark A. Yarhouse, *Counseling Couples in Conflict* (Downers Grove, Ill.: InterVarsity Press, 2011), for contextual family therapy. For theological perspectives see for example, M. Kathryn Armistead, Brad D. Strawn and Ronald W. Wright, eds., *Wesleyan Theology and Social Science: The Dance of Practical Divinity and Discovery* (Newcastle upon Tyne, U.K.: Cambridge Scholars, 2010), for Wesleyan theology; Alvin Dueck and Cameron Lee, eds., *Why Psychology Needs Theology* (Grand Rapids: Eerdmans, 2005), for Anabaptist theology.

[10]Saing-Yang Tan, "Developing Integration Skills: The Role of Clinical Supervision," *Journal of Psychology and Theology*, 37, no. 1 (2009): 54-61.

[11]N. T. Wright, *After You Believe: Why Christian Character Matters* (New York: HarperOne, 2010), p. 151.

[12]Michael Polanyi, *The Tacit Dimension* (Chicago: University of Chicago Press, 2009).

[13]Edward E. Decker Jr., "The Holy Spirit in Counseling: A Review of Christian Counseling Journal Articles (1985-1999)," *Journal of Psychology and Christianity* 21, no. 1 (2002): 21-28.

[14]For example see the American Psychological Association video series *Spirituality* and Mark R. McMinn's 2006 contribution to that series, "Christian Counseling."

[15]Edward E. Decker Jr., "Teaching Couples to Pray Together: A Spiritual Application Consistent with the Social Learning-Cognitive Approach to Marital Therapy," *Marriage and Family: A Christian Journal* 4, no. 2 (2001): 131-37; and Siang-Yang Tan, "Integrating Spiritual Disciplines into Psychotherapy: Ethical Issues and Guidelines," *Journal of Psychology and Theology* 31, no. 1 (2003): 14-23.

[16]Stephen Parker, "Faith Development Theory as a Context for Supervision of Spiritual and Religious Issues," *Counselor Education and Supervision* 49, no. 1 (2009): 39-53.

[17]Douglas H. Sprenkle, Sean D. Davis and Jay L. Lebow, *Common Factors in Couple and Family Therapy: The Overlooked Foundation for Effective Practice* (New York: Guilford, 2009).

[18]Sean D. Davis and Fred P. Piercy, "What Clients of Couple Therapy Model Developers and Their Former Students Say About Change, Part I: Model-Dependent

Common Factors Across Three Models," *Journal of Marital and Family Therapy* 33 (2007): 318-43; Davis and Piercy, "What Clients of Couple Therapy Model Developers and Their Former Students Say About Change, Part II: Model-independent Common Factors and An Integrative Framework," *Journal of Marital and Family Therapy* 33 (2007): 344-63.

[19]Alexandra Bachelor and Adam Horvath, "The Therapeutic Relationship," in *The Heart and Soul of Change: What Works in Therapy*, ed. Mark A. Hubble, Barry L. Duncan and Scott D. Miller (Washington, D.C.: American Psychological Association, 1999), pp. 133-78.

[20]Tom Strong and Nathan R. Pyle, "Constructing a Conversational 'Miracle': Examining the 'Miracle Question as It Is Used in Therapeutic Dialogue,'" *Journal of Constructivist Psychology* 22 (2009): 328-53.

[21]Kenneth I. Pargament, *The Psychology of Religion and Coping: Theory, Research, Practice* (New York: Guilford, 1997).

[22]We are "all theologians": see Grenz and Olson, *Who Needs Theology?* "Ultimate concerns" intersect with life: see Robert A. Emmons, *The Psychology of Ultimate Concerns: Motivation and Spirituality in Personality* (New York: Guilford, 1999); Kenneth I. Pargament, Gina M. Magyar, Ethan Benore and Annette Mahoney, "Sacrilege: A Study of Sacred Loss and Desecration and Their Implications for Health and Well-Being in a Community Sample," *Journal for the Scientific Study of Religion* 44, no. 1 (2005): 59-78.

[23]Miroslav Volf, *Free of Charge: Giving and Forgiving in a Culture Stripped of Grace* (Grand Rapids: Zondervan, 2005).

[24]See William Hasker, *The Triumph of God over Evil: Theodicy for a World of Suffering* (Downers Grove, Ill.: InterVarsity Press, 2008); N. T. Wright, *Evil and the Justice of God* (Downers Grove, Ill.: InterVarsity Press, 2009).

[25]For a more thorough model of religious or spiritual assessment at intake see P. Scott Richards and Allen E. Bergin, *A Spiritual Strategy for Counseling and Psychotherapy* (Washington, D.C.: American Psychological Association, 2005). Also see William L. Hathaway, Stacey Y. Scott and Stacey A. Garver, "Assessing Religious/Spiritual Functioning: A Neglected Domain in Clinical Practice?" *Professional Psychology: Research and Practice* 35, no. 1 (2004): 97-104.

[26]Margaret L. Keeling, Megan L. Dolbin-MacNab, James Ford and Susan N. Perkins, "Partners in the Spiritual Dance: Learning Clients' Steps While Minding All Our Toes," *Journal of Marital and Family Therapy* 36, no. 2 (2010): 229-43.

[27]W. Paul Jones, *Theological Worlds: Understanding the Alternative Rhythms of Christian Belief* (Nashville: Abingdon, 1989); W. Paul Jones, *Worlds Within a Congregation: Dealing with Theological Diversity* (Nashville: Abingdon, 2000).

[28]David M. Durst, e-mail to author, July 28, 2011.

[29]Joshua N. Hook, et al., "Empirically Supported Religious and Spiritual Therapies," *Journal of Clinical Psychology*, 66, no. 1 (2010): 46-72; Timothy B. Smith, Jeremy Bartz, and P. Scott Richards, "Outcomes of Religious and Spiritual Adaptations to Psychotherapy: A Meta-Analytic Review," *Psychotherapy Research* 17, no. 6 (2007): 643-55, doi:10.1080/10503300701250347.

[30]Sprenkle, Davis, and Lebow, *Common Factors*, p. 127

[31]John M. Gottman, *The Science of Trust: Emotional Attunement for Couples* (New York: W. W. Norton, 2011).

[32]Sprenkle, Davis, and Lebow, *Common Factors*, p. 127.

[33]See, for example, F. LeRon Shults and Steven J. Sandage, *The Faces of Forgiveness: Searching for Wholeness and Salvation* (Grand Rapids: Baker Academic, 2003), pp. 168-221.

[34]Steve Wilkens and Mark L. Sanford, *Hidden Worldviews: Eight Cultural Stories that Shape Our Lives* (Downers Grove, Ill.: InterVarsity Press, 2009), pp. 14-15.

[35]Jill Duba Onedera, *The Role of Religion in Marriage and Family Counseling* (New York: Routledge, 2006).

[36]W. Paul Jones, *Theological Worlds: Understanding the Alternative Rhythms of Christian Belief* (Nashville: Abingdon, 1989), p. 16.

[37]Durst renamed Jones' five worlds. The first term is Jones's original label and the term following the backslash is Durst's label: Alien or Orphan/Foreigner, Outcast/Faint, Warrior/Fighter, Fugitive/Fugitive, Victim or Refugee/Flattened.

[38]David M. Durst, e-mail message to author, January 26, 2011. I am indebted to David M. Durst for his insights into Jones's theological worlds.

[39]Ibid.

[40]Ibid.

[41]Ibid.

[42]Ibid.

[43]Ibid.

[44]Jones, *Theological Worlds*, p. 27.

[45]F. LeRon Shults and Steven J. Sandage, *Transforming Spirituality: Integrating Theology and Psychology* (Grand Rapids: Baker Academic, 2006), p. 267, emphasis added.

[46]Edward P. Shafranske, "Religious Beliefs, Affiliations, and Practices of Clinical Psychologists," in *Religion and the Clinical Practice of Psychology*, ed. Edward P. Shafranske (Washington, D.C.: American Psychological Association, 1996), pp. 149-64; Scott J. Young, Craig Cashwell, Marsha Wiggins-Frame and Christine Belaire, "Spiritual and Religious Competencies: A National Survey of CACREP-Accredited Programs," *Counseling and Values* 47, no. 1 (2002): 22-33.

[47]John C. Gonsiorek, P. Scott Richards, Kenneth I. Pargament and Mark R. McMinn, "Ethical Challenges and Opportunities at the Edge: Incorporating Spirituality and Religion in Psychotherapy," *Professional Psychology: Research and Practice* 40, no. 4 (2009): 389.

[48]Linda A. Hunter and Mark A. Yarhouse, "Considerations and Recommendations for Use of Religiously-based Interventions in a Licensed Setting," *Journal of Psychology and Christianity* 28, no. 2 (2009): 164-65.

[49]Saing-Yang Tan, *Counseling and Psychotherapy: A Christian Perspective* (Grand Rapids: Baker Academic, 2011), p. 380.

Chapter 3: A Theologically Reflective Counseling Relationship

[1]Neil Pembroke, "A Trinitarian Perspective on the Counseling Alliance in Narrative Therapy," *Journal of Psychology and Christianity* 24, no. 1 (2005): 13-20.

[2]Michael J. Lambert, "Implications of Outcome Research for Psychotherapy Integration," in *Handbook of Psychotherapy Integration*, ed. John C. Norcross and Marvin R. Goldfried (New York: Basic Books, 1992), pp. 94-129.

[3]Stanley J. Grenz and Roger E. Olson, *Who Needs Theology?* (Downers Grove, Ill.: InterVarsity Press, 1996), p. 116.

[4]Mildred Bangs Wynkoop, *A Theology of Love: The Dynamic of Wesleyanism* (Kansas City: Beacon Hill, 1972), p. 21.

[5]John Wesley, "On the Trinity," *The Sermons of John Wesley*, The United Methodist Church, http://new.gbgm-umc.org/umhistory/wesley/sermons/55.

[6]Kenneth J. Collins, *The Theology of John Wesley: Holy Love and the Shape of Grace* (Nashville: Abingdon, 2007), p. 145.

[7]Clark H. Pinnock, *Flame of Love: A Theology of the Holy Spirit* (Downers Grove, Ill.: InterVarsity Press, 1996), p. 36.

[8]Dennis F. Kinlaw, *Let's Start with Jesus: A New Way of Doing Theology* (Grand Rapids: Zondervan, 2005), p. 30.

[9]W. Paul Jones, *Theological Worlds: Understanding the Alternative Rhythms of Christian Belief* (Nashville: Abingdon, 1989).

[10]Ibid., p. 47.

[11]Douglas H. Sprenkle, Sean D. Davis and Jay L. Lebow, *Common Factors in Couple and Family Therapy: The Overlooked Foundation for Effective Practice* (New York: Guilford, 2009), pp. 95-97.

[12]Ibid., pp. 45-59.

[13]Karen Tallman and Arthur C. Bohart, "The Client as a Common Factor: Clients as Self-Healers," in *The Heart and Soul of Change: What Works in Therapy*, ed. Mark A. Hubble, Barry L. Duncan and Scott D. Miller (Washington, D.C.: American Psychological Association, 1999).

[14]Lambert, "Implications of Outcome Research for Psychotherapy Integration," pp. 94-129; Karen B. Helmeke and Douglas H. Sprenkle, "Clients' Perceptions of Pivotal Moments in Couples Therapy: A Qualitative Study of Change in Therapy," *Journal of Marital and Family Therapy* 26 (2000): 469-84.

[15]Sprenkle, Davis and Lebow, *Common Factors*, p. 53.

[16]See Linda A. Hunter and Mark A. Yarhouse, "Considerations and Recommendations for Use of Religiously-based Interventions in a Licensed Setting," *Journal of Psychology and Christianity* 28, no. 2 (2009).

[17]Everett L. Worthington, "Understanding the Values of Religious Clients: A Model and Its Application to Counseling," *Journal of Counseling Psychology* 35 (1988): 166-74; Everett L. Worthington, Taro A. Kurusu, Michael E. McCullough and Steven J. Sandage, "Empirical Research on Religion and Psychotherapeutic Processes and Outcomes: A 10-Year Review and Research Prospectus," *Psychological Bulletin* 119 (1996): 448-87; and Michael D'Andrea and Elizabeth Foster Heckman, "A 40-Year Review of Multicultural Counseling Outcome Research: Outlining a Future Research Agenda for the Multicultural Counseling Movement" *Journal of Counseling and Development* 86 (2008): 346-63.

[18]Todd W Liebert, Julia B. Smith and Vaibhavee R. Agaskar, "Relationship Between the Working Alliance and Social Support on Counseling Outcomes," *Journal of Clinical Psychology* 67 (2011): 709-19.

[19]C. R. Snyder, Scott T. Michael and Jennifer S. Cheavens, "Hope as a Psychotherapeutic Foundation of Common Factors, Placebos, and Expectancies," in *The Heart and Soul of Change: What Works in Therapy*, ed. Mark A. Hubble, Barry L. Duncan, and Scott D. Miller (Washington, D.C.: American Psychological Association, 2000), pp. 329-60; Kaethe Weingarten, "Reasonable Hope: Construct, Clinical Applications, and Supports," *Family Process* 49 (2010): 5-25; Denise J. Larsen and

Rachel Stege, "Hope-Focused Practices During Early Psychotherapy Sessions: Part I: Implicit Approaches," *Journal of Psychotherapy Integration* 20 (2010): 271-92; Denise J. Larsen and Rachel Stege, "Hope-Focused Practices During Early Psychotherapy Sessions: Part II: Explicit Approaches," *Journal of Psychotherapy Integration* 20(2010): 293-311.

[20]Sprenkle, Davis, and Lebow, *Common Factors,* p. 127.

[21]Ibid., p. 65.

Chapter 4: Responsible Living

[1]An early version of this material was presented at the annual meeting of the Society for the Study of Psychology and Wesleyan Theology, Kansas City, Missouri, March 2, 2006. It was subsequently published as "Wesleyan Holiness and Differentiation of Self: A Systems Approach," in K. Amistead, B. D. Strawn and R. W. Wright, *Wesleyan Theology and Social Science* (Newcastle-upon-Tyne, U.K.: Cambridge Scholars, 2010), pp. 83-93. The song lyrics I reference in this first sentence are from the song "Take My Life (Holiness)" by Micah Stampley, www.lyricsmania.com/take_my_life_holiness_lyrics_micah_stmpley.html.

[2]Wesley D. Tracey, "Spiritual Direction in the Wesleyan-Holiness Movement," *Journal of Psychology and Theology* 30, no. 4 (2002): 323-35.

[3]Ken Blue, *Healing Spiritual Abuse: How to Break Free from Bad Church Experiences* (Downers Grove, Ill.: InterVarsity Press, 1993).

[4]James R. Beck, "Self and Soul: Exploring the Boundary Between Psychotherapy and Spiritual Formation," *Journal of Psychology and Theology* 31, no. 1 (2003): 24-36; Siang-Yang Tan, "Integrating Spiritual Direction into Psychotherapy: Ethical Issues and Guidelines," *Journal of Psychology and Theology* 31, no. 1 (2003): 14-23.

[5]J. Muilenburg, "Holiness," *Interpreter's Dictionary of the Bible* (Nashville: Abingdon, 1962), 2:616-26, emphasis added.

[6]T. Runyon and J. R. Burck, "Sanctification/Holiness," *Dictionary of Pastoral Care and Counseling,* ed. Rodney J. Hunter (Nashville: Abingdon, 1990), pp. 1112-15, emphasis added.

[7]Brad D. Strawn and Warren S. Brown, "Wesleyan Holiness Through the Eyes of Cognitive Science and Psychotherapy," *Journal of Psychology and Christianity* 23, no. 2 (2004): 121-29.

[8]Virginia T. Holeman and Steve L. Martyn, *Inside the Leader's Head* (Nashville: Abingdon, 2008).

[9]Randy L. Maddox, *Responsible Grace: John Wesley's Practical Theology* (Nashville: Abingdon, 1994); Mark H. Mann, *Perfecting Grace: Holiness, Human Being, and the Sciences* (New York: T & T Clark International, 2006).

[10]This link between holiness and love is expanded in Mildred Bangs Wynkoop, *A Theology of Love* (Kansas City, Mo.: Beacon Hill, 1972); and Kenneth J. Collins, *The Theology of John Wesley: Holy Love and the Shape of Grace* (Nashville: Abingdon, 2007).

[11]Wynkoop, *A Theology of Love.*

[12]See Mann, *Perfecting Grace.*

[13]Ibid., p. 155.

[14]Warren S. Brown, "Nonreductive Physicalism and Soul: Finding Resonance between Theology and Neuroscience," *American Behavioral Scientist* 45, no. 12 (August 2002): 1812-21.

[15]See Mann, *Perfecting Grace*, p. 140.

[16]Ronald W. Wright, Greg Dimond, and Philip Budd, "Experienced Presence: An Intersubjective Perspective on John Wesley's Early Theology," *Journal of Psychology and Christianity* 23, no. 2 (Summer 2004): 155-64.

[17]For a full discussion of differentiation of self, see Michael E. Kerr and Murray Bowen, *Family Evaluation* (New York: W. W. Norton, 1988).

[18]Jack Balswick and Judith Balswick apply differentiation of self within the context of marriage in terms of "differentiated unity." See Jack O. Balswick and Judith K. Balswick, *A Model for Marriage: Covenant, Grace, Empowerment, and Intimacy* (Downers Grove, Ill.: InterVarsity Press, 2006).

[19]Wesley did not include challenging automatic negative thoughts in his list, but I think this would be consistent, especially if the client used biblical truth as the counter.

[20]Edwin Friedman, *Generation to Generation* (New York: Guilford, 1985).

[21]Maddox, *Responsible Grace*.

[22]Ibid., p. 54.

[23]Jerry L. Walls and Joseph R. Dongell, *Why I Am Not a Calvinist* (Downers Grove, Ill.: InterVarsity Press, 2004).

[24]W. Paul Jones, *Worlds Within a Congregation* (Nashville: Abingdon, 2000).

[25]See for example, Balswick and Balswick, *A Model for Marriage;* Aida B. Spenser, William D. Spenser, Steve Tracy and Celestia Tracy, *Marriage at the Crossroads* (Downers Grove, Ill.: InterVarsity Press, 2009).

[26]Virginia T. Holeman, *Reconcilable Differences: Hope and Healing for Troubled Marriages* (Downers Grove, Ill.: InterVarsity Press, 2004).

[27]James N. Sells and Mark A. Yarhouse, *Counseling Couples in Conflict: A Relational Restoration Model* (Downers Grove, Ill.: InterVarsity Press, 2011).

[28]Jennifer S. Martinez, Timothy B. Smith and Sally H. Barlow, "Spiritual Interventions in Psychotherapy: Evaluations by Highly Religious Clients," *Journal of Clinical Psychology* 63, no. 10 (2007): 903-7.

Chapter 5: Out of the Office and into the Streets

[1]John Wesley, Preface to *List of Poetical Works*, in *The Works of John Wesley*, vol. 14 (Peabody, Mass.: Hendrickson, 1872), p. 321.

[2]To be faithful to John Wesley I want to underscore that Wesley's concern centered on living out one's faith within the community of believers. The social justice accent is a logical extension of this, supported by Wesley's ministry to the poor.

[3]N. T. Wright, *After You Believe* (New York: HarperOne, 2010), p. 247.

[4]Courtland C. Lee, *Counseling for Social Justice*, 2nd ed. (Alexandria, Va.: American Counseling Association, 2007), p. vii.

[5]Avery Calhoun and William Pelech, "Responding to Young People Responsible for Harm: A Comparative Study of Restorative and Conventional Approaches," *Contemporary Justice Review* 13, no. 3 (2010): 287-306, doi:10.1080/10282580.2010.498 238; Anne-Marie McAliden, "'Transforming Justice': Challenges for Restorative Justice in an Era of Punishment-based Corrections," *Contemporary Justice Review* 14, no. 4 (2011): 383-406; Katherine van Wormer, "Restorative Justice as Social Justice for Victims of Gendered Violence: A Standpoint Feminist Perspective," *Social Work* 54, no. 2 (2009): 107-16.

[6]I give credit to my colleague David Thompson for his generous sharing of his insights about justice in the Old Testament. Any misconceptions are entirely my own.

[7]Theodore W. Jennings Jr., "Transcendence, Justice, and Mercy: Toward a (Wesleyan) Reconceptualization of God," in *Rethinking Wesley's Theology for Contemporary Methodism*, ed. Randy L. Maddox (Nashville: Kingswood, 1998), p. 65.

[8]Steven C. Roy, "Embracing Social Justice: Reflections from the Storyline of Scripture," *Trinity Journal* 30 (2009): 3-48.

[9]William N. Grosch and David C. Olsen, *When Helping Starts to Hurt: A New Look at Burnout Among Psychotherapists* (New York: W. W. Norton, 1994).

[10]Roy, "Embracing Social Justice," p. 18.

[11]The bystander effect reveals that people are less inclined to provide help when other bystanders are present.

[12]"Green Dot Strategy," Violence and Prevention Center, www.uky.edu/Student Affairs/VIPCenter/learn_greendot.php.

[13]Roy, "Embracing Social Justice," p. 18.

[14]"The Program," Refuge for Women, accessed April 24, 2012, www.refugefor women.org/the-program.

[15]Roy, "Embracing Social Justice," p. 48.

[16]M. Douglas Meeks, "Sanctification and Economy: A Wesleyan Perspective on Stewardship," in *Rethinking Wesley's Theology for Contemporary Methodism*, ed. Randy L. Maddox (Nashville: Kingswood, 1998), p. 91.

[17]Ibid., p. 94.

[18]Donald E. Gowan, "Wealth and Poverty in the Old Testament: The Case of the Widow, the Orphan, and the Sojourner," *Interpretation* 41 (1987): 341-53.

[19]N. T. Wright, *Evil and the Justice of God* (Downers Grove, Ill.: InterVarsity Press, 2009).

[20]"John Wesley Quotes," ThinkExist.com, accessed June 30, 2011, http://thinkexist.com/ quotation/do_all_the_good_you_can-by_all_the_means_you_can/148152.html.

[21]Meeks, "Sanctification and Economy," p. 87.

[22]John Wesley, "On Visiting the Sick," sermon 98, *The Sermons of John Wesley*, The United Methodist Church, accessed June 30, 2011, www.umcmission.org/Find-Resources/Global-Worship-and-Spiritual-Growth/John-Wesley-Sermons/ Sermon-98-On-Visiting-the-Sick.

[23]John Wesley, "The Reformation of Manners," sermon 52, *The Sermons of John Wesley*, The United Methodist Church, accessed June 30, 2011, http://new.gbgm-umc.org/ umhistory/wesley/sermons/52.

[24]Howard A. Snyder, *The Radical Wesley and Patterns for Church Renewal* (Eugene, Ore.: Wipf & Stock, 1996), p. 2.

[25]Rebecca L. Toporek, Judith A. Lewis and Hugh C. Crethar, "Promoting Systemic Change Through ACA Advocacy Competencies," *Journal of Counseling & Development* 87, no. 3 (2009): 267-68.

[26]Manivong J. Ratts, "Social Justice Counseling: Toward the Development of a Fifth Force Among Counseling Paradigms," *Journal of Humanistic Counseling, Education, and Development* 48, no. 2 (2009): 160.

[27]"What is Social Justice Counseling?" Counselors for Social Justice, accessed April 28, 2011, http://counselorsforsocialjustice.com.

[28]Judith A. Lewis, Michael D. Lewis, Judy A. Daniels and Michael J. D'Andrea,

Community Counseling: Empowerment Strategies for a Diverse Society, 3rd ed. (Pacific Grove, Calif.: Brooks/Cole, 2003).

[29]See Alvin Dueck and Kevin Reimer, *A Peaceable Psychology* (Grand Rapids: Brazos, 2009).

[30]Mark A. Noll, *The New Shape of World Christianity* (Downers Grove, Ill.: Inter-Varsity Press, 2009), p. 22.

[31]Ibid., p. 30.

[32]The other four marks of mission include (1) proclaiming the good news of the kingdom, (2) teaching, baptizing and nurturing new believers, (3) responding to human need by loving service, and (4) striving to safeguard the integrity of creation and sustain and renew the life of the earth. (See Andrew Walls and Cathy Ross, eds., *Mission in the 21st Century: Exploring the Five Marks of Global Mission* [Maryknoll, N.Y.: Orbis, 2008]).

[33]Valdir Raul Steuernagel, "To Seek to Transform Unjust Structures of Society," in *Mission in the 21st Century: Exploring the Five Marks of Global Mission*, eds. Andrew Walls and Cathy Ross (Maryknoll, N.Y.: Orbis, 2008), p. 67.

[34]Urie Bronfenbrenner, "Toward an Experimental Ecology of Human Development," *American Psychologist* 32 (1977): 513-31.

[35]Laurie D. McCubbin and Thu A. Dang, "Native Hawaiian Identity and Measurement," in *Handbook of Multicultural Counseling*, ed. Joseph G. Ponterotto et al., 3rd ed. (Los Angeles: Sage, 2010), p. 275.

[36]Ibid., p. 276.

[37]Ibid.

[38]Ibid.

[39]See for example, William J. Doherty, Tai J. Mendenhall, and Jerica M. Berge, "The Families and Democracy and Citizen Health Care Project," *Journal of Marital and Family Therapy* 36 (2010): 389-402, doi:10.1111/j.1752-0606.2009.00142.x.

[40]Harry Aponte, *Bread and Spirit: Therapy with the New Poor* (New York: W. W. Norton, 1994).

[41]To learn more about Step by Step go to www.sbslex.org.

[42]Lewis et al., *Community Counseling*, p. 23.

[43]Nancy Boyd-Franklin, *Reaching Out in Family Therapy: Home-based, School, and Community* (New York: Guilford, 2000); Sanna Thompson, Kimberly Bender, Janet Lantry, and Patrick Flynn, "Treatment Engagement: Building Therapeutic Alliance in Home-Based Treatment with Adolescents and Their Families," *Contemporary Family Therapy: An International Journal* 29, no. 1/2 (2007): 39-55.

[44]Take a moment to make as long a list as possible of words that come to mind when you think of the following: cancer, heart disease and mental illness. Chances are that more negative terms are associated with mental illness than with cancer or heart disease.

[45]W. Paul Jones, *Theological Worlds* (Nashville: Abingdon, 1989), pp. 57-70; W. Paul Jones, *Worlds Within a Congregation* (Nashville: Abingdon, 2000), pp. 59-60.

[46]For more information see www.newbeginnings.org.

[47]For more information on NAMI Walks, see www.nami.org/walkTemplate .cfm?section=namiwalks.

[48]For complete lyrics see "Did You Feel the Mountains Tremble?" by Martin Smith and Matt Redman, www.metrolyrics.com/did-you-feel-the-mountains-tremble-lyrics-sonicflood.html.

Chapter 6: Just Forgive?

[1]John M. Gottman, *The Science of Trust: Emotional Attunement for Couples* (New York: W. W. Norton, 2011).

[2]These two stories are excerpted from Virginia T. Holeman, *Reconcilable Differences: Hope and Healing for Troubled Marriage* (Downers Grove, Ill.: Intervarsity Press, 2004).

[3]Randy L. Maddox, *Responsible Grace: John Wesley's Practical Theology* (Nashville: Kingswood, 1994), p. 97.

[4]Joel B. Green and Mark D. Baker, *Recovering the Scandal of the Cross: Atonement in New Testament and Contemporary Contexts* (Downers Grove, Ill.: InterVarsity Press, 2000).

[5]You can read well-developed comparisons of atonement theories in the following books: Green and Baker, *Recovering the Scandal of the Cross*; James Beilby and Paul R. Eddy, eds., *The Nature of the Atonement: Four Views* (Downers Grove, Ill.: Inter-Varsity Press, 2006); and John Driver, *Understanding the Atonement for the Mission of the Church* (Scottdale, Penn.: Herald Press, 1986).

[6]N. T. Wright, *Evil and the Justice of God* (Downers Grove, Ill.: InterVarsity Press, 2004), pp. 95, 114.

[7]Ibid., pp. 98-99.

[8]Green and Baker, *Recovering the Scandal of the Cross*, pp. 192-209.

[9]Henry H. Knight III, "Amazing Love! The Atonement in John and Charles Wesley," *Circuit Rider*, September-October, 2004, p. 7, accessed June 30, 2011, www.umph .org/pdfs/circuitrider/P101ALov.pdf.

[10]Jerry L. Walls and Joseph R. Dongell, *Why I Am Not a Calvinist* (Downers Grove, Ill.: InterVarsity Press, 2004).

[11]Maddox, *Responsible Grace*, p. 106.

[12]Ibid., p. 107.

[13]Ibid., p. 109.

[14]Miroslav Volf, *Exclusion and Embrace* (Nashville: Abingdon, 1996).

[15]Robert D. Enright and Richard P. Fitzgibbons, *Helping Clients Forgive: An Empirical Guide for Resolving Anger and Restoring Hope* (Washington, D.C.: American Psychological Association, 2000), p. 38; Everett L. Worthington Jr., *Forgiving and Reconciling: Bridges to Wholeness and Hope* (Downers Grove, Ill.: InterVarsity Press, 2003).

[16]Everett L. Worthington Jr., *A Just Forgiveness: Responsible Healing Without Excusing Injustice* (Downers Grove, Ill.: InterVarsity Press, 2009), pp. 74-75.

[17]Ibid., p. 75.

[18]Ibid., p. 78.

[19]Wayne E. Hill, Cathy Hasty, and Carol Moore, "Differentiation of Self and the Process of Forgiveness: A Clinical Perspective for Couple and Family Therapy," *Australian & New Zealand Journal of Family Therapy* 32, no. 1 (2011): 43-57; Virginia T. Holeman, Janet B. Dean, Lise DeShea, and Jill D. Duba, "Forgiveness, Sacred Loss/Desecration, and Differentiation of Self," *Journal of Psychology and Theology*, 39, no. 1 (2011): 31-43; Steven J. Sandage and Peter J. Jankowski, "Forgiveness, Spiritual Instability, Mental Health Symptoms, and Well-being: Mediator Effects of Differentiation of Self," *Psychology of Religion and Spirituality* 2, no. 3 (2010): 168-80; Rachel Dekel, "Couple Forgiveness, Self-Differentiation and Secondary

Traumatization Among Wives of Former POWs," *Journal of Social & Personal Relationships* 27, no. 7 (2010): 924-37.

[20]Worthington, *Just Forgiveness*, pp. 102-5.

[21]A version of this section was published in Virginia Todd Holeman, *Reconcilable Differences: Hope and Healing for Troubled Marriages* (Downers Grove, Ill.: InterVarsity Press, 2004), pp. 121-46.

[22]Worthington, *Just Forgiveness*.

[23]While I believe that reconciliation is the biblical bias, I am painfully aware that many relationships cannot bear the weight of reconciliation because of the depth of injury that people inflict on one another and the risks associated with reconciliation. Prior to reconciliation, injured parties must carefully consider issues of safety. Not all people will reconcile, and Christians who counsel must respect clients' choices in this regard.

[24]John Gottman argues that married couples who experience betrayal can move into pathways of forgiveness and reconciliation if their relationship has been characterized by moments of turning toward one another, emotional attunement, effective repairs and positive sentiment override, or if these couple behaviors can be developed. See Gottman, *Science of Trust*, pp. 331-85.

[25]Michael J. Wohl, Lise DeShea and Rebekah L. Wahkinney, "Looking Within: Measuring State Self-Forgiveness and Its Relationship to Psychological Well-Being," *Canadian Journal of Behavioural Science* 40, no. 1 (2008): 1-10, doi:10.1037/0008-400x.40.1.1.1.

[26]Ann Macaskill, "Differentiating Dispositional Self-Forgiveness from Other-Forgiveness: Associations with Mental Health and Life Satisfaction," *Journal of Social & Clinical Psychology* 31, no. 1 (2012): 28-50, doi: 10.1521/jscp.2012.21.1.28.

[27]Julie J. Exline et al., "Reparative Behaviors and Self-Forgiveness: Effects of a Laboratory-based Exercise," *Self & Identity* 10, no. 1 (2011): 101-26, doi: 10.1080/15298861003669565.

[28]Worthington, *Just Forgiveness*, p. 28. See also pp. 62-64.

Chapter 7: Seeing Now in Light of the Not Yet

[1]Roberto E. Mercadilloa, José Luis Diazb, Erick H. Pasayea and Fernando A. Barriosa, "Perception of Suffering and Compassion Experience: Brain Gender Disparities," *Brain and Cognition* 76, no. 1 (2011): 5-14, doi:10.1016/j.bandc.2011.03.019; Loran F. Nordgren, Kasia Banas and Geoff MacDonald, "Empathy Gaps for Social Pain: Why People Underestimate the Pain of Social Suffering," *Journal of Personality and Social Psychology* 100, no. 1 (2011): 120-28, doi:10.1037/a0020938.

[2]Ronnie Janoff-Bulman, *Shattered Assumptions* (New York: Free Press, 1992).

[3]Kenneth I. Pargament, G. M. Magyar, E. Benore and Annette Mahoney, "Sacrilege: A Study of Sacred Loss and Desecration and Their Implications for Health and Well-Being in a Community Sample," *Journal for the Scientific Study of Religion*, 44, no. 1 (2005): 59-78, doi:10.1111/j.1468-5906.2005.00265.x; Annette Mahoney, Mark S. Rye and Kenneth I. Pargament, "When the Sacred Is Violated: Desecration as a Unique Challenge to Forgiveness," in *Handbook of Forgiveness*, ed. Everett L. Worthington Jr. (New York: Routledge, 2005), pp. 57-71.

[4]Don E. Davis, Joshua N. Hook and Everett L. Worthington, "Relational Spirituality and Forgiveness: The Roles of Attachment to God, Religious Coping, and

Viewing the Transgression as a Desecration," *Journal of Psychology and Christianity* 27, no. 4 (2008): 293-301; Virginia T. Holeman, Janet B. Dean, Lise DeShea and Jill D. Duba, "Forgiveness, Sacred Loss/Desecration, and Differentiation of Self," *Journal of Psychology and Theology*, 39, no. 1 (2011): 31-43.

[5]Ray S. Anderson, *The Shape of Practical Theology: Empowering Ministry with Theological Praxis* (Downers Grove, Ill.: InterVarsity Press, 2001), p. 103.

[6]Joel B. Green, *1 Peter*, The Two Horizons New Testament Commentary (Grand Rapids: Eerdmans, 2007), p. 142.

[7]N. T. Wright, *Surprised by Hope: Rethinking Heaven, the Resurrection, and the Mission of the Church* (New York: HarperOne, 2008), pp. 18- 19.

[8]Kenneth J. Collins, *The Theology of John Wesley: Holy Love and the Shape of Grace* (Nashville: Abingdon, 2007), p. 314.

[9]Current neuroscientific discoveries have led several noteworthy theologians and biblical scholars to call into question the dualistic construct of an immortal soul. My intent is not to argue for or against such proposals in this book. I refer readers who are interested in these discussions to Warren S. Brown, Nancey Murphy and H. Newton Malony, eds., *Whatever Happened to the Soul? Scientific and Theological Portraits of Human Nature* (Minneapolis: Fortress, 1998); Joel B. Green, ed., *What About the Soul? Neuroscience and Christian Anthropology* (Nashville: Abingdon, 2004); Joel B. Green and Stuart L. Palmer, eds., *In Search of the Soul: Four Views of the Mind-Body Problem* (Downers Grove, Ill.: InterVarsity Press, 2005); and Joel B. Green, *Body, Soul, and Human Life: The Nature of Humanity in the Bible* (Grand Rapids: Baker, 2008).

[10]Collins, *Theology of John Wesley*, pp. 325-26.

[11]Wright, *Surprised by Hope*, p. 122.

[12]Ibid., p. 46. Wright credits Dominic Crossan with this phrase.

[13]See especially, N. T. Wright, *Evil and the Justice of God* (Downers Grove, Ill.: InterVarsity Press, 2006).

[14]Wright, *Surprised by Hope*, p. 46.

[15]Miroslav Volf, *The End of Memory: Remembering Rightly in a Violent World* (Grand Rapids: Eerdmans, 2006), p. 26.

[16]Ibid., p. 28.

[17]Ibid., p. 42.

[18]Ibid., p. 201.

[19]Richard K. James, *Crisis Intervention Strategies*, 6th ed. (Pacific Grove, Calif.: Brooks/Cole-Thompson Learning, 2008); Rick A. Myer, *Assessment for Crisis Intervention* (Pacific Grove, Calif.: Brooks/Cole-Thompson Learning, 2001).

[20]John Briere and Catherine Scott, *Principles of Trauma Therapy: A Guide to Symptoms, Evaluation, and Treatment* (Thousand Oaks, Calif.: Sage, 2006); Laurence J. Kirmayer, Robert Lemelson, and Mark Barad, eds., *Understanding Trauma: Integrating Biological, Clinical and Cultural Perspectives* (New York: Cambridge University Press, 2007).

[21]Joseph D. Tariman et al., "Physician, Patient, and Contextual Factors Affecting Treatment Decisions in Older Adults with Cancer and Models of Decision Making: A Literature Review," *Oncology Nursing Forum* 39, no.1 (2012): E70-E83; Mary Miller Lewis, "Spirituality, Counseling, and Elderly: An Introduction to the Spiritual Life Review," *Journal of Adult Development* 8, no. 4 (2001): 231-40.

[22]Julie J. Exline, Virginia T. Holeman and Lise DeShea, "Is Apology Worth the Risk? Predictors, Outcomes, and Ways to Avoid Regret," *Journal of Social and Clinical Psychology*, 26, no. 4 (2006): 479-504.

[23]Stanley Hauerwas and Jean Vanier, *Living Gently in a Violent World* (Downers Grove, Ill.: InterVarsity Press, 2008); Miroslav Volf, *Free of Charge: Giving and Forgiving in a Culture Stripped of Grace* (Grand Rapids: Zondervan, 2005); Wright, *Evil and the Justice of God*.

[24]Christine A. Courtois, *Healing the Incest Wound: Adult Survivors in Therapy* (New York: W. W. Norton, 1988); Suzanne R. Freedman and Robert D. Enright, "Forgiveness as an Intervention Goal with Incest Survivors," *Journal of Consulting and Clinical Psychology*, 64, no. 5 (1996): 983-92, doi:10.1037/0022-006X.64.5.983.

[25]Jamie D. Aten, "Equipping Faith Communities for Disaster: The Church Disaster Mental Health Project Website," *Journal of Applied Research in Economic Development* 5 (2008): 56-57; Jamie D. Aten, Sharon Topping, Ryan M. Denney and John M. Hosey, "Helping African American Clergy and Churches Address Minority Disaster Mental Health Disparities: Training Needs, Model, and Example," *Psychology of Religion and Spirituality* 3 (2011): 15-23.

[26]Green, *1 Peter*.

[27]Kenneth S. Kantzer, "The Cut-rate Grace of a Health and Wealth Gospel," *Christianity Today* 29, no. 9 (1985): 14-15; Bruce Barron, *The Health and Wealth Gospel: What's Going on Today in a Movement That Has Shaped the Faith of Millions?* (Downers Grove, Ill.: InterVarsity Press, 1987).

[28]Julie J. Exline and Joshua B. Grubbs, "'If I Tell Others About My Anger Toward God, How Will They Respond?' Predictors, Associated Behaviors, and Outcomes in an Adult Sample," *Journal of Psychology and Theology* 39, no. 4 (2011): 304-15.

[29]"Non-anxious presence" is a category that I first learned from Edwin Friedman's classic text *Generation to Generation* (New York: Guildford, 1985). We model "non-anxious presence" when we do not allow the anxieties of others to become our own anxiety, but we can still remain emotionally connected and available to those anxious others, in spite of their anxiety.

Postscript

[1]John H. Coe and Todd W. Hall, *Psychology in the Spirit* (Downers Grove, Ill.: InterVarsity Press, 2010).

[2]See Eric L. Johnson, ed., *Psychology and Christianity: Five Views*, Spectrum Multiview Books (Downers Grove, Ill.: InterVarsity Press, 2010).

Bibliography

𝔇

Anderson, Ray S. *Christians Who Counsel*. Pasadena, Calif.: Fuller Seminary Press, 1990.

———. *The Shape of Practical Theology: Empowering Ministry with Theological Praxis*. Downers Grove, Ill.: InterVarsity Press, 2001.

Armistead, M. Kathryn, Brad D. Strawn and Ronald W. Wright, eds. *Wesleyan Theology and Social Science: The Dance of Practical Divinity and Discovery*. Newcastle upon Tyne, U.K.: Cambridge Scholars Press, 2010.

Aten, Jamie D., Mark R. McMinn and Everett L. Worthington, eds. *Spiritually Oriented Interventions for Counseling and Psychotherapy*. Washington, D.C.: American Psychological Association, 2011.

Green, Joel B., and Mark D. Baker., *Recovering the Scandal of the Cross: Atonement in New Testament and Contemporary Context*. Downers Grove, Ill.: InterVarsity Press, 2011.

Beilby, James, and Paul R. Eddy, eds. *The Nature of the Atonement: Four Views*. Downers Grove, Ill.: InterVarsity Press, 2006.

Browning, Don S. *Religious Thought and the Modern Psychologies*. Philadelphia: Fortress, 1987.

Carlson, Thomas D., Dwight Kirkpatrick, Lorna Hecker and Mark Killmer. "Religion, Spirituality, and Marriage and Family Therapy: A Study of Family Therapists' Beliefs about the Appropriateness of Addressing Religious and Spiritual Issues in Therapy." *American Journal of Family Therapy* 30, no. 2 (2002): 157-71.

Cashwell, Craig S. *Integrating Spirituality and Religion into Counseling: A Guide to Competent Practice*. Alexandria, Va.: American Counseling Association, 2011.

Coe, John H., and Todd W. Hall. *Psychology in the Spirit: Contours of a Transformational Psychology*. Downers Grove, Ill.: InterVarsity Press, 2010.

Collins, Kenneth J. *The Theology of John Wesley: Holy Love and the Shape of Grace*. Nashville: Abingdon, 2007.

Cornish, Marilyn A., and Nathaniel G. Wade. "Spirituality and Religion in Group Counseling: A Literature Review with Practice Guidelines." *Professional Psychology: Research and Practice* 41, no. 5 (2010): 398-404.

Driver, John. *Understanding the Atonement for the Mission of the Church.* Scottdale, Penn.: Herald Press, 1986.

Dueck, Alvin, and Cameron Lee, eds. *Why Psychology Needs Theology.* Grand Rapids: Eerdmans, 2005.

Dunnington, Kent J. *Addiction and Virtue: Beyond the Models of Disease and Choice.* Downers Grove, Ill.: InterVarsity Press, 2011.

Entwistle, David N. *Integrative Approaches to Psychology and Christianity: An Introduction to Worldview Issues, Philosophical Foundations, and Models of Integration.* Eugene, Ore.: Wipf & Stock, 2004.

Erickson, Martin J., Lorna Hecker, Dwight Kirkpatrick, Mark Killmer and Edassery James. "Clients' Perceptions of Marriage and Family Therapists Addressing the Religious and Spiritual Aspects of Clients' Lives: A Pilot Study." *Journal of Psychotherapy and the Family* 13 (2002): 109-25. doi: 10.1300/J085v13n01_06.

Friedman, Edwin. *Generation to Generation.* New York: Guilford, 1985.

Gonsiorek, John C., P. Scott Richards, Kenneth I. Pargament and Mark R. McMinn. "Ethical Challenges and Opportunities at the Edge: Incorporating Spirituality and Religion into Psychotherapy." *Professional Psychology: Research and Practice* 40 (August 2009): 385-95. doi:10.1037/a0016488.

Grenz, Stanley, J. *The Social God and the Relational Self.* Louisville: Westminster John Knox, 2001.

Grenz, Stanley J., and Roger E. Olson. *Who Needs Theology? An Invitation to the Study of God.* Downers Grove, Ill.: InterVarsity Press, 1996.

Hall, M. Elizabeth Lewis, Jennifer S. Ripley, Fernando L. Garzon and Michael W. Mangis. "The Other Side of the Podium: Student Perspectives On Learning Integration." *Journal of Psychology & Theology* 37, no. 1 (2009): 15-27.

Hoffman, Marie T. *Toward Mutual Recognition: Relational Psychoanalysis and the Christian Narrative.* New York: Routledge, 2010.

Holeman, Virginia Todd. *Reconcilable Differences: Hope and Healing for Troubled Marriages.* Downers Grove, Ill.: InterVarsity Press, 2004.

Hubble, Mark A., Barry L. Duncan and Scott D. Miller, eds. *The Heart and Soul of Change: What Works in Therapy.* Washington, D.C.: American Psychological Association, 1999.

Johnson, Eric L., ed. *Psychology and Christianity: Five Views.* 2nd ed.

Downers Grove, Ill.: InterVarsity Press, 2010.

———. *Worlds Within a Congregation: Dealing with Theological Diversity.* Nashville: Abingdon, 2000.

Jones, Stanton L., and Richard E. Butman. *Modern Psychotherapies: A Comprehensive Christian Appraisal.* Downers Grove, Ill.: InterVarsity Press, 1991.

Jones, W. Paul. *Theological Worlds: Understanding the Alternative Rhythms of Christian Belief.* Nashville: Abingdon, 1989.

Maddox, Randy L. *Responsible Grace: John Wesley's Practical Theology.* Nashville: Abingdon, 1994.

Mann, Mark H. *Perfecting Grace: Holiness, Human Being, and the Sciences.* New York: T & T Clark, 2006.

McMinn, Mark R., and Clark D. Campbell. *Integrative Psychotherapy: Toward a Comprehensive Christian Approach.* Downers Grove, Ill.: InterVarsity Press, 2007.

McMinn, Mark R., Ryan C. Staley, Kurt C. Webb and Winston Seegobin. "Just What Is Christian Counseling Anyway?" *Professional Psychology: Research and Practice* 41 (2010): 391-97.

Miller, William R., ed. *Integrating Spirituality into Treatment: Resources for Practitioners.* Washington, D.C.: American Psychological Association, 1999.

Miller, William R., and Harold D. Delaney, eds. *Judeo-Christian Perspectives on Psychology: Human Nature, Motivation, and Change.* Washington, D.C.: American Psychological Association, 2005.

Myers, David G., and Malcolm A. Jeeves. *Psychology Through the Eyes of Faith.* San Francisco: Harper & Row, 1987.

Richards, P. Scott, and Allen E. Bergin, eds. *A Spiritual Strategy for Counseling and Psychotherapy.* 2nd ed. Washington, D.C.: American Psychological Association, 2005.

Richards, P. Scott, Jeremy D. Bartz and Karl A. O'Grady. "Assessing Religion and Spirituality in Counseling: Some Reflections and Recommendations." *Counseling & Values* 54, no. 1 (2009): 65-79.

Roberts, Robert C., and Mark R. Talbot, eds. *Limning the Psyche: Explorations in Christian Psychology.* Grand Rapids: Eerdmans, 1997.

Ross, George R. *Evaluating Models of Christian Counseling.* Eugene, Ore.: Wipf & Stock, 2011.

Sandhu, Daya Singh. *Spirituality as a Fifth Force in Counseling and Psychology: Implications for Practice, Training, and Research.* Alexandria, Va.: American Counseling Association, in press.

Sells, James N., and Mark A. Yarhouse. *Counseling Couples in Conflict.* Downers Grove, Ill.: InterVarsity Press, 2011.

Shafranske, Edward P., ed. *Religion and the Clinical Practice of Psychology.* Washington, D.C.: American Psychological Association, 1996.

Shults, F. LeRon, and Steven J. Sandage. *Transforming Spirituality: Integrating Theology and Psychology.* Grand Rapids: Baker Academic, 2006.

Sorenson, Randall Lehmann, Kimberly R. Derflinger, Rodger K. Bufford and Mark R. McMinn, "National Collaborative Research on How Students Learn Integration: Final Report," *Journal of Psychology and Christianity* 23, no. 4 (2004): 355-65.

Sprenkle, Douglas H., Sean D. Davis and Jay L. Lebow, *Common Factors in Couple and Family Therapy: The Overlooked Foundation for Effective Practice.* New York: Guilford, 2009.

Stevenson, Daryl H., Brian E. Eck and Peter C. Hill, eds. *Psychology and Christianity Integration: Seminal Works that Shaped the Movement.* Batavia, Ill.: Christian Association for Psychological Studies, 2007.

Stoltenberg, Carl, and Ursula Delworth. *Supervising Counselors and Therapists: A Developmental Approach.* San Francisco: Jossey-Bass, 1987.

Tan, Siang-Yang. *Counseling and Psychotherapy: A Christian Perspective.* Grand Rapids: Baker Academic, 2011.

Thompson, David L., and Gina Thompson Eickoff. *God's Healing for Hurting Families: Biblical Principles for Reconciliation and Recovery.* Indianapolis: Wesleyan Publishing House, 2004.

Volf, Miroslav. *The End of Memory: Remembering Rightly in a Violent World.* Grand Rapids: Eerdmans, 2006.

———. *Exclusion and Embrace.* Nashville: Abingdon, 1996.

Wright, N. T. *After You Believe: Why Christian Character Matters.* New York: HarperOne, 2010.

———. *Evil and the Justice of God.* Downers Grove, Ill.: InterVarsity Press, 2004.

———. *Surprised by Hope: Rethinking Heaven, the Resurrection, and the Mission of the Church.* New York: HarperOne, 2008.

Worthington, Everett L., Jr. *A Just Forgiveness: Responsible Healing Without Excusing Injustice.* Downers Grove, Ill.: InterVarsity Press, 2009.

Wynkoop, Mildred Bangs. *A Theology of Love: The Dynamic of Wesleyanism.* Kansas City, Mo.: Beacon Hill, 1972.

Yarhouse, Mark A., and Brant T. VanOrman. "When Psychologists Work with Religious Clients: Applications of the General Principles of Ethical Conduct." *Professional Psychology: Research and Practice* 30 (1999): 557-62. doi:10.1037/0735-7028.30.6.557.

Yarhouse, Mark A., and James N. Sells. *Family Therapies: A Comprehensive Christian Appraisal.* Downers Grove, Ill.: InterVarsity Press, 2008.

Young, J. Scott, Marsha Wiggins-Frame and Craig S. Cashwell. "Spirituality and Counselor Competence: A National Survey of American Counseling Association Members." *Journal of Counseling and Development* 85 (2007): 47-52.

Index

Abelard, Peter, 139, 142
abuse, 11, 30, 90, 94, 103, 104, 117, 118, 159, 171, 172
academic preparation, 18-21
addressing, 44, 45, 48, 50
advocacy, 13, 35, 99, 104, 113-21, 123, 124, 126, 130, 135
affect, 50, 77
aligning, 44, 45, 50-51
American Counseling Association, 39, 40, 114
American Psychological Association, 39
Anselm of Canterbury, 138-39
anxiety, 77, 88-92, 98, 127, 130, 169, 172, 174, 175
apology, 144, 148, 150
Aponte, Harry, 119
assessment, 36, 47, 59, 195n25
Aten, Jamie, 172
atonement, 35, 134, 135-43, 149-51
attaining, 44, 45, 51
attending, 44, 45, 46-48, 69
Baker, Mark D., 22, 136, 138
behavioral shifts, 50, 76
Bohart, Arthur, 70
Bowen, Murray, 88, 89, 92
Bronfenbrenner, Urie, 117-18, 121
Calvin, Calvinism, 16, 92
case conceptualization, 33, 35, 36, 87, 117
Christian counseling, 8, 9, 11, 13, 17, 19, 21, 28, 34, 41, 58, 62, 115, 116, 117
Christian theology, definition of, 21-22
Christian worldview, 28
Christus Victor, 137-38, 144
client characteristics, 70-72
client expectancy, 75-76
Coe, John, 26, 180
cognition(s), 50
cognitive reframing, 50, 76, 77
collaboration, 29, 34, 46, 48, 50, 59, 67, 68, 72, 73, 86, 172, 174, 180
collaborative eschatology, 165-66, 178

Collins, Ken, 15, 163, 164
common factors, 17, 35, 44, 50, 63, 64, 69, 70, 71, 72, 75, 76, 77, 78
community, 12, 14, 15, 24, 30, 49, 66, 70, 91, 102, 106, 107, 108, 109, 110, 111, 112, 114, 115, 117, 118, 119, 120, 123, 124, 126, 129, 130, 132, 143, 161, 172, 177
competency, 27, 28, 29, 59, 60
    professional, 28
    theological, 29
consultation. See supervision
consummation, 106, 108-9
Counselors for Social Justice, 114-15
Courtland, C. Lee, 103
Creation, 32, 86, 104, 105, 106-7, 120, 164, 167, 170
crisis, 13, 35, 159, 168, 169-70, 173, 174, 175, 178
critical thinking, 26
    strong sense, 27
    weak sense, 26-27
C.R.O.S.S., 122-30
cross of Christ, 16, 104, 134, 135, 142-44, 149-53, 165, 167, 168
cutoff, 89, 90, 91, 95, 146, 148
D'Andrea, Michael, 121
Daniels, Judy, 121
Davis, Sean, 17, 44, 50, 70, 77
desecration, 159, 176
differentiating holiness, 89-93, 96
differentiation of self, 87-89, 145-46, 148, 192n36, 199n18
discipleship, 32, 38, 43, 152
domestic violence, 94, 103, 118
Durst, David M., 49, 53-55, 196n37
ecosystem, 118
ecosystemic, 119, 127
emotional reactivity, 89, 91, 96, 145, 146, 149
emotional regulation, 50, 76, 77
empathy, 29, 148

environment, 87, 107, 115-19, 129, 177
epiphania, 52, 53, 55, 69, 92, 93, 125, 151, 177
eschatological perspective, 161, 177, 178
eschatology, 35, 161, 162-69, 178
ethical, 17, 31, 33, 34, 35, 36, 38, 39, 41, 42, 44, 50, 52
ethics codes, 28, 56, 58, 60, 77, 95, 106, 119, 174, 181
evidence-based, 38
evil 11, 32, 52, 54, 111, 125, 126, 136, 137, 146, 164, 165, 167, 168, 171, 173, 178
Exline, Julie, 173
faint. See theological worlds
faith, 13, 14, 15, 20, 21, 24, 25, 32, 47, 49, 51, 59, 70, 72, 74, 112, 137, 139
faithfulness, 12, 44, 51, 76, 105, 128, 138, 149, 165, 172, 178
"Fall," 106, 107-8, 170, 172
fighter. See theological worlds
flattened. See theological worlds
forces in counseling, 39-40
foreigner. See theological worlds
forgive, 11, 58, 138, 171, 176, 177
forgiveness, 13, 16, 35, 43, 49, 54, 57, 58, 124, 129, 133-35, 139-55, 159, 166, 170, 172
    decisional, 145
    emotional, 145
formation, 32, 34, 79, 141
Frank, Ked, 108
Friedman, Edwin, 91
fugitive. See theological worlds
fusion, 89, 90, 91, 92, 96, 146
goals, 16, 34, 36, 43, 44, 50, 51, 52, 60, 72, 73, 74, 86, 88, 102, 103, 120, 135, 176
God, 10, 11, 15, 16, 21, 22, 29, 31, 2, 33, 34, 36, 38, 40, 43, 47, 49, 51, 53, 54, 62-69, 71, 75, 82, 83,

85-88, [90, 91, 92], 95, 97, 104, 105-12, 120, 121, 125, 128, 136, 137, 138-47, 150, 159, 160, 162, 163, 164, 165, 167, 168, 170, 173, 174
Gowan, Donald E., 109, 110
grace, 15, 24, 30, 31, 32, 49, 65, 71-72, 85-86, 90, 91, 92, 95, 96, 99, 102, 129, 141, 142, 146, 147, 163, 164, 165
    prevenient, 32, 71-72
Green, Joel B., 22, 136, 138, 161
Green Dot, 107, 108
Gregory of Nyssa, 137-39
Grenz, Stanley, 21, 22, 23, 28, 29, 30, 38, 64, 65
Grubbs, Joshua, 173
Hall, Elizabeth Lewis, 20
Hall, Todd, 26, 180
Heber, Reginald, 62
Helmeke, Karen, 70
hermeneutics, 48, 56-58
holiness, 32, 64, 81-99, 102-4, 111-12, 129, 130, 135, 140, 164
    personal, 14, 35, 49, 81-99, 101, 102, 104, 130
    relational, 84, 87
    social, 14, 35, 49, 85, 99, 101-30, 135
holiness movement, 82
holy, 82, 84, 102, 150, 165
holy love, 63, 64, 65, 82, 85, 112, 141, 142, 163, 164
Holy Spirit, 10, 15, 16, 17, 24, 31-32, 34, 41, 42, 43, 44, 45, 46, 50, 65, 66, 69, 72, 76, 77, 85, 91, 92, 102, 104, 121, 125, 141, 142, 146, 147, 163, 165, 168, 174
hope, 43, 44, 49, 51, 54, 63, 70, 75, 76, 78, 88, 93, 106, 119, 128, 129, 162, 163, 165, 166, 176, 177
"I" position, 88, 89, 90, 96, 97, 98, 127, 146, 148, 154, 178
image of God, 16, 77, 85, 90, 106, 141, 158
imagination
    Christian, 161
    conversion of, 12
    theologically reflective, 167

informed consent, 14, 34, 36, 43, 47, 48, 50, 59, 66, 73, 74 115, 117, 180
injustice, 49, 54, 103, 104, 107, 109, 117, 121, 154-55, 168,
    gap, 153, 154
integration, 7, 12, 13, 14, 17, 18, 19, 20, 21, 35, 39-41, 75, 77, 102, 116
    explicit, 17, 19, 34, 36, 43, 47, 48, 50, 56, 59, 66, 73, 76, 103, 191n23
    implicit, 34, 35, 43, 50, 66, 191n23
interpretive strategy, 57
interpretive tradition, 56
Irenaeus, 137
Janoff-Bulman, Ronnie, 29, 158, 166
Jennings, Theodore, Jr., 105
Jesus Christ, 11, 15, 16, 21, 25, 32, 38, 40, 41, 44, 47, 49, 57, 62, 65, 73, 77, 82, 83, 84, 85, 86, 92, 103, 110, 111, 117, 121, 126, 133, 134, 135, 136, 137, 138, 139, 140, 144, 151, 159, 160, 161, 162, 165, 168, 169, 171, 172, 173, 176, 177
Jones, W. Paul, 49, 52, 53, 55, 68, 92
justice, 83, 94, 95, 98,102, 116, 140, 152, 165, 167, 171, 177
    counseling, 121-22
    distributive, 104
    of God, 11, 13, 54, 104, 105-11, 142, 168, 169, 178
    restorative, 104, 108
    retributive, 104
    social, 13, 14, 35, 36, 102, 103, 113, 121
    and Wesley, 111-13
Kinlaw, Dennis F., 66, 67
Knight, Henry H., III, 141
Lambert, Michael, 63, 70, 77
Lebow, Jay, 44, 70,77
Lewis, Judith, 121
Lewis, Michael, 121
licensure, 20,28,29,191
love, 15, 16, 26, 32, 49-52, 62-69, 71, 75, 82, 84-87, 90, 92, 96, 98, 102, 105, 112, 121, 128, 137, 139,

141, 147, 143-47, 151, 158, 163-64, 167-68
macrosystem, 118, 119
Maddox, Randy, 92, 111, 112, 135, 142-43
Mann, Mark H., 85, 87
Martyn, Steve, 84
maturity, 32, 36, 44, 56, 72, 82, 152, 154, 173, 174, 192n36
means of grace, 16, 91
Meeks, M. Douglas, 109, 110, 112
memory
    explicit, 24
    implicit, 24
mesosystem, 117
meta, 44, 51, 128
microsystem, 117, 118, 128, 177
model, specific
    interventions, 50, 77
models of therapy, 77
Moltmann, Jürgen, 65
moral influence model, 136, 139, 142, 143
National Alliance on Mental Illness, 123, 124
New Testament, 10, 110, 136, 160, 161
Noll, Mark A., 116
nonanxious presence, 91, 174
nonspecific mechanisms of change, 76-77
obsessio, 52, 53, 55, 69, 92, 93, 125, 151, 177
Old Testament, 105, 109, 110, 200n6
Olson, Roger, 21, 22, 23, 28, 29, 30, 38, 64
oral-based cultures, 24
pain, 51, 90,92, 128, 130, 134, 137, 140, 143, 145, 148, 150, 151, 160, 161, 163, 164, 165, 170-95
Pannenberg, Wolfhart, 65
patterns of behavior, 50
peace, 50, 54, 55, 90, 91, 96, 97, 104, 108, 117, 178
penal substitution model, 139-40
perichoresis, 67
person-in-environment, 119
person-in-relationships, 13, 119
Polyani, Michael, 42
poverty, 55, 103, 110, 117, 119, 120, 158

practical divinity, 14, 15, 64
practical theology, 14, 22,
   141
prayer, 18, 43, 50, 59, 60, 66,
   102, 111, 122, 127
prevenient grace. *See* grace,
   prevenient
process model, 17, 50, 51
REACH model of
   forgiveness, 146-47
reconciliation, 35, 49, 95,
   104, 133, 134, 135, 136,
   139, 140, 141, 142, 143,
   144, 145, 149-50, 151, 153,
   154, 155, 166, 172
redemption, 88, 106, 108,
   136, 137, 166, 167
Refuge for Women, 108
repentance, 49, 58, 94, 96,
   133, 135, 139, 140, 143,
   144, 145, 147-48, 150,
   151, 153, 154, 171
Richard of St. Victor, 65
righteousness, 32, 105, 110,
   112
Roberts, Dana, 116
Ross, Cathy, 116
Roy, Steven, 106-9
sacred loss, 159, 176
salvation, 16, 49, 91, 112,
   113, 135, 136, 141, 142,
   163, 166
Sandage, Steve, 56, 189n1
Sanford, Mark, 52
satisfaction model, 136,
   138-39, 143
Scripture, 15, 22, 23, 26, 27,
   38, 47, 48, 50, 56, 57, 59,
   66, 77, 82, 96, 109, 116,
   141, 170
self-responsibility, 48, 51,
   88, 89, 90, 92, 96, 97, 101,
   109, 11, 119, 127, 146,
   148, 149, 155
self-soothing, 91, 127, 146,
   149
Shults, F. LeRon, 56, 189n1
sin, 16, 26, 32, 47, 54, 86,
   88, 90, 95, 107, 112, 134,
   137, 138, 139, 140, 141,
   142, 143, 144, 146, 151,
   152, 153, 164, 165, 168,
   170, 171, 172, 173
social change agent, 118
social justice, 13, 14, 35, 36,
   102, 105, 109, 113-24,
   126, 129, 130, 135, 152,
   199n2

Sorenson, Randall, 19
soteriology, 10, 135
spiritual formation, 17, 20,
   180
Sprenkle, Douglas H., 44,
   70, 77
Step By Step, 120, 201n41
Steuernagel, Valdir, 117
suffer, suffering, 11, 13, 25,
   30, 54, 55, 105, 111, 113,
   117, 122, 123, 129, 130,
   134, 137, 158, 159, 161,
   162, 163, 164, 166, 167,
   168, 169, 170, 172, 173,
   177, 178
supervision, 19, 29, 42, 43,
   58, 180
tacit knowledge, 42, 43
Tallman, Karen, 70
Tan, Siang-Yang, 60
teaching, 18
professional form, 44, 191
spiritual formation, 17, 20,
   180, 192n33
theological formation, 27,
   32, 38, 180
"tear and repair," 69, 75, 86
theodicy, 11
theological themes, 36, 43,
   44, 45, 48, 49, 50, 73, 76,
   95, 98, 125, 152, 176, 180
theological/theology
   cognitive dissonance, 11
   constructive task, 22
   continuum, 23-26
   critical task, 22
   discernment, 29
   disequilibrium, 11
   empathy, 29
   explicit, 11, 24, 26,
      30-36, 55, 56
   as a hidden bias, 14
   implicit, 20, 23, 26,
      30-35, 55, 56
   integration, 12, 18, 21,
      22, 25, 27, 30, 38, 41,
      44, 45, 46, 50, 56, 102,
      170, 174
   reflection, 7, 9, 10
theological worlds, 49,
   52-55, 68-69, 92, 125-26,
   144, 151, 177, 196n37
   faint, 49, 53-54, 68, 92,
      125
   fighter, 49, 53-54, 68,
      125-26
   flattened, 50, 53, 54, 55,
      68, 125, 177

foreigner, 49, 53, 68-69,
   125
fugitive, 49, 53, 54, 68,
   125, 151
theologically reflective
   counseling, 17
   commitments, 36, 38,
      41, 48, 50, 59, 63, 64,
      76
   prerequisites, 31-35
therapeutic alliance, 46, 48,
   63, 67, 68, 70, 72, 73-75,
   78, 174
therapist characteristics,
   72-75
trauma, 35, 158, 159, 160,
   161, 166, 167, 168, 169-70,
   172, 173, 174, 175
Trinity, 13, 62, 64-69, 75,
   78, 90, 96, 106, 135, 144,
   167
trust, 75, 147-51, 168
truth(s), 14, 15, 22, 23, 26,
   27, 38, 40, 43, 55, 65, 82,
   84, 90, 105, 108, 133, 136,
   159, 166, 167
types of theology/
   theologians
   academic, 25-26
   folk, 23-26
   lay, 25
   ministerial, 25
   professional, 25-26
Violence Intervention
   Program, 107-8
Volf, Miroslav, 65, 144, 163,
   166-68
Walls, Andrew, 22, 116
Wesley, Charles, 9, 37, 61,
   81, 131, 157
Wesley, John, 14-16, 17, 32,
   64, 65, 82, 84, 85, 91, 92,
   102, 104, 111, 112, 113,
   121, 135, 141, 142, 163,
   164, 165
Wilkins, Steve, 52
worldview, 11, 28, 39, 49,
   52, 53, 74, 158, 170
Worthington, Everett, Jr.,
   145, 146, 153
Wright, N. T., 42, 102, 137,
   162, 163, 164, 165
Wynkoop, Mildred Bangs,
   64, 85
WYSIWYG ("what you see
   is what you get"), 56-57